INHERITANCE TAX ON LIFETIME GIFTS

AUSTRALIA AND NEW ZEALAND
The Law Book Company Ltd.
Sydney : Melbourne : Perth

CANADA AND U.S.A.
The Carswell Company Ltd.
Agincourt, Ontario

INDIA
N.M. Tripathi Private Ltd.
Bombay
and
Eastern Law House Private Ltd.
Calcutta and Delhi
M.P.P. House
Bangalore

ISRAEL
Steimatzky's Agency Ltd.
Jerusalem : Tel Aviv : Haifa

MALAYSIA : SINGAPORE : BRUNEI
Malayan Law Journal (Pte.) Ltd.
Singapore and Kuala Lumpur

INHERITANCE TAX
ON
LIFETIME GIFTS

By

THOMAS IVORY, M.A. (CANTAB.)
of Lincoln's Inn, Barrister;
Fellow of St. Catharine's College, Cambridge

RICHARD BRAMWELL, LL.M. (LOND.)
of Middle Temple, Barrister

STEPHEN COOKE, Solicitor
Partner, Withers

PAUL CLARK, B.A. (OXON.), Solicitor,
Partner, Withers

LONDON
SWEET & MAXWELL
1987

Published in 1987 by
Sweet & Maxwell Limited of
11 New Fetter Lane, London
Computerset by Promenade Graphics Limited, Cheltenham
Printed in Great Britain by
Hazell Watson & Viney Limited, Member of BPCC Group
Aylesbury, Bucks

British Library Cataloguing in Publication Data
Inheritance tax on lifetime gifts.
1. Inheritance and transfer tax—Great Britain
I. Ivory, Thomas
336.2'76 HJ5813.G7

ISBN 0-421-37910-3

PREFACE

The advent of inheritance tax has been something of a mixed blessing for practitioners. The good news is the much greater scope for tax saving which is provided by the concept of the Potentially Exempt Transfer ("PET"), all the more so after the Finance (No. 2) Act 1987 which brought interest in possession settlements within the PETS regime. The bad news is the resurrection of the "gift with reservation" provisions from the days of estate duty, whose width and obscurity was notorious and has been criticised at the hightest judicial level. (*St. Aubyn* v. *Att-Gen.* [1952] A.C. 15 at page 44 *per* Lord Radcliffe).

This book does not pretend to provide all the answers to the gifts with reservation problems that arise in practice. All the authors can hope to do is to explain where the potential traps lie or may lie, and how best to avoid them. The object of the book is to give the reader guidance as to how to take maximum advantage of the opportunities which inheritance tax presents whilst steering a reasonably safe course through the minefield of gifts with reservation. If we have achieved that object, we will be well satisfied.

Needless to say the authors welcome any comments and suggestions from readers.

CONTENTS

TABLE OF CASES

TABLE OF STATUTES

TABLE OF STATUTORY INSTRUMENTS

LIST OF ABBREVIATIONS

C.G.T.	Capital Gains Tax
C.G.T.A.	Capital Gains Tax Act
C.T.T.	Capital Transfer Tax
F.A.	Finance Act
I.C.T.A.	Income and Corporation Taxes Act
I.H.T.	Inheritance Tax
I.H.T.A.	Inheritance Tax Act
PET	Potentially Exempt Transfers

CHAPTER 1

Inheritance Tax on Lifetime Gifts

I. THE SCOPE OF THIS BOOK

1–01 This book is not offered as a comprehensive study of inheritance tax. As the title indicates, the tax treatment of death is not covered (except incidentally). Further, given that in many respects inheritance tax is capital transfer tax (C.T.T.) with another name, a basic knowledge of principle is assumed, so that, for example, the reader is taken to be familiar with the idea that a chargeable transfer is measured by reference to the extent to which the transferor's estate is diminished, where this exceeds the value of what is given away. **1–01**

Inheritance tax offers enormous scope for tax saving by means of lifetime gifts, and the object of this book is first, to acquaint the reader with those parts of inheritance tax which differ from C.T.T., and second, to discuss the ways and means of getting the most out of the opportunities that now present themselves.

In a little over a decade, the tax treatment of gifts has almost come full circle. Up to 1974, there was Estate Duty, which was with some justice referred to as a voluntary tax, because if a donor survived seven years, his gift was free of duty (provided he reserved no benefit out of the gift). Then came the first version of C.T.T., with the concept of lifetime cumulation, few reliefs, and rates up to 75 per cent. on lifetime gifts. Had it continued in force, this form of tax would have eventually absorbed much of the private property in this country. In the second version of C.T.T., lifetime cumulation was replaced by 10 year cumulation, and rates on lifetime gifts were reduced to half those on death throughout the scale; but in principle, most forms of gift were taxable. Now, inheritance tax makes tax on some gifts at least once more a voluntary matter, for certain types of gift are free of tax if the donor survives for seven years (and reserves no benefit out of the gift). For taxpayers who leave things too late, rates of tax go up to 60 per cent. on death.

II. TWO TYPES OF LIFETIME GIFTS

1–02 There are two main categories of lifetime gifts for inheritance tax purposes: (a) potentially exempt transfers and (b) other lifetime gifts. 1–02

(a) Potentially Exempt Transfers

The first (and by far the most advantageous) comprises those types of gift which qualify as "potentially exempt transfers" ("PETS" for short), of which the most common types are outright gifts to another individual, gifts into interest in possession settlements (which are treated as gifts to another individual) and gifts into exempt accumulation and maintenance settlements for beneficiaries under the age of 25 years. The magic of PETS is that they are free of all tax if the donor survives for seven years.[1] If the donor dies within the seven year period, the gift will be charged to inheritance tax at the death rates but subject to a reduction in the full death rate depending upon how long the donor did survive after making the gift:

Years between date of gift and date of death	Percentage of full death rate charged
0–3 years	100%
3–4 ,,	80%
4–5 ,,	60%
5–6 ,,	40%
6–7 ,,	20%[2–3]

This percentage reduction at first sight appears to be very similar to the taper relief under the old estate duty (the predecessor of capital transfer tax). The similarity, however, is purely superficial. Under estate duty taper relief operated as a percentage reduction in the amount of *the gift*. Taper relief under inheritance tax is much less favourable. It does *not* reduce the amount of the chargeable transfer; it simply reduces the *rate of charge*. The amount of the chargeable transfer itself remains unchanged. That is of crucial importance in determining the rate of charge on the rest of the donor's estate on death. The point may be illustrated by considering a PET up to but not exceeding the donor's nil rate band. If that PET becomes a chargeable transfer as a result of the donor's death within the following seven years, taper relief would be of no effect whatsoever. It cannot reduce the rate of charge, because the rate of charge would be nil anyway, the chargeable transfer being within the nil rate band. The amount of the chargeable transfer itself would be unaffected. So the rest of the estate passing on death would not enjoy any benefit from the donor's nil rate band which is already entirely consumed by the earlier chargeable transfer.

1–03 A number of other points may be noted here. Firstly, the amount upon which tax is charged is calculated by reference to values *as at the date of the gift*, rather than at the date of death. This again is in contrast to the estate duty position, the inheritance tax treatment this time being more favour- 1–03

[1] I.H.T.A. 1984, s.3A(4).
[2–3] *Ibid.*, s.3A(4), ss.7(1) and (4).

able at any rate in the usual case where the value of the property increases between the date of the gift and the date of death. (In the exceptional case where the value of the property has decreased by the time of the death, there is a specific relief allowing the lower value at the date of death to be taken: para. 4–19 below).

Secondly, there is no question of the concept of "grossing up" (whereby the amount of a lifetime chargeable transfer is increased by the amount of any tax borne by the donor) applying to PETS (see para. 4–05 below).

Thirdly, although the potentially exempt transfer becomes retrospectively a chargeable transfer on the donor's death within the following seven years, the tax is payable and interest starts to run at the same time as on a chargeable transfer on death.[4] The rates of tax chargeable will also be the rates in force at the date of death.[5]

(b) **Other lifetime gifts**

1–04 The second category of lifetime gifts covers all other lifetime gifts of which the most common examples are the creation of discretionary settlements. These are chargeable transfers from the outset, and as such are chargeable immediately (as under capital transfer tax) at one half of the full death rate.[6] If, however, the donor dies within the following seven years, the rate of charge may be increased (but not decreased) to the death rate subject to taper relief (the effect of taper relief and the amount subject to the charge on death following the same principles as on the death charge for PETS as already explained).[7] The additional charge on death would normally arise if the death occurs within five years after the chargeable transfer. After five years, taper relief would normally reduce the death charge to below the lifetime rate (50 per cent.) so there would be no further charge. There are, however, some circumstances in which the charge on death between five and seven years after the gift could still be higher than the lifetime charge (see para. 4–08 below). 1–04

Summary

1–05 It will be seen that the basic C.T.T. structure has by and large been preserved under inheritance tax in the second category of gifts (all gifts other than PETS), although the position is more penal in so far as there could be an increased charge if the donor dies within the following five (or in some cases seven) years. (Contrast C.T.T. where the lifetime rate could not be increased once the donor survived three years). But the most radical change is of course the introduction of a separate category of potentially exempt transfers which are free of tax if the donor survives seven years. That is the really attractive feature of inheritance tax and means that the advantages of lifetime gifts under inheritance tax can be much greater than under C.T.T. 1–05

[4] *Ibid.*, s.226(3A) and para. 4–05 below.
[5] *Ibid.*, s.8(1A).
[6] *Ibid.*, s.7(2).
[7] *Ibid.*, ss.7(4) and (5).

III. RESERVATION OF BENEFITS

1–06 It should, however, also be noted at this early stage that although lifetime gifts can achieve greater savings under inheritance tax, it will in many cases be much more difficult to make a lifetime gift which is effective for inheritance tax purposes. 1–06

This is because of the introduction of the old estate duty reservation of benefits rules.[8] These rules (which had no counterpart under C.T.T.) are considered in detail in Chapter 6 below. For the time being, suffice it to say that they are intended to prevent a person from "having his cake and eating it," that is to say giving away his property more than seven years before his death to avoid tax whilst continuing to enjoy benefits from it. Under C.T.T. it was, for example, possible for a person to give away his house to his children whilst continuing to live in it for the rest of his life; or to settle investments upon a discretionary trust for beneficiaries including himself and continue to enjoy the income from the investments at the discretion of the trustees. These and other popular strategies under capital transfer tax will in most cases be rendered ineffective for inheritance tax purposes as a result of the reservation of benefit rules. The rules are technical and in many cases it will be possible to circumvent them by careful planning, as will be seen later. But in general it is much more difficult to make an effective gift of property for inheritance tax purposes whilst continuing to enjoy the benefit of the property than in the days of capital transfer tax.

1–07 Where a gift falls foul of the reservation of benefits rules the consequences can be disastrous. The property which is comprised in the gift will still be treated as comprised in the donor's estate at death if the reservation of benefit continues until death, and accordingly will be brought into charge at the full death rate *on its value at the time of death*.[9] If the reserved benefit ceases before the donor's death he will be treated as making a potentially exempt transfer at that time, which will become chargeable if he were to die within the seven years following the cessation of the reservation of benefit.[10] (The original gift would also be a chargeable transfer or potentially exempt transfer as the case may be, and could give rise to a separate charge in its own right, although relief is provided by statutory regulations from the double charge which would otherwise arise in such circumstances.[11] The regulations, with examples, are to be found in Appendix 2.) At all events, the message to the would-be inheritance tax planner must be: avoid the reservation of benefits rules at all costs. 1–07

IV. PERIOD FOR CUMULATING CHARGEABLE TRANSFERS

1–08 One other change from C.T.T. which may be noted briefly here is the reduction in the period for cumulating chargeable transfers from 10 years to seven years.[12] So if a person makes a chargeable transfer, it will fall out 1–08

[8] F.A. 1986, s.102 and Sched. 20.
[9] *Ibid.*, s.102(3).
[10] *Ibid.*, s.102(4).
[11] *Ibid.*, s.104(1)(b) and S.I. 1987 No. 1130.
[12] I.H.T.A. 1984, s.7(1). The anniversary charges on discretionary trusts however are still every 10 years (para. 3–04 below).

of account after seven years, and his nil rate and lower rate bands will then revive for the benefit of the rest of his estate.

V. WHEN TO MAKE A GIFT

1–09 As the saving of tax depends upon how long the donor survives after making the gift, the general principle must be to make the gift as soon as possible. Apart from anything else, the sooner the gift is made, the cheaper the cost of insuring the liability on death within the following seven years. 1–09

The age of the donor is of course one of the most important factors. A comparatively young man in his 30's or 40's and in good health may not be too concerned about inheritance tax for the time being. He can give away his property at any time up until seven years before his death free of inheritance tax. On that basis he might well take the view that he can afford to wait say 10–15 years before making gifts. If he should happen to die unexpectedly in the meantime, he can always leave his estate to his widow and let her give it away during her lifetime.

The one great imponderable in all this is how long inheritance tax will last. In particular the authors doubt whether the concept of a potentially exempt transfer would survive long after a change of government. For that reason many people will be well advised to take advantage of the inheritance tax regime while the going is good, even if they are still comparatively young.

1–10 One major difficulty in practice, however, has already been touched upon, namely whether the person contemplating a gift can actually afford to give away his property. Under capital transfer tax this was not in practice a major problem because it was possible to make an effective gift of one's property for tax purposes whilst still enjoying the benefit of the property: many of the insurance schemes in their various forms achieved this, as did the simple discretionary trust under which the settlor was a beneficiary. But these are by and large no longer possible under inheritance tax because of the reservation of benefit rules. Many people will now be in a position where they should be making gifts for inheritance tax purposes as soon as possible but they simply cannot afford to give much away. There is indeed a certain level of wealth (possibly the £250,000–£500,000 bracket for a married couple) which one might call the inheritance tax "poverty trap." The value of the estates will be large enough to attract a substantial charge to inheritance tax, but not large enough to enable them to "offload" during their lifetime, particularly if, as in many cases, much of the total value of the estates is represented by the matrimonial home which cannot be given away (or is at least very difficult to give away). This area is a very important one in practice and is much more difficult to deal with under inheritance tax. 1–10

VI. C.G.T. DISADVANTAGES OF PETS AND OTHER LIFETIME GIFTS

1–11 One disadvantage of PETS (and all other lifetime gifts) is the loss of the C.G.T. uplift in base cost on death. Suppose a prospective donor has an asset pregnant with gains. If he retains the asset until his death, his personal representatives would acquire the asset for C.G.T. purposes at mar- 1–11 ket value at the date of death without charge.[13] That should eliminate the chargeable gain and the asset can then be sold free of C.G.T. If, however, the donor gives away the asset during his lifetime, it will *prima facie* be a disposal at market value under Capital Gains Tax Act (C.G.T.A.) 1979, s.29A (transactions otherwise than by way of bargain at arm's length), so that a chargeable gain will arise. In some cases where the asset in question is for example a business or shares in a family trading company and the donor is over 60, retirement relief may be available under Finance Act (F.A.) 1985, ss.69, 70 and Sched. 20 which will exempt the chargeable gain (up to £100,000). But where retirement relief is not available (or is not sufficient to cover the chargeable gain), it will be necessary to claim "hold-over" relief under F.A. 1980, s.79 (gifts between individuals as extended by F.A. 1982, s.82 to trustees) to avoid a chargeable gain accruing on the gift. The effect of "hold-over" relief broadly speaking will be that the disposal is deemed to be on a no gain/no loss basis, so that no chargeable gain accrues to the donor, and the donee takes over the asset at the donor's original base cost. The gain will thus be "held over" until a subsequent disposal by the donee, when it will come into charge.

1–12 In many cases the loss of the C.G.T. uplift in basecost on death is not so important in practice as to deter the owner from making a gift to save inheritance tax. Often the asset to be given away will not be pregnant with gain (whether because it is not a chargeable asset at all, or because the base cost plus indexation is already not far below market value). Moreover, where the asset is pregnant with gain in theory, it may be highly unlikely that the gain would ever be realised in practice, or at least not for a very long time, as for example where the asset is a business which is being handed down from a father to his son who is working full time in the business. Even if it is eventually sold, the chargeable gains may be "rolled over" by reinvesting the proceeds of sale in further business assets[14] and so on.

1–13 In some cases, however, the loss of the C.G.T. uplift can be very serious indeed and in an extreme case can completely undo any inheritance tax savings achieved by the gift. This is particularly the case with assets qualifying for 50 per cent. business or agricultural relief where the maximum rate of inheritance tax on the gross value of the property is effectively 30 per cent.—which equates with the rate of C.G.T. Where such assets are likely to be sold shortly after the donor's death, the inheritance tax savings achieved by the gift may well be totally eliminated by the C.G.T. charge arising on the subsequent sale (which could have been avoided had the donor retained the asset until death). Indeed, it is possible to get the worst of all possible worlds if the donor dies shortly after making the gift. There will then be no inheritance tax savings (because he did not live long enough) and the C.G.T. uplift in base cost is lost. That unhappy scenario is all too common in the authors' experience, and they cannot emphasise strongly enough that the C.G.T. position must be considered carefully when contemplating an *inter vivos* gift, particularly where the prospective donor is very elderly and may or may not survive for long enough to

[13] C.G.T.A. 1979, s.49(1).
[14] C.G.T.A. 1979, ss.115 *et seq*.

achieve significant inheritance tax savings. In such a case, if the client is married, it may be much better for him simply to retain the asset until death, leave it to his wife under his will and let her give it away during the remainder of her lifetime. That way, one gets the benefit of the C.G.T. uplift in base cost on the donor's death, whilst still leaving a chance of saving inheritance tax via the subsequent gift by the surviving spouse.

VII. STAMP DUTY

1–14 With the abolition of the charge under the heading voluntary dispositions, a gift will not give rise to any *ad valorem* charge to stamp duty.[15] 1–14

[15] F.A. 1985, s.82. The instrument should be certified in accordance with the Stamp Duty (Exempt Regulations) 1987, S.I. 1987 No. 516.

CHAPTER 2

Potentially Exempt Transfers

I. INTRODUCTION

2–01 As was seen in the last chapter, one of the most important and attractive features of inheritance tax is the concept of a potentially exempt transfer which is free of all tax if the donor survives for seven years (in contrast to any other form of gift which is a chargeable transfer from the outset). The definition of what constitutes a potentially exempt transfer is obviously of crucial importance in the field of inheritance tax planning, and will now be examined in detail. 2–01

II. THE DEFINITION OF POTENTIALLY EXEMPT TRANSFERS

2–02 The definition of a potentially exempt transfer is contained in I.H.T.A. 1984, s.3A(1) which reads as follows: 2–02

> "3A. Potentially exempt transfers
> (1) Any reference in this Act to a potentially exempt transfer is a reference to a transfer of value—
>
> (a) which is made by an individual on or after March 18, 1986; and
> (b) which, apart from this section, would be a chargeable transfer (or to the extent to which, apart from this section, it would be such a transfer); and
> (c) to the extent that it constitutes either a gift to another individual or a gift into an accumulation and maintenance trust or a disabled trust;
>
> but this subsection has effect subject to any provision of this Act which provides that a disposition (or transfer of value) of a particular description is not a potentially exempt transfer."

Condition (a) is relatively straightforward and requires little comment at this stage, except to note that the termination of an interest in possession to which an individual was beneficially entitled under a settlement is treated as a transfer of value made by an individual for this purpose. This is explained in detail later (para. 2–04A).

2–03 Condition (b) is also straightforward, the rationale for it being that if the transfer is unconditionally exempt under some other provision, it is neither necessary nor even desirable to treat it as *potentially* exempt under section 3A. The one exception is the annual £3,000 exemption which is the subject of a special provision. The effect of the provision is somewhat obscure, but the intention appears to be that in determining whether a transfer is a PET, the annual exemption is disregarded.[1] This preserves the annual exemption intact for the benefit of any chargeable transfers made in the course of that year. Should the PET subsequently become a chargeable transfer in the event of the donor's death within the following seven years, the annual exemption is first allocated to any other chargeable transfers in the year and any balance is set against the PET which has now become a chargeable transfer.[2] **2–03**

Example:

X makes a gift of £10,000 to his son absolutely. He then pays a £2,000 premium on a life assurance policy held on discretionary trusts. The whole of the £10,000 gift will be a PET. The payment of the premium would be exempt under the annual exemption. If X dies within the following seven years the remainder of the annual exemption would be set against the PET which has become a chargeable transfer, reducing it to £9,000. (For the sake of simplicity it is assumed that there is no annual exemption carried forward from the previous year).

2–03A Condition (c) is at the heart of the definition of PETS and requires close examination. **2–03A**

It will be seen that in order to qualify as a potentially exempt transfer under condition (c) the transfer of value must take one of three forms:

(a) a gift to another individual (which for this purpose includes a gift into a settlement under which another individual is beneficially entitled to an interest in possession: see para. 2–04A below);
(b) a gift into an accumulation and maintenance trust; or
(c) a gift into a disabled trust.

Of the three, the first two are by far the most important in practice and will be examined in detail. The last of the three (gift into a disabled trust) is a reference to settlements within I.H.T.A. 1984, s.89 (trusts for disabled persons). As these are comparatively rare and of little general application, they are not discussed further in this book.

[1] I.H.T.A. 1984, s.19(3A)(*a*). The difficulty is that s.19(3A) does not actually say that. What it does say is that any PET shall be ignored for the purposes of the annual exemption. But of course under s.3A, a transfer is only a PET in the first place if it is not otherwise exempt (*Sic* including exempt under the annual exemption). This is completely circular.

[2] *Ibid.*, s.19(3A)(*b*).

III. GIFT TO ANOTHER INDIVIDUAL

2–04 A transfer of value qualifies as a gift to another individual as defined in section 3A(2) which reads as follows: 2–04

"(2) Subject to subsection (6) below, a transfer of value falls within subsection (1)(*c*) above, as a gift to another individual—

(a) to the extent that the value transferred is attributable to property which, by virtue of the transfer, becomes comprised in the estate of that other individual, . . . , or
(b) so far as that value is not attributable to property which becomes comprised in the estate of another person, to the extent that, by virtue of the transfer, the estate of that other individual is increased . . . ."

Before going any further, it should be noted that subsection (2) is in terms an exhaustive definition of the phrase "gift to another individual." In the authors' opinion it is therefore unnecessary to determine for this purpose whether a transfer of value is a "gift" in the ordinary meaning of that word. If the transfer of value satisfies the requirements of subsection (2)(*a*) or (2)(*b*), it will be "a gift to another individual" as defined whether or not it could be described as a "gift" on general principles. It is understood that this is also the Revenue's view.

2–04A The section as originally enacted required, under limb (a), the property to have become comprised in another individual's estate *otherwise than as settled property* or, under limb (b), an increase in the value of another individual's estate *otherwise than by an increase in the value of settled property comprised in his estate*. The words in italics prevented a gift into a settlement under which another individual was beneficially entitled to an interest in possession from qualifying as a PET, under the heading "gift to another individual," notwithstanding the basic concept that a person who is beneficially entitled to an interest in possession in settled property is deemed to be beneficially entitled to the settled property in which that interest subsists. Happily the words in italics have been deleted with respect to gifts made on or after March 17, 1987. Consequently, a transfer of property into a settlement under which another individual is beneficially entitled to an interest in possession (or a transfer of value which increases the value of property comprised in such a settlement) can now qualify as a PET in exactly the same way as a transfer by way of absolute gift to another individual. The whole topic of PETS in the context of interest in possession settlements is examined further below (paras. 2–07 *et seq.*, below). 2–04A

2–05 One point which is not entirely clear on the wording of the subsection is the exact extent of the exemption where the transfer of value exceeds the value of the property transferred, typically where the transfer also has the effect of reducing the value of the property retained by the transferor. 2–05

Suppose for example A owns a 51 per cent. shareholding in a company which is valued as a controlling shareholding at £50,000. He transfers 2 per cent. to B by way of outright gift. A 2 per cent. holding on its own has a value of £500. A's remaining 49 per cent. is valued as a minority holding at say £30,000. The amount of the transfer of value is the reduction in the value of A's estate, *i.e.* £20,000. But the value of the property transferred (the 2 per cent. holding) is only £500.

The transfer of value of £20,000 is only potentially exempt to the extent that:

> "it is attributable to property which, by virtue of the transfer, becomes comprised in the estate of that other individual."

It is a possible view that only £500 of the transfer of value is so attributable, that being the value of the property transferred, the remaining £19,500 of the value transferred being attributable to the reduction in value of the property retained by the transferor. On that basis only £500 would qualify as a potentially exempt transfer, the remaining £19,500 being a chargeable transfer.

Such a result would seem very harsh, and the better view is probably that the whole of the £20,000 would be exempt in these circumstances. The test is the extent to which the value transferred is attributable to *the property* which becomes comprised in the transferee's estate, not *the value* of that property. The whole of the transfer of value is attributable to that property (the 2 per cent. holding) in the sense that it is the transfer of that property *and nothing else* which is responsible for the whole of the reduction in the value of the transferor's estate.

A similar point arises in connection with I.H.T.A. 1984 s.18 (transfers between spouses) where the wording is very similar. On the latter provision the Revenue's practice is to treat the whole of the value transferred as exempt even though it exceeds the value of the property transferred to the spouse. It is understood that the Revenue take the same view of s.3A(2).[3] On that basis, in the above example the Revenue should in practice accept that the whole of the transfer of value of £20,000 qualifies as a potentially exempt transfer.

2–06 Although the usual case of a gift to another individual will be a transfer 2–06 of property to the donee (or to the trustees of an "interest in possession" settlement), it is also possible to have a "gift to another individual" which does not involve any transfer of property to the donee, but where there is nonetheless an increase in the value of the "donee's" estate.[4] An example would be where the "donor" pays for repairs or improvements to a house owned by the donee. Again a question could arise as to the extent of the exemption where the amount of the transfer of value (the reduction in the value of the donor's estate) exceeds the amount of the increase in the value of the donee's estate (*e.g.* if in the above example, the cost of the repairs or improvements exceeded the increase in value of the house). Here it is thought that on the wording of subsection (2)(*b*), the exemption must be limited to the increase in the value of the donee's estate.

Interest in Possession Settlements

2–07 As already seen, under inheritance tax as originally enacted, a gift into 2–07 an interest in possession settlement did not qualify as a PET because of the specific exclusion of settled property from the definition of "gift to another

[3] See also s.23(1) (gifts to charities) where again similar wording is used.
[4] *Ibid.*, s.3A(2)(*b*).

individual." This was despite one of the basic principles of inheritance tax which is to treat a person who is beneficially entitled to an interest in possession under a settlement as beneficially entitled to the settled property in which that interest subsists.

The result was to discriminate heavily against the creation of an interest in possession settlement in favour of an outright gift to another individual. Indeed the discrimination against interest in possession settlements went further than that, because the termination of an interest in possession under a settlement could not be a PET either. The termination of an interest in possession *inter vivos* is an occasion upon which tax is charged *as if* the (ex) life tenant had made a transfer of value; and the legislation as originally enacted directed that all such notional transfers of value were not to be treated as PETS.

2–08 Fortunately Parliament has recognised, albeit somewhat belatedly, that it was fundamentally inconsistent with the basic principles of settled property to exclude "interest in possession" settlements from the PET regime in this way. The exclusions of settled property from the definition of "gift to another individual" in italics above have been deleted so that a gift into a settlement under which another individual is beneficially entitled to an interest in possession (or which increases the value of property comprised in such a settlement) is now treated as a gift to another individual and so can qualify as a PET. Moreover, although the general rule that notional transfers of value are not to be treated as PETS is preserved, there is now a specific exception for notional transfers of value arising under I.H.T.A. 1984, s.52 on the *inter vivos* termination of an interest in possession. The termination of the interest in possession will be treated as a transfer of value made by an individual (the ex life tenant) and can thus qualify as a PET if and to the extent that the trusts which arise on the termination of the interest in possession are of the appropriate character, *i.e.* one or more of the following: 2–08

(a) another individual becomes absolutely entitled to the property; or
(b) another individual becomes beneficially entitled to an interest in possession in the property; or
(c) the property becomes subject to exempt accumulation and maintenance trusts; or
(d) the property becomes subject to a disabled trust under section 89.

2–09— 2–10 The result is that a gift into an "interest in possession" settlement can now be just as advantageous for inheritance tax purposes as an absolute gift to another individual, and may be an attractive alternative where it is desired not to give away the property to the intended donee absolutely. 2–09— 2–10

One particularly attractive feature of the interest in possession settlement as a vehicle for making the gift is the scope for flexibility which it can provide through overriding powers of appointment vested in the trustees (or other persons). In that regard, to qualify as a PET, the requirement is merely that another individual is entitled to an interest in possession *at the time of the gift.* It matters not that the individual's interest in possession might be terminated at any time thereafter by the exercise of an overriding power of appointment. So a gift into a settlement under which an individual is beneficially entitled to a life interest which is subject to a wide overriding power of appointment vested in the trustees in favour of other persons will still be a PET. Moreover if the trustees subsequently exercise the power of appointment to terminate the life interest, that would also be a PET, so long as the effect of the appointment is to make another individual absolutely entitled, or to confer an interest in possession on another individual, or to create exempt accumulation and maintenance trusts or disabled trusts. What one cannot do by way of a PET is to terminate the life interest by appointing the property on discretionary trusts. The termination of the life interest in such circumstances would be a chargeable transfer by the (ex) life tenant (and there are special rules for calculating the rate of charge in such circumstances: see para. 3–26 below).

IV. GIFTS INTO ACCUMULATION AND MAINTENANCE TRUSTS

2–11 The second of the two common forms of potentially exempt transfers is "a gift into an accumulation and maintenance trust." This is defined in section 3A(3) as follows: 2–11

> "Subject to subsection (6) below, a transfer of value falls within subsection (1)(*c*) above as a gift into an accumulation and maintenance trust . . . , to the extent that the value transferred is attributable to property which, by virtue of the transfer, becomes settled property to which section 71 . . . of this Act applies."

Section 71 is the provision which exempts accumulation and maintenance trusts from the periodic and exit charges which would arise on the settlement under the discretionary trust charging regime. Accumulation and maintenance trusts are examined in detail below.

Several of the points mentioned in connection with the definition of "gift to another individual" arise equally with this definition, *viz.*:

(a) the subsection is a comprehensive definition of the phrase "gift into an accumulation and maintenance trust," so it is unnecessary to consider whether the transfer of value could otherwise be described as a "gift" within the ordinary meaning of that word;
(b) the question as to the extent of exemption arises equally here where the amount of the transfer of value exceeds the value of the property transferred. It is thought that the wider approach would be taken here as under the first limb of the definition of "gift to another individual."

In one respect the definition of "gift into an accumulation and maintenance trust" is narrower than the definition of "gift to another individual." Under subsection (3) the property to which the transfer of value is attributable must "become settled property to which section 71 . . . applies," *i.e.* it must be transferred into the settlement. It is not enough to show that the value of the settled property has been increased if property has not been transferred into the settlement. Contrast the definition of "gift to another individual" which is satisfied if *either* the property has become comprised in the transferee's estate *or*, if it has not, the value of his estate has been increased.

2–12 This point should be noted in particular when considering the payment of premiums in respect of life assurance premiums on a policy which is held upon accumulation and maintenance trusts. If the settlor pays the premiums directly to the insurance company, the payments will not qualify as potentially exempt transfers. Often it will not matter, because the payments would in any event be covered by the "normal expenditure out of income" or annual exemptions. But where it is not covered by those exemptions and it is desired to make the payments as potentially exempt transfers, it would be necessary for the settlor to pay the money over to the trustees of the settlement and let them pay the premiums. (This could, however, have income tax disadvantages in a case where income tax relief is available on the premiums. To qualify for the tax relief the premiums must be paid by the settlor to the insurance company, not by the trustees: see para. 5–14 below). 2–12

Accumulation and Maintenance Trusts

Introduction

2–13 An accumulation and maintenance trust (A&M trust) is a trust of the kind defined by section 71 of the I.H.T.A. The detailed provisions of section 71 are considered below, but the general idea is that initially, property is held upon trust for one or more persons under the age of 25, the income (if any) to be accumulated if not applied for their maintenance. From an age not exceeding 25, one or more of the beneficiaries must become entitled either to the property outright or to an interest in possession in it. Where the requirements of section 71 are met: 2–13

(a) the gift into the A&M trust is a PET;
(b) there is no charge to tax when the beneficiaries take the property or interests in possession in the property.

2–14 Because A&M trusts have to begin as trusts in favour of persons under the age of 25, they carry their own set of problems: donors are often reluctant to confer irrevocable benefits on young people who have yet to demonstrate their ability to handle wealth responsibly. Depending on particular circumstances, much flexibility can be incorporated within an A&M trust so that benefits can be switched from one beneficiary to another below the age of 25 without any tax charge. As a last resort there is no objection to the reservation of a power to revoke a beneficiary's interest after he has attained 25: such a revocation will either result in a PET or a chargeable transfer depending upon the nature of the succeeding interest (see para. 2–08 above). It is usually found that the best procedure is to provide for interests in possession only after the initial accumulation period, but to confer on the trustees the power to appoint capital absolutely if they see fit. This ensures that at least the capital is preserved unless and until it is evident that a beneficiary is a worthy recipient. 2–14

An illustration may help to make clear these introductory remarks:

Example

G is the grandfather of X and Y who are 16 and 14 respectively. G settles property upon A&M trusts for X and Y, with equal life interests from the age of 25. The trustees have power to vary or abrogate the interests of X or Y, provided that the power can be exercised only when they are both under 25 and so that any diminution in one share is matched by a corresponding increase in the other. The trustees also have power to appoint to either beneficiary the capital representing his share.

When Y is 22 it becomes evident that he is addicted to heroin, and the trustees exercise their power to remove him as a beneficiary. Accordingly, upon attaining 25, X becomes entitled to a life interest in the whole fund. When X attains 30, the trustees exercise their power of appointment to distribute the whole of the capital to him. None of the events described above would attract a charge to I.H.T. (at least if G survived for seven years after creating the settlement).

2–15 One problem which is sometimes encountered is that of a non-existent class: a settlor wishes to make a settled gift for the benefit of his grandchildren, but he has none as yet. If he had *one* it would be a simple matter to make a class gift that would benefit all his grandchildren whenever born, but it will be seen that an A&M trust must have at least one living beneficiary when it is created. The difficulty of there being no members of the intended class can be overcome by including, as beneficiaries, one or more young children who are (say) the children of nephews or nieces of the settlor. When a grandchild is born, the initial beneficiaries can be excluded so that, thereafter, only grandchildren will benefit. It will be seen that the drawback to this type of arrangement (where all the persons who have ever been beneficiaries are not grandchildren of a common grandparent) is that the trust ceases to enjoy the tax exemptions of A&M trusts after 25 years: see para. 2–35 below. The common grandparent test does not of course imply that a grandparent must be a settlor, so that, for example, a parent may create an A&M trust for his children, without the 25 year restriction applying. **2–15**

The detail of section 71 will now be examined.

The Requirements for Exemption Under Section 71 (Accumulation and Maintenance Settlements)

2–16 A transfer of value will only qualify as gift into an accumulation and maintenance settlement if the settlement is one which meets the requirements of section 71 (Exempt Accumulation and Maintenance Settlements). These are unchanged from the days of capital transfer tax. **2–16**

There are two main requirements for exemption under section 71:

(a) one or more persons (referred to as "beneficiaries") *will*, on or before attaining a specified age not exceeding 25, become beneficially entitled to the settled property or to an interest in possession therein; and
(b) no interest in possession subsists for the time being and the income is to be accumulated so far as not applied for the maintenance, education or benefit of a beneficiary.[5]

Where the beneficiaries are not all grandchildren of a common grandpar-

[5] I.H.T.A. 1984, s.71(1).

ent, there is a third requirement, namely that not more than 25 years have elapsed since the settlement commenced ("the 25 year rule"). This is considered in detail later.

2–17 Accumulation and maintenance trusts can take the form of a single gift to one individual, *e.g.* 2–17

> "The Trust Fund shall be held upon trust for X if he attains the age of 18 years";

or separate gifts to each of a number of individuals, a part of the trust fund being held separately for each individual, *e.g.*

> "The Trust Fund shall be divided into three equal parts, one such equal part to be held upon trust for A if he attains the age of 18 years, a second such equal part to be held upon trust for B if he attains the age of 18 and the remaining third equal part to be held upon trust for C if he attains the age of 18 years."

Each individual will then have his own part of the trust fund to which he will be prospectively entitled, and section 71 will apply separately to each individual's part.

Alternatively, there can be a class gift, a gift of the whole of the trust fund to a class of beneficiaries, *e.g.*

> "The Trust Fund shall be held upon trust for such of my children as shall attain the age of 18 years and if more than one in equal shares."

This, which is much the most common form of accumulation and maintenance trust, is a single gift to the class of beneficiaries. Each beneficiary will be prospectively entitled to a proportionate share of the trust fund, which may vary from time to time depending upon how many beneficiaries are in existence. If a beneficiary dies before the specified age, his share would accrue to the other surviving beneficiaries (normally without charge). Correspondingly if he lives but someone else dies, his share may be increased by a proportionate part of the share of the deceased beneficiary which would accrue to his share.

2–18 The beneficiaries can include unborn persons (although there must be at least one beneficiary in existence before the settlement can qualify as an exempt A&M trust under section 71).[6] Again, the existing beneficiaries' shares would be *pro tanto* decreased by the birth of a further beneficiary prospectively entitled to a share. 2–18

If it is desired to include unborn beneficiaries without limit, regard must be had to the rule in *Andrews* v. *Partington*.[7] The effect of this rule is to exclude as beneficiaries under a class gift any person born *after* the first beneficiary becomes entitled to his share of the gift, in the absence of a contrary contention.

Example:

Trust Fund is held upon trust for such of the children of S as attain the age of 18 years and if more than one in equal shares absolutely. At the date of the settlement there are three children of S in existence, A aged 6, B

[6] *Ibid.*, s.71(7).

[7] (1791) 3 Bro.C.C. 401.

aged 4, and C aged 2. When A attains 18, he will become entitled to his share. The class will then close under the rule in *Andrews* v. *Partington*[8] in the absence of a contrary intention. The effect will be to exclude any further children of S born after A's eighteenth birthday from taking. But it will not of course affect B and C (or any other child of S born before A's eighteenth birthday) from becoming entitled to his prospective share.

2–19 In some cases, it may be important to exclude the rule in *Andrews* v. *Partington*,[9] for example, where a settlor who has recently re-married wishes to set up an A&M trust both for the children of his first marriage and any children he may have from his second marriage. If the children of the first marriage are already close to the specified age, the rule in *Andrews* v. *Partington*[10] should be excluded to allow for the children of the second marriage to take, even if they are born after the first child has become entitled to his share. This can be done quite simply by expressing a clear contrary intention, for example by inserting the words "whenever born": **2–19**

> "For such of the children of S *whenever born* as shall attain the age of 18 years etc."[11]

This would enable beneficiaries born after the first child has become entitled to his share to take. It will be noted that this may have further tax implications, because the share of the child who has already taken would be *pro tanto* decreased by the subsequent birth of a further beneficiary, and that would be a transfer of value by that child.[12] However, that transfer of value would itself now be a PET,[12a] so this is much less serious than it used to be prior to the F.A. 1987 amendments, when it was automatically a chargeable transfer. (There is no tax charge in the converse case where shares or prospective shares of existing beneficiaries are increased on the death of another beneficiary below the specified age who has not yet attained an interest in possession).[13]

2–20 Of the two main requirements, the one which requires most care is the first, namely that one or more of the beneficiaries will become entitled to the settled property or to an interest in possession in it on or before attaining the specified age not exceeding 25. **2–20**

It should be noted at the outset that this requirement can be satisfied by the beneficiaries becoming entitled to the settled property on attaining the specified age, *either* absolutely *or* for a life interest (or other interest in possession). It is indeed quite common when drafting A & M trusts to provide that on attaining the specified age, each beneficiary's share shall not vest in him absolutely but shall be retained by the trustees upon trust to pay the income to him for life, the trustees having a power at their discretion to advance the capital of his share to him, with remainders over to his chil-

[8] *Ibid.*
[9] *Ibid.*
[10] *Ibid.*
[11] *In re Edmondson's Will Trusts* [1972] 1 W.L.R. 183 (C.A.).
[12] I.H.T.A. 1984, s.52(1).
[12a] Under *ibid.* s.3A(1)(c).
[13] *Ibid.*, s.71(4)(*b*).

dren, etc.[14] The advantages of this type of A & M trust, and the use of the power of advancement at the discretion of the trustees, have already been explained (paragraph 2–14 above).

2–21 However, whether the beneficiaries are to become entitled to the settled property absolutely or for life interests only, one must be able to predicate *with absolute certainty* that they will become so entitled on or before a specified age not exceeding 25. Of course it is perfectly possible that all the beneficiaries may die below the specified age so that no-one becomes entitled. But that is neither here nor there for the purposes of section 71 because the possibility of the beneficiaries' death under the specified age is inherent in section 71 itself, *viz.* that the beneficiaries will become entitled "on or before attaining the specified age not exceeding 25." The point is that if they *do* survive, one or more of them must become entitled. 2–21

It is not of course necessary that all the beneficiaries will become entitled to the trust fund. It is enough that one or more will do so if they survive. It is therefore permissible to give the trustees (or even the settlor) power to vary the shares of any beneficiaries who are under the specified age *inter se*, even to the extent of cutting out one or more beneficiaries completely; or (which comes to much the same thing) giving the trustees (or other persons) the power to select those beneficiaries who are to take and in what proportions, and in default of selection to all who attain the specified age equally.

2–22 Whether it is desired to include a power to vary shares or a power of selection will be a matter for the settlor to decide in consultation with his advisers. Many settlors wish to provide for complete equality between the beneficiaries in all circumstances, so that everyone has an equal opportunity. Others prefer to give trustees (or someone else) a discretion so that preference can be given to one or more of the beneficiaries who have more need of the trust fund than others, or who will use the money more wisely. That may be particularly the case if the beneficiaries are very young at the time when the settlement is created, when no one can predict the personality and circumstances of the beneficiaries when they attain the specified age many years in the future. 2–22

A power to select beneficiaries or a power to vary shares (including cutting someone out altogether) will be essential when a "token" beneficiary has been included at the outset to satisfy the rule that there must be at least one beneficiary in existence before section 71 can apply: see paragraph 2–26 below.

If a power to vary shares or a power of selection is included, care should be taken to ensure that the power is not exercisable in any way which would increase the share of a beneficiary who has already attained the specified age at the expense of the share of a beneficiary who has not. A suitable power will be found at clause 4 in precedent B in Appendix 1.

2–23 In determining whether one or more of the beneficiaries will become entitled on or before attaining the specified age, regard is had purely to the terms of the settlement, all matters extraneous to the settlement being ignored. So it matters not that a beneficiary might assign his interest to a 2–23

[14] The power of advancement has to be expressly provided. The statutory power under s.32 of the Trustee Act 1925 would not apply if the beneficiary's entitlement is to income only.

third party; or that he could be deprived of his interest on bankruptcy; or that his interest might be prevented from vesting by a variation approved by the court under the Variation of Trusts Act 1958.[15]

Subject to that, however, there must be *absolute certainty* that one or more beneficiaries *will* become entitled under the terms of the settlement. Given the strictness of this requirement, great care must be exercised in that regard when drafting an accumulation and maintenance settlement. In particular, if there is a power of appointment or advancement under the terms of the settlement before the beneficiaries have attained the specified age, it must not be exercisable in any way which would or might prevent the beneficiaries' shares from vesting in possession by the specified age at the latest. The mere existence of such a power of appointment (and the mere possibility that it might be exercised with that effect) would prevent the settlement from satisfying this requirement (even if it is never intended that the power would be exercised in that way).[16]

2–24 If it is desired to include such a power of appointment or advancement which could be exercised in that way, it must be made subject to a proviso that the power will not be exercised in any way which would or might prevent the beneficiaries' shares from vesting on or before the age of 25. An example will be found at clause 5(*b*) in precedent A in Appendix 1. **2–24**

No such objection can be taken to an overriding power of appointment which is only exercisable over a beneficiary's share after he has attained the specified age and become entitled to an interest in possession. The existence of the power of appointment would not prevent the beneficiary's share vesting in possession on or before attaining the specified age, which is all that section 71 requires. For the purposes of section 71, it is irrelevant that that power of appointment might be exercised after the beneficiary's interest in possession has arisen to take it away from him (although of course if it were to be exercised in that way, there would be a PET or chargeable transfer on the termination of the beneficiary's interest in possession (depending on the nature of the succeeding interest: para. 2–08 above).[17]

2–25 Great care is also necessary with some of the wider forms of administrative powers, which again might conceivably be exercised in a way which would prevent the beneficiaries from becoming entitled to interests in possession on or before 25. Examples which might be vulnerable are: **2–25**

(a) a power to pay life assurance premiums out of income; or
(b) a power to apply capital in purchasing a house as a residence for a beneficiary.

The first of these powers is considered in detail in the chapter on insurance

[15] *Inglewood* v. *I.R.C.* [1983] S.T.C. 133 at p. 138f–h.

[16] In theory even the statutory power of advancement might be objectionable in that regard because it could be exercised in such a way as to defer the beneficiaries' entitlement beyond the specified age (or even remove it altogether: see *Re Hampden* [1977] T.R. 177). However, the Court of Appeal have said *obiter* that the statutory power of advancement does not prejudice the requirements of s.71 (apparently on the basis that it is an administrative power rather than a dispositive power), *Inglewood* [1983] S.T.C. at p. 139; and the Revenue in practice have no objections to it.

[17] I.H.T.A. 1984, s.52(1).

(paragraphs 5–14 *et seq*. below). The second power could prejudice the requirements of section 71 if it could be exercised to apply capital in which there is as yet no interest in possession subsisting to buy a residence for a beneficiary over the specified age. That would (at least arguably) give the beneficiary over the age of 25 an interest in possession in the capital so applied, and correspondingly prevent any beneficiary under the age of 25 from taking an interest in possession in it. The mere existence of such a power (and the possibility that it might be exercised in that manner) on that basis could be enough to breach the requirements of section 71 at the outset. If such powers are to be included in the settlement, they should be specifically restricted so that they cannot offend the conditions of section 71. For example, the power to purchase a house as a residence could be restricted to a residence for a beneficiary who was for the time being entitled to, or to an interest in possession in, the capital so applied. Alternatively, a general proviso can be inserted to all the administrative powers that they cannot be exercised in any way which would or might prevent interests in possession arising in the trust fund. An example of such a proviso will be found at clause 10 in precedent A in Appendix 1.

2–26 Before leaving this condition, one other point may be noted here. "Persons" in sub-section 1(*a*) includes unborn persons; but a settlement cannot be exempt under section 71 unless there is (or has been) at least one beneficiary in existence.[18] If, for example, the beneficiaries are "the grandchildren of X," the settlement will not be exempt unless and until one of the grandchildren is born. Where none of the beneficiaries is yet born, it is often possible to get around this difficulty by including a "token" beneficiary, who is in existence, in the class of beneficiaries with a view to "cutting him" out at a later date after the first "genuine" beneficiary is born. For that purpose it will of course be necessary to include in the settlement a power to select beneficiaries or a power to vary shares (including cutting out a beneficiary completely) of the type described at paragraph 2–21 above. This is also one of the instances where the 25 year rule will apply: see paragraphs 2–31 and 2–32 below where an example of this class of case is considered. 2–26

Provisions for the Trust Income Before the Beneficiaries Become Entitled

2–27 The second condition lays down requirements as to how the income of the trust fund must be dealt with pending the beneficiaries becoming entitled to the settled property or to interests in possession in it. To meet these requirements there must be a *trust* to accumulate the income, subject to a power to apply the income for the maintenance, education or benefit of the beneficiaries who have not yet attained the specified age.[19] The Revenue do not in practice object to a simple accumulation trust, so the power of maintenance can be dispensed with if desired (although it would be very unusual to do so, and probably unwise unless there is a special reason for it). The Revenue do, however, insist upon the *trust* to accumu- 2–27

[18] *Ibid.*, s.71(7).
[19] *Ibid.*, s.71(1)(*b*).

late the income (with or without the power of maintenance). A mere power to accumulate will not suffice.

The simplest way of meeting these requirements is to incorporate section 31 of the Trustee Act 1925 with the usual modifications (see clauses 8 and 9 in precedent A in Appendix 1).[20] Under section 31, while the beneficiary is under the age of 18, the trustees will have power to apply the income of his share for his maintenance, education or benefit, and the balance of the income not so applied must be accumulated.[21] If, however, the beneficiaries' interests are still contingent at 18 (*e.g.* if a specified age is chosen of 21 or 25) the beneficiary will be entitled to the income from his share from the age of 18 until his interest vests (at 21, or as the case may be 25).[22] The result would be that a beneficiary would have an interest in possession in his share at 18, rather than the specified age. (If his share were to accrue to someone else after he has attained 18, *e.g.* on his death or on the exercise of a power to vary shares, there would be a termination of his interest in possession, and a chargeable transfer or PET would arise accordingly).

2–28 If it is desired to defer the beneficiaries' entitlement to income beyond 18, it will be necessary to provide an express trust to accumulate the income, with a power of maintenance, pending the beneficiaries attaining the specified age. Care must be taken with the rule against excessive accumulations, which only permits income to be accumulated for one of six possible periods:

(a) the life of the settlor;
(b) 21 years from the death of the settlor;
(c) the duration of the minorities of any persons living at the death of the settlor;
(d) the duration of the minorities of any persons who if of full age would be entitled under the terms of the settlement to the income directed to be accumulated;
(e) 21 years from the date of the settlement;
(f) the duration of the minorities of any persons alive at the date of the settlement.[23]

Only one of the periods can be chosen, and the choice must be made at the outset (normally by defining the accumulation period expressly in the settlement). The one most commonly chosen is (e), 21 years from the date of the settlement, which will be satisfactory in most cases. But problems can arise if a high specified age is chosen, and the beneficiaries include very young children or unborns. If, for example, the specified age is 25, and the beneficiaries include children under the age of four at the date of the settlement and/or unborns, it would not be possible to provide a trust to accumulate the income from their shares right up until the specified age under a 21

[20] When the interests of the beneficiaries are contingent, s.31 only applies if the gift carries the intermediate income (s.31(3)).
[21] But with power to treat past accumulations as income for the current year so long as the beneficiary is still under the age of 18 and his interest still subsists (s.31(2)).
[22] Trustee Act, 1925, s.31(1)(ii).
[23] L.P.A. 1925, s.164(1). Perpetuities and Accumulations Act 1964, s.13. These restrictions do not apply in Northern Ireland, where accumulation is permitted for the entirety of the perpetuity period.

year accumulation period. It is, of course, possible to choose a different accumulation period: *e.g.* if the settlor is relatively young and in good health, it may be better to choose his life as the accumulation period, which might well give a longer period. But of course there is no guarantee in that regard, and it might actually give a shorter accumulation period if he were to die prematurely.

2–29 Where there is a danger that the express trust to accumulate income will (or might) exceed the accumulation period, it will in practice be necessary to confine the accumulation trust to the accumulation period (whatever accumulation period has been chosen), and leave section 31 of the Trustee Act to apply (with the usual modifications) after the expiry of the accumulation period to any share which has not yet vested in possession. If a child is over the age of 18 at the expiry of the accumulation period, he will be entitled to the income of his share until his share vests on attaining the specified age.[24] If he is under the age of 18 at the expiry of the accumulation period, there will be the statutory trust to accumulate (not affected by the rule against excessive accumulations) and power of maintenance until he attains 18, when he will again become entitled to the income pending his attaining the specified age.[25] **2–29**

The 25 Year Rule

2–30 As mentioned above, there is a third requirement for exemption under the Inheritance Tax Act 1984 section 71.[26] This requirement can be satisfied in one of two ways: **2–30**

Either

(a) all the persons who are or have been beneficiaries are grandchildren of a common grandparent (or the children, widowers or widows of such grandchildren who were beneficiaries but died before they could take). This will be referred to as "the common grandparent" test;

or

(b) not more than 25 years have elapsed since the settlement commenced (or since it last satisfied the common grandparent test). This will be referred to as the "25 year rule."

In the majority of cases, the common grandparent test will be satisfied and there will be no need to worry about the 25 year rule. The test would clearly be satisfied if the beneficiaries are—

"the grandchildren of X."

So also if the beneficiaries are—

"the children of X,"

the children of X being, of course, children of a common grandparent, namely X's parents.

[24] Trustee Act 1925, s.31(1)(ii).
[25] *Ibid.*
[26] I.H.T.A. 1984, s.71(2).

2–31 Some care is needed when dealing with first cousins. If the beneficiaries are all first cousins of each other, the test would be satisfied *e.g.* "the children of X and the children of X's brother." But all the first cousins of an individual might not satisfy the test *inter se*, *e.g.* "the children of the marriage of Mr and Mrs X, the children of Mr X's brother, and the children of Mrs X's brother." There would be no common grandparent between the children of X's brother and the children of Mrs X's brother, although they would all be first cousins of Mr and Mrs X's children. 2–31

More generally, a common instance when the test is not satisfied is where the beneficiaries cover more than one generation, *e.g.*—"X's children and grandchildren." This would not satisfy the common grandparent test because the children would not have the same grandparents as the grandchildren (the grandparents of X's grandchildren being the *parents* of X's children).

This type of case is often encountered where it is desired to create an accumulation and maintenance settlement in favour of grandchildren, but there are no grandchildren yet in existence. As has already been explained, this creates a difficulty because a settlement cannot be an accumulation and maintenance settlement unless at least one of the beneficiaries is or has been in existence. If there are no grandchildren in existence, but there is a child under the age of 25, it is quite common to include that child as a beneficiary, so as to satisfy this requirement. But in that event, the common grandparent test would not be satisfied, and the 25 year rule will apply.

Example:

Suppose X has three children, A (aged 27), B (aged 25), and C (aged 16). X wishes to create an A & M trust in favour of his grandchildren, but no grandchild yet exists. X could create an A & M trust in favour of C and X's future grandchildren, the inclusion of C meeting the requirement that there is at least one beneficiary in existence. But in that event, the 25 year rule would apply, the common grandparent test not being satisfied.

2–32 *A fortiori*, the common grandparent test would not be satisfied if a non-related person is used as the "peg" beneficiary, as is sometimes done (para. 2–26 above). 2–32

It will also be noted that the common grandparent test requires all persons who are or *have been* beneficiaries to be grandchildren of a common grandparent. So, in the above example, if X is included as a beneficiary at the outset, the settlement will never satisfy the common grandparent test, even if C is subsequently excluded at a later date when a grandchild is born.

Substitution Provisions

2–33 When drafting A & M trusts, it is common to provide that if a beneficiary dies below the specified age leaving a child or children surviving him, his surviving children should step into his shoes, and take the share which the deceased beneficiary would have taken had he survived to the specified age. Such a provision would not offend the common grandparent test, there being a specific extension of the "grandchildren of common grandparents" test to include the children, widows or widowers of such deceased 2–33 grandchildren who would have taken had they survived to the specified age.[27] It will be noted that the extension only covers *children* or widows or widowers of deceased beneficiaries, *not* remoter issue.

Substitution provisions of the type described may not be very important if the specified age chosen is low (say 18) where the chances of a beneficiary dying below the specified age leaving a child or children surviving him may be quite low. The importance of a substitutional provision increases, however, if the specified age chosen is high. If the maximum specified age (25) is chosen, there may be a distinct possibility that a beneficiary might die under the specified age leaving a child surviving him, when it may be desirable to have a substitutional provision of the type described.

Illegitimate, Adopted and Step Children

2–34 It is specifically provided that a person's children include his illegitimate, adopted and step children.[28] It follows that a person's parents would be the grandparents of his child, so an adopted child of a person would share the same grandparents as the person's natural children. **2–34**

The 25 Year Rule

2–35 Where the common grandparent test is not satisfied, then, as stated above, the 25 year rule will apply.[29] Under the 25 year rule, the settlement itself will be exempt under section 71 for the first 25 years; so that[29]: **2–35**

(a) the creation of the settlement (and any transfers of property into it within the first 25 years) would be potentially exempt transfers;
(b) there would be no charge if the beneficiaries become entitled to their shares (whether absolutely or on interest in possession trusts) within the 25 year period. If they do not do so, there would be a charge to tax on the expiry of the 25 year period when the settlement ceases to be an exempt A & M settlement.[30]

In practice what this means is that the beneficiaries' shares will have to vest in possession within 25 years to avoid a charge, which can be provided for either automatically under the terms of the settlement or by the trustees' exercising a power of appointment under the settlement. (See the drafting notes to the precedents in Appendix 1.)

V. GIFTS VIA SPOUSE WITH BETTER LIFE EXPECTANCY

2–36 The prospective tax saving which can be achieved by means of a PET depends of course upon the donor surviving seven years, or at least for more than three years when the rate of charge will be reduced by taper relief. If a prospective donor has a poor life expectancy, but his wife has a rather better life expectancy, it might be worth considering transferring **2–36**

[27] *Ibid.*, s.71(2)(*b*)(ii). There is no actual requirement that the children should take the *same* share as their deceased parent, although it is usually provided thus.
[28] *Ibid.* s.71(8).
[29] *Ibid.* s.71(2)(*a*).
[30] *Ibid.* s.71(3)(*a*).

part of his estate to his wife, thus enabling his wife to make a PET so that the tax saving depends upon her life expectancy rather than his.

The danger is that the transfer from husband to wife and the onward gift by the wife could be regarded as a transfer of value by associated operations by the husband directly to the ultimate donee, so that the relevant life expectancy is still the husband's.[31]

In the days of capital transfer tax, the Revenue did not normally seek to invoke the associated operations rule against a transfer between spouses and a subsequent gift by the transferee spouse, at least in straightforward cases, provided that it was not actually a condition of the transfer between spouses that the onward gift should be made by the recipient spouse.[32] However, in the authors' view, it would be unwise to place too much reliance upon this, and it is only sensible to take precautions to reduce the risk of an attack under the associated operations rule. If possible a transfer between the spouses should be seen in the context of a general strategy of equalising estates, facilitating future gifts by either spouse, without any precise intention being formed at that stage of precisely who will give what to whom, and when. A reasonable interval should then be allowed to lapse before considering a PET by the transferee spouse out of the property transferred (even at the expense of delaying the date when time starts to run for the purposes of the tax saving).

2–36A It is considered that the problem of dispositions by associated operations may be avoided by means of a short-term settlement on the spouse with the better life expectancy: *e.g.* "upon trust for W for life or the period of two years, whichever shall be the less, remainder to S absolutely". Here there would appear to be no "operations" capable of being asssociated, since W's interest terminates by the effluxion of time, and, of course, the termination of the life interest operates as a PET. In the case of *very* short term interests, the question may arise of whether the new approach to the avoidance of tax entitles the courts to disregard the life interest: see the discussion at para. 3–24 below. **2–36A**

2–37 One other point should be noted in this connection. If the property transferred between the spouses is agricultural or business property, the transferee spouse would not be entitled to agricultural or business property relief on a subsequent gift of that property unless she has held it for long enough to satisfy the relevant minimum period of ownership or occupation in her own right. There is provision for one spouse who acquires property *on the death of* the other spouse to be credited with the other spouse's period of ownership or occupation[33]; but there is no such provision where the property was acquired by way of a lifetime gift. **2–37**

[31] *Ibid.* s.268(3).

[32] Inland Revenue Press Notice dated April 8, 1975.

[33] I.H.T.A. 1984, s.108 (business property relief) and s.120 (agricultural relief).

Chapter 3

Discretionary Trust—Chargeable Transfers

I. Introduction

3–01 In this book, the term "discretionary trust" is used to describe a settlement which is subject to I.H.T.A. 1984 Pt. III, Chap. III (settlements with no interests in possession), that is to say a settlement of property in which there is for the time being no interest in possession to which an individual is beneficially entitled, and which does not enjoy exempt status. **3–01**

Under such a trust the settled property will typically be held upon trust for a class of beneficiaries ("the discretionary beneficiaries"), the income being payable to all or any one or more of the beneficiaries as the trustees in their discretion think fit and the trustees also having wide powers of appointment over capital and income. Such a trust is to be distinguished from the other two principal forms of settlement:

(a) the "interest in possession" settlement under which one or more beneficiaries is for the time being entitled to the income (whether for life or some shorter period), paras. 2–07 *et seq*. above; and
(b) the exempt accumulation and maintenance trust to which I.H.T.A. 1984, s.71 applies (paras. 2–13 *et seq*. above).

Some accumulation and maintenance trusts to which section 71 applies could be classified under trust law as discretionary trusts, particularly those of the more flexible type where for example the income of the trust fund may be payable at the discretion of the trustees while the beneficiaries are under the specified age, and the trustees may have powers of appointment over capital. The discretionary powers of the trustees will however inevitably be restricted because of the necessity of complying with the requirements of section 71, in particular that one or more of the beneficiaries must become entitled to the settled property or at least to an interest in possession therein on or before attaining a specified age not exceeding 25. This is in contrast to a full discretionary trust of the traditional type where the trustees are often given the widest powers of appointment over income and capital, only limited by the requirements of trust law to comply with the rules against perpetuities and excessive accumulations. At all events for inheritance tax purposes, accumulation and maintenance settlements are entirely different from "normal" discretionary trusts because transfers into A & M settlements are PETS, and the trusts themselves are in general exempt from the charges which would otherwise arise under the discretionary trust regime. They are thus best classified for inheritance tax purposes as *sui generis*, and not as discretionary trusts. That classification is adhered to throughout this book.

II. Gifts into Discretionary Trusts: A Chargeable Transfer ab Initio

3–02 A transfer of property into a discretionary trust will be a chargeable transfer from the outset, chargeable at one half the full death rates (with the possibility of an increase in the rate of charge if the donor dies within the following five, or in some cases, seven years after the gift).[1–3] That will not in fact matter very much if the amount transferred into the settlement does not cause the settlor to exceed his nil rate band (£90,000 for the year 1987–88) because no tax would be payable on such a chargeable transfer anyway. If the donor survives for seven years it will then fall out of account under the seven year limit to the cumulative total of chargeable transfers. 3–02

Thus the creation of discretionary settlement within the nil rate band should be every bit as effective in saving tax as a PET of the same amount. In both cases the tax saving is achieved by the donor surviving the seven year period (in the case of the chargeable transfer because it then falls out of account, and in the case of a potentially exempt transfer because it is then irrevocably exempt). No tax saving is achieved in *either* case if the donor dies within the seven year period. Taper relief would have no effect because it does not reduce the amount of the chargeable transfer, but only the rate of tax charged on the chargeable transfer (which was nil anyway being within the nil rate band).

In this context it should be remembered that in the case of a married couple, each spouse has his own nil rate band to make use of. So they can each make a chargeable transfer of up to £90,000 (the figure for the year 1987–88) without incurring any charge to tax. Moreover if the property in question qualifies for 50 per cent. agricultural or business property relief, that figure is effectively doubled when looking at gross values (before the relief). So a married couple with property qualifying for such relief could between them make transfers into discretionary settlements of £360,000 in terms of gross value (before the relief), all within the nil rate band.

Where, however the amount transferred causes the settlor to exceed his

[1–3] I.H.T.A. s.7(2), (4), (5).

nil rate band so that tax is actually payable, a gift into a discretionary settlement will be at a serious disadvantage as compared with other forms of gift which qualify as PETS and which would accordingly be free of charge if the donor survives for seven years.

III. SUBSEQUENT CHARGES ON THE DISCRETIONARY TRUST

3–03 As has already been mentioned briefly, a discretionary trust suffers from a further disadvantage as compared with an accumulation and maintenance settlement, because not only is the initial transfer of the property into the settlement a chargeable transfer, but there will also eventually be a further occasion (or even occasions) of charge on the property within the settlement under the discretionary trust regime. (In contrast there would be no subsequent occasions of charge on property within an exempt accumulation and maintenance settlement, except in unusual circumstances). The discretionary trust charging regime is somewhat complicated, and will have to be considered at some length. But it is worth noting at the outset that the maximum rate of any one charge under the discretionary trust regime will be 9 per cent., and it will only be in very exceptional cases (where the trust fund is very large or where the settlor had a substantial cumulative total before making the settlement) that the rate of charge would be even close to that maximum. In the vast majority of cases the rate will be much lower than 9 per cent. and indeed in many cases will be nil. 3–03

"Exit" and "Anniversary" Charges

3–04 There are two main types of charge on discretionary trusts: "exit" charges and "anniversary" charges. 3–04

An "exit" charge arises on each and every occasion when property comprised in the settlement ceases to be "relevant property," *i.e.* ceases to be subject to the discretionary trust regime.[4] This could be either because the property ceases to be comprised in the settlement altogether, for example where beneficiaries have become absolutely entitled; or it could be that the property remains within the settlement but it is no longer subject to the discretionary trust regime, as where beneficiaries have become entitled to life interests or other interests in possession, or where the property becomes subject to exempt accumulation and maintenance trusts. Any of these events could happen automatically in accordance with the terms of the trust. But in the vast majority of cases such an event will have been brought about by the action of the trustees (or someone else), normally by exercising a power of appointment or advancement. The term "breaking the trust" is often used to describe this process whereby trustees exercise a power of appointment or advancement so that the settled property ceases

[4] *Ibid.*, s.65(1)(*a*); alternatively, if the trustees make a disposition which reduces the value of the relevant property (s.65(1)(*b*)). There are various exceptions, *e.g.* for payments of income (s.65(5)(*b*)), payments of costs and expenses (s.65(5)(*a*), dispositions by trustees which were not intended to confer a gratuitous benefit, and grants of agricultural tenancies for full consideration (s.65(6)).

to be subject to the discretionary trusts (whether or not the property remains comprised within the settlement).

An "anniversary" charge arises on every 10th anniversary of the commencement of the settlement, if there is still "relevant property" (*i.e.* property subject to the discretionary trust regime) comprised in the settlement at that time.[5]

It will be noted that the exit charge and the anniversary charge are complementary in nature. If the trust is broken before the first 10 year anniversary, the trust fund would at that time be subject to the exit charge and there would be no subsequent anniversary charge (except in the unusual case where the property again becomes subject to discretionary trusts). Correspondingly if the trust is not broken before the first 10 year anniversary, it would then be subject to the anniversary charge. If it is broken within the 10 years following the first 10 year anniversary, it would be subject to an exit charge at that point. Otherwise it would be subject to another anniversary charge on the second 10 year anniversary; and so on. (If of course the trust is broken as to part of the settled property only, that part would be subject to the exit charge, and the balance of the settled property would in due course become subject to the anniversary charge). A simple example will help to illustrate the principles.

Example

3–05 Suppose S, who has made no previous chargeable transfers, settles £150,000 upon discretionary trusts for the benefit of his family. The property is retained upon discretionary trusts for 25 years, and is then broken by an appointment of the whole of the trust fund in favour of the settlor's children absolutely. In addition to the chargeable transfer on the making of the settlement, the following charges would arise within the settlement. (For the sake of simplicity it is assumed that the value of the property and the rates of charge remain constant): 3–05

(a) after 10 years there would be an anniversary charge on the value of the property. The rate of charge would be approximately 1·9 per cent., giving an actual charge to tax of £2,850;
(b) after 20 years there would be another anniversary charge which would be of the same amount (the value of the property and the rates of charge being assumed to remain constant);
(c) on the making of the appointment after 25 years, there would be an exit charge at a rate equal to one half of the last anniversary charge, giving an actual charge of £1,425.

The total of the charges within the settlement would thus be £7,125 or 4·75 per cent. of the value of the property.

Calculation of Exit and Anniversary Charges

3–06 To calculate an exit or anniversary charge it is necessary to know two things: (a) the amount which is subject to the charge and (b) the rate of charge. 3–06

[5] *Ibid.*, s.64.

The Amount Subject to the Charge

3–07 The amount which is subject to the charge is straightforward in both instances. 3–07

In the case of the anniversary charge, the charge is simply on the value of the relevant property (*i.e.* the property subject to discretionary trusts) at the anniversary in question.[6]

In the case of an exit charge, the amount subject to the charge is the value of relevant property comprised in the settlement immediately before the exit charge less the value of any relevant property in the settlement immediately after the exit charge.[7] Where the trust is broken in respect of the whole of the trust fund this will simply be the value of the trust fund at the date of the charge. Where the trust is broken as to part only of the trust fund, the amount subject to the charge will be the value of the trust fund immediately before the charge less the value of the part of the trust fund remaining subject to the discretionary trusts immediately after the charge. In many cases this will be the same as the value of the part of the trust fund in respect of which the trust was broken; but not in all cases. The value of the whole may be greater than the sum of its parts, for example where the trustees break the trust as regards part of a majority shareholding in a private company, leaving a minority holding subject to the discretionary trusts. If the tax is borne out of the balance of the trust fund remaining subject to the discretionary trusts, the amount subject to the charge is grossed up to take account of the tax.[8]

Rates of Charge

3–08 Determining the rate of charge is a complicated process, and there are fundamental differences not just between exit charges and 10 year anniversary charges, but also between exit charges before the first 10 year anniversary of the settlement and exit charges after the first 10 year anniversary. It will be necessary to consider each of these separately. 3–08

(a) **Rate of exit charge before the first 10 year anniversary.** The rate of an exit charge before the first 10 year anniversary is a fraction of the rate which would be chargeable on a notional chargeable transfer.[9]

The amount of the notional chargeable transfer is normally the value, immediately after the settlement commenced, of the property comprised in it, that is to say the initial value of the settled property, *not* its value at the date of the charge (see further para. 3–13 below).[10]

It will be noted that account is taken for this purpose of *all* the property

[6] *Ibid.*, s.64. This will include accumulations of income which are regarded as part of the settled property from the date when the accumulation is made. Income which has neither been accumulated nor distributed at the date of the charge is not regarded as part of the settled property and is thus outside the charge (Nor will it be subject to the exit charge if it is distributed in due course as income: s.65(5)(*b*) and note 4 above). See generally SP8/86, [1986] S.T.I. 708.

[7] I.H.T.A. 1984, s.65(2)(*a*). For the treatment of undistributed income, etc. see note 6 above.

[8] *Ibid.*, s65(2)(*b*).

[9] *Ibid.*, s.68(1).

[10] *Ibid.*, ss.68(4)(*a*) and (5)(*a*).

comprised in the settlement immediately after its commencement even if it was not all subject to discretionary trusts; *e.g.* if part was to be held upon interest in possession or exempt accumulation and maintenance trusts, account must nevertheless be taken of the initial value of that part.

The amount of the notional chargeable transfer will be increased beyond the initial value of the settled property in either of the following circumstances:

(a) if there is a "related settlement", that is to say a settlement made by the same settlor commencing on the same day.[11] The notional chargeable transfer is then increased by the initial value of the settled property in the related settlement, again whether or not the property comprised in the related settlement was subject to discretionary trusts[12]; (See further para. 3–20 below.)

(b) if further property is added to the settlement after its commencement (and before the event giving rise to the exit charge). The notional chargeable transfer is then increased by the value of the added property at the time of its addition to the settlement.[13]

The notional chargeable transfer is assumed to have been made on top of a cumulative total equal to the total chargeable transfers made by the settlor within the seven years ending on the day the settlement commenced but disregarding the chargeable transfer arising from the creation of the settlement itself and any other chargeable transfers made on that day.[14]

3–09 Tax is then calculated on the notional chargeable transfer on top of that cumulative total at one half the full death rates.[15] One then takes the average rate of charge on the notional chargeable transfer, and the actual rate of charge is the "appropriate fraction" of that rate, the appropriate fraction being: 3–09

$$\tfrac{3}{10}\text{ths X } \frac{\text{the period which has elapsed since the settlement commenced (calculated in complete quarters of a year)}}{\text{40 (the number of quarters in 10 years)}^{16}}$$

The rate of charge thus depends *inter alia* upon how long has expired since the settlement commenced, the appropriate fraction rising gradually from nil (if the settlement is broken within the first three months) to just under 30 per cent. if the settlement is broken in the last quarter before the first 10 year anniversary. As the maximum charge on the notional chargeable transfer would also be 30 per cent. (1/2 of 60 per cent., the top rate on death), the maximum rate of an exit charge within the last quarter before the 10th anniversary would be (just under) 30 per cent. x 30 per cent., *i.e.* 9 per cent. In fact it would only be in exceptional cases that the rate would

[11] *Ibid.*, s.62.
[12] *Ibid.*, s.68(5)(*b*).
[13] *Ibid.*, s.68(5)(*c*). This applies whether or not the further property has remained comprised in the settlement.
[14] *Ibid.*, s.68(4)(*b*).
[15] *Ibid.*, s.68(4)(*c*).
[16] *Ibid.*, ss.68(1) and (2).

come anywhere close to that maximum (where the initial value of the trust fund was very large indeed, or where the settlor had a substantial cumulative total of chargeable transfers in the seven years preceding the day of commencement of the settlement.)

3–10 **The rate of the anniversary charge.** The rate of the anniversary charge is again a fraction (this time a flat 3/10ths) of the rate which would be chargeable on a notional chargeable transfer.[17] 3–10

The amount of the notional chargeable transfer is normally simply the amount which is subject to the anniversary charge (*i.e.* the value of the "relevant property" at the date of the charge).[18] The amount of the notional chargeable transfer may however be increased in the following circumstances:

(a) If other property became comprised in the settlement which was not then relevant property (*i.e.* was not subject to discretionary trusts) and has not subsequently become relevant property while remaining comprised in the settlement.[19] In that case the value of such other property immediately after it became comprised in the settlement would be added to the notional chargeable transfer. This would happen if for example part of the trust fund had from the outset been held upon interest in possession or exempt accumulation and maintenance trusts. Although that part of the trust fund would not itself be subject to any charge under the discretionary trust regime (unless it subsequently became subject to discretionary trusts), it would nevertheless adversely affect the rate of anniversary charge on that part of the trust fund which was subject to the discretionary trusts, being included in the notional chargeable transfer by reference to which the rate of anniversary charge is calculated. (That is also the case with the rate of an exit charge before the first 10 year anniversary: see para. 3–08 above).

(b) If there is a "related settlement" the notional chargeable transfer is then increased by the value of the property comprised in the related settlement immediately after its commencement, again whether "relevant property" or not.[20]

3–11 The notional chargeable transfer is assumed to have been made on top of a cumulative total equal to the aggregate of the following: 3–11

(a) the total chargeable transfers made by the settlor in the seven years ending with the day the settlement commenced but disregarding the chargeable transfer arising on the creation of the settlement itself and any other chargeable transfers made on that day.[21] If the settlor has made a further chargeable transfer between the commencement of the settlement and the anniversary in question adding property to the settlement or otherwise increasing its value, the total of his

[17] Ibid., s.66(1).
[18] *Ibid.*, s.66(3), s.66(4)(*a*).
[19] *Ibid.*, s.66(4)(*b*).
[20] *Ibid.* s.66(4)(*c*).
[21] *Ibid.*, s.66(3)(*b*), s.66(5)(*a*).

chargeable transfers in the seven year period ending with the date of the addition will be taken, if greater than the total chargeable transfers in the seven years ending with the commencement of the settlement.[22] Again the chargeable transfer comprising the addition itself and other chargeable transfers made on the same day are disregarded for this purpose, as are chargeable transfers in the seven year period which are attributable to property which has already been taken into account in computing the notional chargeable transfer or the cumulative total.[22a]

(b) the amount subject to exit charges (if any) within the 10 years preceding the anniversary in question.[23]

The tax on the notional chargeable transfer is calculated (at half the full death rates[24]) on top of the cumulative total, and the average rate of charge taken. The actual rate of charge is then simply 3/10ths of that rate.[25] Again the maximum rate of anniversary charge will be 3/10 x 3/10, *i.e.* 9 per cent.

3–12 **The rate of an exit charge after the first 10 year anniversary.** The rate of an exit charge after the first or subsequent anniversary charges is the "appropriate fraction" of the rate of the last preceding anniversary charge, the appropriate fraction being: 3–12

$$\frac{\text{the period (measured in complete quarters) between the last anniversary charge and the exit charge}}{\text{40 (being the number of quarters in a 10 year period)}^{26}}$$

So the exit charge will normally simply be a fraction of the rate of the last anniversary charge, rising from nil (where the trust is broken within the quarter immediately following an anniversary charge) to almost 100 per cent. of the rate of the last anniversary charge in the final quarter before the next anniversary charge.

3–13 **Nil rate band discretionary trusts.** As already explained, the transfer of property into a discretionary trust will be a chargeable transfer *ab initio*, but this will not normally matter if the chargeable transfer is within the settlor's nil rate band; there will be a nil rate of charge, and the chargeable transfer will fall out of account after seven years. 3–13

[22] *Ibid.*, s.67(1), (3). Additions to the settlement are disregarded for this purpose if they were not primarily intended to increase the value of the settled property and did not result in more than a 5 per cent. increase (s.67(2)).

[22a] I.H.T.A. 1984, ss.67(3)(*b*), (5).

[23] If the property which was subject to an exit charge is again relevant property at the anniversary date (*i.e.* it ceased to be held upon discretionary trusts and then subsequently became again held upon discretionary trusts) the double counting which would otherwise arise is prevented by s.67(6).

[24] *Ibid.*, s.66(3)(*c*).

[25] *Ibid.* s.66(1).

[26] *Ibid.*, ss.69(1) and (4). If property has been added to the settlement between the last anniversary charge and the date of the exit charge (or alternatively if property which was comprised in the settlement at the date of the last anniversary but was not then relevant property has since become relevant property) the rate of the last anniversary charge is adjusted for this purpose to take account of such property: ss.69(2) and (3).

Moreover, with very few exceptions mentioned below, it will always be possible to break such a trust at any time before the first 10 year anniversary without incurring any actual charge to tax. Although that will be theoretically the occasion of an exit charge under the discretionary trust regime, the rate of charge should be nil. That will be the case even if the value of the property at the date of the exit charge has multiplied many times. The reason for this is as follows. Although the *amount* subject to the exit charge will be the value of the property at *the date of the charge*, the *rate* of the exit charge will be determined by reference to the value of the settled property *immediately after the settlement commenced*, that being the notional chargeable transfer by reference to which the actual rate of charge is calculated (para. 3–08 above).

3–14 *Example* 3–14

Suppose S, who has an existing cumulative total of chargeable transfers of £10,000, transfers £80,000 cash into a discretionary trust. Just before the 10th anniversary of the settlement, the whole of the fund is appointed on accumulation and maintenance trusts, giving rise to an exit charge. At the time of the appointment, the trust fund is worth £1 million.

Assuming that there are no complications such as related settlements or subsequent additions to the settlement, the notional chargeable transfer will be the initial value of the trust fund at the commencement of the settlement (£80,000),[27] on top of the settlor's cumulative total of chargeable transfers immediately prior to the settlement (£10,000).[28] The notional chargeable transfer will be entirely within the nil rate band and so will have a nil rate of charge. Correspondingly the actual rate of charge will be nil too, even though the value of the property at the date of the charge was £1 million.

Contrast however the position if the trust had not been broken, and was allowed to become subject to the anniversary charge after 10 years. The rate of the anniversary charge, unlike the exit charge before the first 10 year anniversary, *does* depend upon the value of the property at *the date of the charge* (in the example £1m), para. 3–10 above. The notional chargeable transfer would then be £1m which, on top of a cumulative total of £10,000 would be charged at an average rate of approximately 25 per cent. The actual rate of charge would then be 3/10ths of that, *i.e.* 7·5 per cent., giving a tax liability of approximately £75,000.[29]

3–14A The strategy just described of setting up a discretionary trust under the nil rate band and breaking it just before the first 10 year anniversary is particularly useful for property which currently has a very low value but is likely to grow substantially in the future. A common example is a shareholding in a new company which is about to or has recently started trading, when the shares are not worth much more than par value, but will multiply 3–14A

[27] I.H.T.A. 1984, s.68(5)(*a*).

[28] *Ibid.*, s.68(4)(*b*).

[29] In this example, there was of course a dramatic increase in the value of the property. In cases where the property does not increase in value by more than inflation over the intervening years, the rate of the anniversary charge will probably be nil, the increase in the value of the property being matched by the indexation of the nil rate band.

in value many times over if the business prospers. By transferring them straightaway into a discretionary settlement, the owner gets them out of his estate under his nil rate band, and he (or his trustees) will not have to decide who is ultimately to get the property until nearly 10 years later, when an appointment can be made breaking the trust without any actual rate of charge.

3–15 This simple strategy which was in widespread use in the final years of capital transfer tax still holds good under inheritance tax. In one respect however the strategy has altered under inheritance tax. In the days of C.T.T. it was standard practice for the settlor to be included as one of the discretionary beneficiaries, so that he could in due course enjoy the income from the shares or other property at the discretion of the trustees. Under inheritance tax it will normally be necessary to exclude the settlor from taking any benefit under the settlement because of the reservation of benefits provisions (Chapter 6). It is however still possible to include the settlor's spouse as one of the beneficiaries (although care will be needed in applying income or capital for the benefit of the spouse in any way which might indirectly benefit the settlor as well). It may even be possible to include the settlor as well by conferring a short initial interest in possession on his spouse, although these days one has to think very carefully before using such an artificial device. These possibilities are considered in more detail later (paras. 3–22—3–23 below). 3–15

Freezing Schemes

3–16 The use of a nil rate band discretionary trust which can be broken at any time up until the first 10 year anniversary without any charge irrespective of the then value of the property can be seen in its most dramatic form in the context of freezing schemes. 3–16

Freezing schemes can take various forms. But the object of most of them, as the name implies, is to freeze the value of an asset in the donor's estate, any future growth in value being taken out of his estate in favour of individual donees or the trustees of a settlement. One type of asset which is pre-eminently suitable for a freezing scheme is a majority shareholding in a family company. The first step is to create a new class of shares which initially have minimal rights in terms of dividends and rights to participate in surplus capital on a winding-up, etc., and will continue to do so so long as the company's profitability and value remain static. But the rights attaching to the new shares are linked to the future growth of the company, so that, for example, the rights to dividends increase as the company's profits increase, and the rights to capital on a winding-up increase in line with the net asset value of the company. The new "future growth" shares are transferred to the next generation or into trust at a time when they have very little value, but any future growth in the value of the company will enure for the benefit of these shares outside the donor's estates.

In the days of C.T.T., a "nil rate band" discretionary trust was often considered the most suitable vehicle to receive the new future growth shares. So long as the initial value of the shares (on top of the settlor's cumulative total prior to making the settlement) is within the nil rate band, the trust can be broken at any time before the 10th anniversary of the settlement without any charge to tax, even if the value of the shares at that time is many millions of pounds.

3–17 This strategy by and large still holds good under inheritance tax, although the discretionary trust will sometimes not be the most suitable vehicle for the gift. One of the problems which was encountered in practice with freezing schemes of the type described was calculating the amount of the chargeable transfer when transferring the new future growth shares into trust. Although the value of the transferred shares at that stage might be low, it was uncertain whether the reduction in value of the old shares was much greater. In other words the fear was that the value of those shares was not so much frozen to its present value but actually substantially reduced because of the lack of any growth potential as a result of the freezing of the rights attaching to the shares. In the case of a multi-million pound company there was a risk of a very substantial immediate chargeable transfer. 3–17

Where such difficulties are encountered under inheritance tax, it may be better to transfer the future growth shares into an accumulation and maintenance or interest in possession settlement or by way of outright gift to individuals rather than a discretionary trust, the advantage of the former being of course that they will be potentially exempt transfers anyway so that the question of the amount of the depreciation in the value of the "frozen" shares will not arise unless the donor dies within the following seven years. (As against that, if the donor does die within the following seven years, the Revenue may be in a stronger position with hindsight when it comes to valuations, if the company has in fact grown much more valuable in the meantime.)

Multiple Settlements

3–18 Because of the structure of the discretionary trust regime, it will usually be advantageous to transfer property into a number of different settlements, rather than put it all into a single settlement. The "multiple settlements" strategy does not reduce the total chargeable transfers on transferring the property into the discretionary settlements; but it should reduce the subsequent charges under the discretionary trust charging regime on the property comprised in the settlements. 3–18

There are a number of variations on the theme. But the one which has the potential for achieving the greatest tax saving is to set up a number of "pilot" settlements on different days with nominal amounts in cash, and then transfer the main property, dividing it equally between the trustees of the pilot settlements. This may secure a nil rate of exit charge before the first 10 year anniversary even where the amount of property being settled is far in excess of the nil rate band.

3–19 *Example* 3–19

Suppose a settlor with no previous chargeable transfers wishes to transfer £350,000 into a discretionary trust.

If he puts the whole of the cash into one settlement, the rate of exit charge before the first 10 year anniversary would be calculated by reference to the rate chargeable on a notional chargeable transfer of £350,000. If the trust was broken immediately before the first 10 year anniversary, the rate of charge would be approximately 5 per cent., giving a tax liability of £17,000 approximately (ignoring changes in the value of the property and the rates of charge).

Contrast the position where the settlor creates four "pilot" settlements with say £50 cash for each one, established on *different days* (to avoid "related settlements": see below); and then pays £87,500 to the trustees of each of the four settlements. Subject to the possible risk of an attack on *Furniss* v. *Dawson*,[30] the rate of an exit charge on breaking any of the four settlements before the first 10 year anniversary should be nil. In the case of each settlement, the notional chargeable transfer would be £87,550,[31] which is assumed to be made on top of a cumulative total ranging from nil for the first settlement to £150 in the case of the fourth settlement (being the chargeable transfers comprising the payment of £50 to each of the first three settlements).[32] In each case therefore the notional chargeable transfer would be covered by the nil rate band so the rate of the charge on the notional chargeable transfer (and correspondingly the actual rate of exit charge) would be nil.

The "multiple settlement" strategy should also reduce the rate of the anniversary charge (and correspondingly the rate of an exit charge after a 10 year anniversary), although it will not necessarily be nil because it will depend upon the value of the property at the date of the charge (paras. 3–10, 3–12 above).

3–19A The "multiple settlements" strategy in its various forms was in widespread use in the later years of capital transfer tax, and the practice is likely to continue under inheritance tax. One cannot of course rule out the possibility of an attack on *Furniss* v. *Dawson*[33] principles. But the worst that can happen is that the strategy simply does not work, all the property being treated under *Furniss* v. *Dawson*[34] as comprised in one settlement (or possibly in four related settlements, which would also be fatal as explained below). There is no downside.

The risk of an attack on *Furniss* v. *Dawson*[35] principles may be reduced by having different trustees and/or different beneficiaries under each of the settlements.

Avoiding "Related Settlements" etc.

3–20 When setting up a discretionary settlement, it will be advisable to avoid having any "related settlements." Settlements are related for this purpose if they are made by the same settlor *and* commence on the same day.[36]

If there is a related settlement, this will adversely affect the rates of charge under the settled property regime on the property comprised in the

[30] [1984] S.T.C. 153.
[31] Comprising £50 (the value of the property comprised in the settlement immediately after it commenced) and £87,500 (the value of the property subsequently added to the settlement): see s.68(5)(*a*) and (*c*) and para. 3–08 above.
[32] I.H.T.A. 1984, s.68(4)(*b*).
[33] [1984] S.T.C. 153.
[34] *Ibid.*
[35] *Ibid.*
[36] I.H.T.A. 1984, s.62.

discretionary settlement. This is because the (initial) value of the property comprised in the related settlement will be included in the notional chargeable transfer by reference to which the actual rate of an exit charge or anniversary charge is computed (see paras. 3–06—3–12 above). This could increase the average rate of charge on the notional chargeable transfer, and correspondingly the rate of the actual charge.

It is important to note that this result follows irrespective of whether the property comprised in the related settlement was itself subject to discretionary trusts. For example the related settlement could comprise "interest in possession" trusts or exempt accumulation and maintenance trusts. The property in such a related settlement would not of course itself be subject to charges under the discretionary trust regime (not being "relevant property"). But it would nonetheless adversely affect the rate of exit and anniversary charges on the property comprised in the discretionary settlement.

A fortiori, it will also be necessary to avoid having property which is not subject to discretionary trusts comprised in the same settlement as property which is held on discretionary trusts. Although not itself chargeable under the discretionary trust regime, it could again adversely affect the rate of charge on the property which was subject to the discretionary trusts (see paras. 3–06—3–12 above).

Provided one is aware of these pitfalls, there should be no difficulty in avoiding them in the context of *inter vivos* settlements. One can avoid having related settlements simply by making sure that the settlements commence on different days. (A settlement commences for inheritance tax purposes when property first becomes comprised in it.)[37] In that regard it matters not that the second one commences the day after the first, so long as it is not the same day.[38]

The Business and Agricultural Relief Trap

3–21 One anomalous point should be noted where the property comprised in a discretionary settlement qualifies for business or agricultural property relief. Where there is an exit charge before the first 10 year anniversary, 3–21

[37] *Ibid.*, s.60.

[38] The "related settlements" provisions can however create a difficult problem under wills. If for example the testator settles part of his estate on discretionary trust and part on (say) life interest trusts, the property subject to the life interest, if not comprised in the same settlement, will nonetheless be property comprised in a "related settlement." (Any settlement arising under a will or intestacy is deemed to commence on the testator's death). The one exception will be where the life interest belongs to the testator's spouse. In that event the property subject to the life interest will be deemed to have been comprised in a separate settlement made by the spouse on the termination of her life interest under the special rules contained in I.H.T.A. 1984, s.80 (initial interest in possession of settlor or spouse).

The "related settlement" problem in wills can be avoided if the testator creates a "pilot" discretionary settlement during his lifetime and then leaves property under his will to the trustees of the *inter vivos* settlement. But this can have other disadvantages owing to the earlier commencement date for the settlement. In particular, the date of the 10 year anniversary charge will be advanced. Also, the rate of an exit charge before the 10 year anniversary could be increased because the "appropriate fraction" will be greater (as a result of the earlier commencement date for the settlement).

the relief will reduce the *amount* which is subject to the exit charge,[39] but it is not taken into account in determining the *rate* of charge. The reason for this is that the notional chargeable transfer by reference to which the actual rate of charge is calculated is basically the value of the property comprised in the settlement immediately after its commencement (para. 3–08). This makes no allowance for the fact that the property may qualify for business or agricultural relief. (The relief reduces not the value of the property as such but rather the amount of the transfer of value insofar as it is attributable to that property).[40]

This point should be noted in particular where one is setting up a nil rate band discretionary trust with property qualifying for business or agricultural relief, intending to break it before the first 10 year anniversary with a nil rate of charge. If the chargeable transfer was brought within the settlor's nil rate band solely because of the business or agricultural relief, and the value of the property itself exceeds the nil rate band, there may well be an effective rate of charge on breaking the trust before the first 10 year anniversary owing to this anomaly.

The anomaly is confined to an exit charge before the first 10 year anniversary. In the case of the 10 year anniversary charge (and correspondingly an exit charge after a 10 year anniversary) the relief will be taken into account both in determining the amount subject to the charge, and the rate of charge.

IV. DISCRETIONARY TRUSTS: SETTLOR OR SETTLOR'S SPOUSE AS BENEFICIARY

3–22 In the later years of the capital transfer tax regime, it was very common practice to transfer property into a discretionary settlement, the settlor (and his spouse) being included as beneficiaries under the trust. This enabled the asset to be removed from the settlor's estate for C.T.T. purposes, but still enabling him to enjoy the income from the property as a beneficiary under the discretionary trust. 3–22

Although the point was not decided under Estate Duty, it is considered that a discretionary trust under which the settlor is a beneficiary would be a gift with reservation under F.A. 1986, s.102 for the reasons explained in para. 6–40 below. It is understood that that is also the Revenue's view. Accordingly for planning purposes it should be assumed that a transfer of an asset into a discretionary trust under which the settlor was a beneficiary would not succeed in removing the asset from the settlor's estate for inheritance tax purposes. (It would however still be a chargeable transfer and could give rise to an immediate charge to tax, so that one could actually be worse off than if no action had been taken. Relief from the double charge which would otherwise arise in due course when the reservation of benefit provisions bite is provided by statutory regulation.)[41]

3–23 There is in principle no objection to the settlor's spouse being included as a beneficiary under the trust because, in contrast to the settlement provisions of the Income Tax Acts, there is no provision under the inheritance tax legislation deeming references to the donor to include the donor's 3–23

[39] I.H.T.A. 1984, ss.103(1) and 105(1).
[40] *Ibid.*, ss.104 and 116.
[41] F.A. 1986, s.104(1)(*b*) and S.I. 1987 No. 1130.

spouse.[41a] If however the settlor's spouse is included as a discretionary beneficiary, care should be taken when paying out any income or capital to or for the benefit of the settlor's spouse that there is no indirect benefit to the settlor, which might be said to be a benefit by associated operations bringing the "gift with reservation" provisions into play. For example there would be no objection to making a payment to the settlor's wife for her to buy a fur coat, or a second car which will be for her exclusive use. It would however be dangerous for the trustees to make a payment to her for the purposes of discharging the rates or mortgage on the family house or to buy a family car, which will benefit the settlor as well as his wife. Depending upon the facts the reservation of benefits provisions might still not bite in such circumstances on the basis that any indirect benefit to the settlor was not at the expense of or to the detriment of his wife's enjoyment of the money (just as in *Oakes* the application of income for the education of the donor's children was held to be unobjectionable even if it indirectly benefitted the donor). Nonetheless this is a dangerous area, and one to be avoided if at all possible. (See further para. 6–02 below.)

3–24 One other possibility, for those brave enough to try it, would be to create a discretionary trust under which the settlor is a beneficiary but which is preceded by a short initial interest in possession (say for six months) to the settlor's spouse. Although a discretionary trust of which the settlor is a beneficiary is probably within the reservation of benefit provisions, technically it would appear not to be caught if the discretionary trust is preceded by a short initial interest in possession to the settlor's spouse. The gift into settlement is an exempt transfer under I.H.T.A. 1984, s.18 (transfers between spouses) and the "gift with reservation" provisions are expressly stated not to apply to gifts which are so exempt.[42] Such artificial devices as this must be treated with considerable caution in the light of the *Furniss* v. *Dawson*[43] principles, although the authors consider that the doctrine as presently formulated might well not apply in these circumstances because there is no "series of transactions" (the termination of the spouse's initial interest in possession occurring automatically with the effluxion of time).[44]

One other point which is often raised in this area is whether the "reservation of benefit" provisions can be avoided if a husband creates a discretionary trust under which his wife is a beneficiary, his wife in turn reciprocating with a settlement under which her husband is a beneficiary. The authors consider that such "reciprocal" settlements would probably be caught by "reservation of benefits" provisions. Although there is no specific provision dealing with reciprocal settlements (in contrast to the settle-

[41a] The trust income would of course be deemed to be the settlor's for income tax purposes: I.C.T.A. 1970, ss.445–457.

[42] *Ibid.* s.102(5)(*a*).

[43] [1984] S.T.C. 153.

[44] If this strategy is used, it will be remembered that the chargeable transfer in putting the asset into the discretionary trust would be made by the settlor's spouse on the termination of her interest in possession (rather than by the settlor). The settlor's spouse would also be deemed to be the settlor of the settlement for the purposes of the discretionary trust charging regime under the special rule in I.H.T.A. 1984, s.80 (initial interest in possession of settlor's spouse). The trust income would of course be treated as the settlor's for income tax purposes: see note 41a above.

ment provisions of the Income Tax Acts) it is considered that the creation of each settlement would probably be a collateral benefit for the settlor of the other settlement.

V. PETs and Chargeable Transfers: the Order of the Gifts

3–25 Where a person is making both a PET and a chargeable transfer, the order of the gifts can be important (see para. 7–19 below for a dramatic illustration in connection with gifts of shares in a family company).[45] 3–25

If the chargeable transfer is a settlement on discretionary trusts, all other things being equal the PET should probably be made *afterwards*. If the PET precedes the settlement, and the settlor dies within the following seven years, the PET will become retrospectively a chargeable transfer. This will increase the settlor's cumulative total of chargeable transfers immediately prior to making the settlement and consequently increase the potential rates of charge within the settlement. This result is avoided if the PET is deferred until after the settlement is made. This point is very important to remember when covering the potential tax liability on a PET by insurance to be held upon discretionary trusts. The policy should normally be taken out and settled *before* the PET is made.

VI. Discretionary Trust Arising on Termination of an Interest in Possession

3–26 It has already been seen that the *inter vivos* termination of an interest in possession on or after March 17, 1987 can be a PET if another individual thereupon becomes absolutely entitled to the settled property or to another interest in possession therein, or if the property thereupon becomes subject to exempt accumulation and maintenance trusts or disabled trusts. If, however, a discretionary trust arises on the termination of an interest in possession, that will be an immediate chargeable transfer by the ex-life tenant. 3–26

Notwithstanding the chargeable transfer on the termination of the interest in possession, however, this could still have been a means of avoiding the charge to tax which would otherwise arise on setting up a discretionary trust exceeding the settlor's nil rate band. The potential planning opportunities here have been restricted (but not completely eliminated) by special charging provisions[46] which apply where a discretionary trust arises following the termination of an interest in possession under a settlement created by way of PET. The rules and the mischief which they are designed to prevent can best be illustrated by considering a few examples.

Examples

[45] The order may affect the total tax payable if the donor dies between five and seven years after the transfer because of s.7(5) (which provides that taper relief in respect of a chargeable transfer cannot reduce the charge to below the lifetime charge). Because of that provision, the total tax is likely to be less in these particular circumstances if the PET was made *first*.

[46] I.H.T.A. 1984, ss.54A, 54B.

3–27 Suppose X with an existing cumulative total of chargeable transfers of £60,000 wishes to transfer £90,000 into a discretionary trust. If he transfers it directly into a discretionary trust, that will be an immediate chargeable transfer of £90,000 which on top of a cumulative total of £60,000 would give rise to a charge to tax of £9,500. Apart from the special charging provisions it would be possible for X to avoid this charge by transferring the property into a settlement under which Y who has no previous chargeable transfers has a life interest, but the trustees have a wide overriding power of appointment. The trustees would then exercise the power of appointment terminating Y's interest in possession and appointing the property on the desired discretionary trusts. Apart from the special charging provisions there would be no charge in such circumstances. The transfer into the interest in possession settlement would be a PET which would be free of all tax if X survived for seven years; and although the termination of Y's interest in possession would be a chargeable transfer, it would be within Y's nil rate band so that no tax would be payable. 3–27

The special charging provisions prevent X from taking advantage of Y's nil cumulative total in that way by effectively charging the chargeable transfer at the rate appropriate to Y's cumulative total at the time, *or, if higher, at the rate applicable to X's cumulative total immediately prior to the settlement.*[47] So in the above example the chargeable transfer would be on top of a cumulative total of £60,000, giving an actual tax charge again of £9,500 (assuming that the value of the property had remained unchanged).

The legislation goes on to provide that if there has been a chargeable transfer within the previous seven years also subject to the special charging provisions in respect of the same settlement (or another settlement made by the same settlor) the amount of the chargeable transfer is added to the cumulative total of the settlor for these purposes.[48] So in the above example it would not be possible to mitigate the effect of the special charging provisions by terminating Y's interest in possession in, say, three successive stages, appointing one-third on discretionary trusts on each occasion. The chargeable transfer of £30,000 on the second appointment would be charged on top of a cumulative total of £90,000 (*i.e.* £60,000 plus the earlier chargeable transfer of £30,000); and the chargeable transfer of £30,000 on the third appointment would be on top of a cumulative total of £12,000 (*i.e.* £60,000 + £30,000 + £30,000), giving the same total tax bill of £9,500. What does not appear to be covered, however, is *simultaneous* chargeable transfers by *different* persons. Suppose in the above example X transfers the £90,000 into a settlement under which Y, X and Q (none of whom have any cumulative total) each have a life interest in one-third, but again subject to the overriding power of appointment. If the trustees make

[47] *Ibid.* s.54A. The provisions can apply where the interest in possession terminates on death, as well as *inter vivos* (s.54A(1)(*b*)). They do not, however, apply if the discretionary trust which arises on the termination of the interest in possession lasts for less than six months and is then followed by another interest in possession or exempt accumulation and maintenance trust, or absolute entitlement (s.54A(2)(*d*)). Nor do they apply if they transfer by the settlor into the settlement was more than seven years before the termination of the interest in possession (s.54A(2)(*a*)); or if the settlor is dead when the interest in possession terminates (s.54(2)(*b*)). Transfers into settlement before March 17, 1987 are also outside the provisions (s.54A(2)(*a*)).

[48] *Ibid.* ss.54B(4)–(7).

a single appointment of the whole of the trust fund on discretionary trusts, the chargeable transfers of £30,000 by each of Y, Z and Q would not give rise to any actual charge, because even under the special charging provisions each transfer of £30,000 is calculated on top of X's original total of £60,000 and thus is within the nil rate band.

It will also be noted that the provisions only apply if the interest in possession subsists at the time of the transfer into settlement.[49] Accordingly the provisions have no application where, for example, X transfers property into an exempt accumulation and maintenance settlement for Y (aged 16) contingently upon his attaining 18, but subject to an overriding power of appointment exercisable after Y has attained 18, and which is duly exercised after his 18th birthday to appoint on discretionary trusts.

[49] *Ibid.* s.54A(2)(*a*).

Chapter 4

Death within Seven Years of Gift

I. Introduction

4–01 Where a transfer of value is made within seven years of the transferor's death, the death will affect the inheritance tax treatment of that transfer of value. There are three main effects: 4–01

(a) if the transfer of value was a PET it will become a chargeable transfer;
(b) if the transfer of value was a chargeable transfer at the outset the rate of tax applicable to it may change;
(c) in either case the value transferred may fall to be recalculated as a result of the limitations on relief for business and agricultural property or a reduction in market value between the date of the transfer of value and the date of death or earlier sale.

These changes can affect the charge on the rest of the estate on death by increasing the applicable cumulative total. They can also produce difficulties in the administration of the estate as awkward questions of liability can arise for the personal representatives.

II. Effects of Death Within Seven Years of Gift

Taking first the effects of the death on the transfer of value itself:

(a) PET made within seven years of transferor's death

4–02 By virtue of I.H.T.A. 1984 s.3A(4) the PET will become a chargeable transfer. The value transferred is to be calculated as at the date of the transfer (subject to the points made at para. 4–19 *infra*). 4–02

Example 1
A (who has made no previous chargeable transfers) gives to his son £150,000 absolutely on January 16, 1988. A dies two years later. No tax is payable at the time of the gift but on death tax is chargeable on the full £150,000 at full rates, *i.e.* tax is £19,000 (assuming Finance Act 1987 rates then still in force).

4–03 The rate of tax will be that applicable after taking into account chargeable transfers made by the transferor in the period of seven years before the PET and using the tables in force at the date of the transferor's death where this serves to reduce the tax because of indexation of the rate bands.[1] 4–03

Example 2
As in Example 1 but assume that at the time of A's death indexation has increased the rate bands by 10 per cent. No tax is payable at the time of the gift but on death tax is chargeable on the full £150,000 at the full rates applicable on January 16, 1990, *i.e.* tax is £15,300.

4–04 Where more than three years have elapsed between the PET and death, the rate of tax will be discounted by taper relief.[2] It is worth emphasising again that the taper relief reduces the rate of charge and not the value transferred. 4–04

Example 3
As in Example 1 but A dies on March 25, 1992. No tax is payable at the time of the gift but on death tax is chargeable on the full £150,000 at 60 per cent.[3] of the full rates, *i.e.* tax is £11,400 (assuming Finance Act 1987 rates then still in force).

4–05 In calculating the tax payable on a PET which has become chargeable annual exemptions for the year in which the gift was made and which are otherwise unused may be set against the value transferred. See para. 2–03 *supra* for a discussion of this point. 4–05

Any tax which is payable on the PET as a result of the transferor's death is due within six months of the end of the month in which death occurred and if not then paid in full interest will run, subject to the availability of interest free instalments. Except in very unusual cases liability for the tax rests primarily with the transferee but if the tax remains unpaid for more than twelve months after the end of the month in which the transferor died the personal representatives will also become liable.[4] The position of personal representatives is considered in more detail at para. 4–22 *infra*.

The transferee may elect to pay the tax by ten equal yearly instalments where the tax is attributable to "qualifying property" in the same way as on any other chargeable transfer.[5] "Qualifying property" is broadly speaking land, controlling shareholdings, shareholdings in unquoted companies of over 10 per cent., or where payment of the tax on such a shareholding in one sum would cause undue hardship and a business or an interest in a business. The transferee must still own the property at the transferor's death (or his own if earlier) and the instalments outstanding become immediately payable on a subsequent sale or gift of the qualifying property.

Where payment is made by instalments these will be interest free if the

[1] I.H.T.A. 1984, ss.8 & 9 & Sched. 2.
[2] I.H.T.A. 1984, s.7(4) and generally para. 1–02 *supra*
[3] I.H.T.A. 1984, s.7(4)(*b*)
[4] I.H.T.A. 1984, ss.199/204(7)/204(8)
[5] See generally I.H.T.A. 1984, ss.227/228/229

qualifying property consists of shares, securities, a business or an interest in a business or attracts agricultural property relief.[6]

(b) Chargeable transfer other than PET made within seven years of transferor's death

4–06 A lifetime chargeable transfer will suffer tax at the time it is made at one half of the full death rates.[7] If the transferor dies within seven years of the transfer the tax bill falls to be recalculated. As with a PET in such circumstances, the value transferred is taken as at the date of transfer (subject to the points made at para. 4–19 *infra*). The rate of tax will be that applicable under I.H.T.A. 1984 s.7(4) so that taper relief applies where more than three years have elapsed between the chargeable transfer and death. This is subject to the proviso that taper relief cannot reduce the tax below that already assessed as at the time of the transfer.[8] The appropriate table of rates will be that applicable at the transferor's death where this serves to reduce the tax because of indexation of rate bands under I.H.T.A. 1984, s.8.[9] 4–06

Example 4

A (who has made no previous chargeable transfers) gives to a discretionary trust £150,000 on January 16, 1988. A dies on March 25, 1991 by which time indexation has increased the rate bands by 10 per cent. Tax payable at the time of the gift would have been one half of the full charge, *i.e.* £9,500. The charge recalculated at the time of death would be on the full £150,000 at the rates applicable on March 25, 1991 discounted by 80 per cent taper relief. This gives a figure of £12,240 and the difference of £2,740 between this and the original charge is payable by reason of the death.

4–07 The rate of tax will also change if the chargeable lifetime transfer was preceded by a PET which was itself made within seven years of the transferor's death. In such a case the PET becomes chargeable and increases the cumulative total applicable to the lifetime chargeable transfer. 4–07

Example 5

A (who has made no previous chargeable transfers) makes a PET of £500,000 on January 16, 1988. On January 21, 1988 he makes a gift of £100,000 to a discretionary trust. A dies on March 28, 1989. At the time of the chargeable lifetime transfer of £100,000 the PET is ignored so the tax payable is at 50 per cent.[10] of the full rate on £100,000 assuming a nil cumulative total, *i.e.* £1,500. The charge recalculated at the time of death, however, is on the full £100,000 at full rates with a cumulative total of £500,000, the PET having become chargeable. The charge on this basis is £60,000 (assuming Finance Act 1987 rates then still in force) and the difference of £58,500 is payable by reason of the death.

[6] I.H.T.A. 1984, s.234
[7] I.H.T.A. 1984, s.7(2)
[8] I.H.T.A. 1984, s.7(5)
[9] I.H.T.A. 1984, s.9 & Sched. 2
[10] I.H.T.A. 1984, s.7(2)

4–08 As seen from the examples, where this recalculation produces a higher tax charge than that at the time of the transfer the higher figure is due with the amount already assessed available as a credit. The rules for time of payment, liability, instalments and interest are in effect the same as for tax due on a PET made within seven years of the transferor's death (see para. 4–05 *supra*). 4–08

Taper relief under I.H.T.A. 1984 s.7(4) reduces the effective rate below 50 per cent. of the full rate where the transferor survives more than five years from the date of transfer. As tax on a chargeable lifetime transfer will have been levied at 50 per cent.[11] of the full rate at the time of the transfer it may be assumed that no extra tax could be payable on the death of a transferor within five years rather than seven years of the transfer. This is not necessarily the case. The rules on Business and Agricultural Property Relief can extend the period in which extra tax is chargeable on death to six years and the possibility of prior PETS coming into charge to the full seven years. For an example of this see para. 4–24 *infra*.

Example 6

As in Example 5 but A dies on January 10, 1995. The tax payable at the time of the chargeable lifetime transfer of £100,000 remains the same, *i.e.* £1,500. On A's death between six and seven years later, however, even with taper relief reducing the effective rate of tax to 20 per cent.[12] of the full rates substantial further tax is due because the recalculation at death assumes a cumulative total of £500,000, the PET having become chargeable. The charge on this basis is £12,000 and the difference of £10,500 is payable by reason of the death.

4–09 Further problems may arise where the chargeable lifetime transfer was into a discretionary trust and was itself preceded by a PET made within seven years of the transferor's death. The fact that the PET becomes chargeable will increase the transferor's cumulative total for the purposes of calculating exit and anniversary charges within the discretionary trust (see paras. 3–04 to 3–15 *supra* for a detailed explanation of these charges). Where an exit charge has occurred before the death it will fall to be recalculated and additional tax will be payable. The rules on liability for the additional tax and the right to pay by instalments are the same as for the exit charge itself as are those on interest save that in deciding the time from which interest runs under I.H.T.A. 1984, s.233 the additional charge is deemed to arise on the death.[13] 4–09

It is possible that where the discretionary trust was preceded by a lifetime chargeable transfer attracting business or agricultural property relief and that relief is lost in whole or in part on the death of the transferor within seven years the cumulative total for the purposes of exit and anniversary charges within the discretionary trust will be increased. This is considered in detail at para. 4–15 *infra*.

[11] I.H.T.A. 1984, s.7(2)
[12] I.H.T.A. 1984, s.7(4)(*d*)
[13] I.H.T.A. 1984, s.236(1A)

(c) Recalculation of value transferred where transferor dies within seven years

Business and agricultural property relief

4–10 Where the value transferred by any transfer of value is attributable in whole or in part to property which at the time of the transfer was "relevant business property" or "agricultural property" the value transferred may be reduced under I.H.T.A. 1984 Part V Chapters I and II respectively. 4–10

"Relevant business property" means[14]:

(i) property consisting of a business or interest in a business;
(ii) shares in or securities of a company which gave the transferor control immediately before the transfer;
(iii) unquoted shares not falling within (ii) above but giving 25 per cent. voting control;
(iv) unquoted shares not falling within (ii) or (iii) above;
(v) land, building, machinery or plant which immediately before the transfer was used wholly or mainly for the purposes of a business carried on by a company of which the transferor then had control or by a partnership of which he was then a partner;
(vi) land, building, machinery or plant which immediately before the transfer was used wholly or mainly for the purposes of the business carried on by the transferor and was settled property in which he was then beneficially entitled to an interest in possession.

Property which falls within categories (i), (ii) or (iii) may be eligible for relief at 50 per cent.[15] and property in the other categories at 30 per cent.[16]

Example 7

On his death A owned a house which together with its contents was valued at £80,000, he had £10,000 in a Building Society and was in business on his own account, the business being valued at £150,000. The value transferred by the notional transfer on his death (assuming no liabilities) would be:

House and contents	£80,000
Building Society account	£10,000
Business	£150,000
	£240,000
Less 50% relief on business	£75,000
	£165,000

4–11 "Agricultural property" means[17] "agricultural land or pasture and includes woodland and any building used in connection with the intensive rearing of livestock or fish if the woodland or building is occupied with agricultural 4–11

[14] I.H.T.A. 1984, s.105
[15] I.H.T.A. 1984, s.104(1)(*a*)
[16] I.H.T.A. 1984, s.104(1)*b*)
[17] I.H.T.A. 1984, s.115(2)

land or pasture and the occupation is ancillary to that of the agricultural land or pasture; and also includes such cottages, farm buildings and farmhouses, together with the land occupied with them, as are of a character appropriate to the property."

Relief for agricultural property is restricted to its agricultural value defined as[18] "the value which would be the value of the property if the property were subject to a perpetual convenant prohibiting its use otherwise than as agricultural property."

Relief for the agricultural value may be given at 50 per cent. where the interest of the transferor in the agricultural property immediately before the transfer carries the right to vacant possession or the right to obtain it within twelve months and in any other case at 30 per cent.[19]

Example 8

As in Example 7 save that instead of the business A owns a farm which he has let on a tenancy and does not have the right to obtain vacant possession within twelve months. The farm is valued, subject to the tenancy, at £150,000 all of which is attributable to its agricultural value. In this case the value transferred by the notional transfer on death would be:

House and contents	£80,000
Building Society account	£10,000
Farm	£150,000
	£240,000
Less relief on the farm at 30%	£45,000
	£195,000

4–12 For the purposes of this chapter it is necessary to consider in outline certain other conditions which have to be satisfied at the time of the transfer for the reliefs to apply. 4–12

Broadly, in the case of business property relief the property must have been owned by the transferor throughout the two years imediately preceding the transfer[20] (with special provisions for replacement property or inherited property)[21] and must not be subject to a binding contract for sale at the time of the transfer.[22]

4–13 Agricultural property relief will be available if either: 4–13

(a) the property was occupied by the transferor for the purposes of agriculture throughout the period of two years ending with the date of the transfer or,[23]
(b) it was owned by the transferor throughout the period of seven years

[18] I.H.T.A. 1984, s.115(3)
[19] I.H.T.A. 1984, s.116(2)
[20] I.H.T.A. 1984, s.106
[21] I.H.T.A. 1984, ss.107/108/109
[22] I.H.T.A. 1984, s.113
[23] I.H.T.A. 1984, s.117(*a*)

ending with the date of the transfer and throughout occupied by the transferor or another for the purposes of agriculture.[24]

As with business property relief, there are special provisions for replacement property or inherited property[25] and the property must not be the subject of a binding contract for sale at the time of the transfer.[26]

Where property will qualify both for business property relief and agricultural property relief the agricultural property relief takes precedence and double relief is not given.[27] There are also provisions for agricultural property relief to apply where the whole or part of the value transferred by a transfer of value is attributable to shares which themselves reflect agricultural value of agricultural property.[28]

4–14 In the case of a PET or a chargeable lifetime transfer where the transferor dies within seven years the business or agricultural property relief available under the above tests may be restricted unless certain further conditions are satisfied at the time of the transferor's death or, if earlier, the transferee's death. Broadly speaking, at the time of the relevant death the property in question must still be owned by the transferee and be either "relevant business property" or "agricultural property" occupied for agricultural purposes. 4–14

If the further conditions are not satisfied at the time of the relevant death the restriction of relief in the case of a PET is total. I.H.T.A. 1984 ss.113A(1) and 124A(1) for business and agricultural property relief respectively state that where the value transferred would otherwise be reduced by the reliefs "it shall not be so reduced." This means that the unreduced value transferred enters into the transferor's cumulative total for all inheritance tax purposes including the charge on the PET, the charge on the transferor's estate at death and the discretionary trust charging regime.

4–15 In the case of chargeable transfers other than PETS which become chargeable the relief is restricted in that "the additional tax chargeable by reason of the death shall be calculated as if the value transferred had not been so reduced."[29] The authors take the view that this means only the charge on the chargeable lifetime transfer itself falls to be recalculated as it is only on this that additional tax will be chargeable "by reason of the death." This seems to be the intention of the legislation as evidenced by the contrast between the wording in I.H.T.A. 1984, ss.113A(1)/124A(1) and 113A(2)/124A(2). It is not impossible, however, to argue that the words "by reason of the death" can bear a much wider meaning and that because loss of the relief can only occur on the death, the relief is then lost for all purposes as additional tax thereby becomes payable "by reason of the death" on the transferor's estate at death and under the discretionary trust charging regime. 4–15

[24] I.H.T.A. 1984, s.117(*b*)
[25] I.H.T.A. 1984, ss.118/120/121
[26] I.H.T.A. 1984, s.124
[27] I.H.T.A. 1984, s.114
[28] I.H.T.A. 1984, s.122
[29] I.H.T.A. 1984, s.113A(2) & 124A(2)

4–16 As mentioned, relief is only restricted where certain conditions are not satisfied at the time of the transferor's death or, if earlier, the transferee's death. In the case of business property relief the conditions are contained in I.H.T.A. 1984, s.113A(3). They are that: 4–16

(a) the property transferred and attracting the relief ("the original property") was owned by the transferee from the time of the transfer to the relevant death and;
(b) immediately before the relevant death on a notional transfer by the transferee the original property would have been relevant business property within I.H.T.A. 1984, s.105 (the minimum period of ownership test of I.H.T.A. 1984, s.106 being disregarded for this purpose).

As regards condition (b) the test only requires that the property qualifies as relevant business property on the notional transfer and not that it so qualifies under the same sub-paragraph of I.H.T.A. 1984, s.105 as on the original transfer. Relief is restricted proportionately where part only of the original property satisfies the s.113A(3) tests.[29a]

Where the transferee disposes of all or part of the original property and reinvests the entire proceeds in other property ("the replacement property") within twelve months of the disposal, relief is still available if[30]:

(a) the replacement property is owned by the transferee immediately before the relevant death and;
(b) either the original property or the replacement property was owned by the transferee from the time of the transfer to the relevant death (excluding any period between the disposal and the acquisition) and;
(c) immediately before the relevant death on a notional transfer by the transferee the replacement property would have been relevant business property within I.H.T.A. 1984, s.105 (the minimum period of ownership test of I.H.T.A. 1984, s.106 being disregarded for this purpose).

If a transferee disposes of the original property before the transferor's death and after that death, but still within twelve months of the disposal, reinvests the entire proceeds in replacement property condition (a) above is disregarded and references to the time of acquisition are substituted for references to the time of the relevant death.[31]

4–17 The conditions which have to be satisfied for agricultural property relief to be available where the transferor dies within seven years of the transfer are similar to those for business property relief. Set out in I.H.T.A. 1984, s.124A(3) they are that: 4–17

(a) the property transferred and attracting the relief ("the original property") was owned by the transferee from the time of the transfer to the relevant death and was not then subject to a binding contract for sale and;

[29a] I.H.T.A. 1984, s.113A(5)
[30] I.H.T.A. 1984, s.113B
[31] I.H.T.A. 1984, s.113B(5)

(b) (except in cases under condition (c) below) immediately before the relevant death the original property is agricultural property (as defined in I.H.T.A. 1984, s.115(2)) and occupied at all relevant times for the purposes of agriculture and;
(c) if the original property is shares or securities in a company the agricultural property to which the relief relates was at all relevant times owned by the company and occupied for the purposes of agriculture.

As with business property relief where part only of the original property satisfies these tests, relief is restricted proportionately.[32] Again, as with business property relief, provision is made to cover a disposal by the transferee of all or part of the original property and reinvestment of the entire proceeds in other property ("the replacement property") within twelve months of the disposal. Relief will then be available if[33]:

(a) the replacement property is owned by the transferee immediately before the relevant death and is not then subject to a binding contract for sale and;
(b) the original property was owned by the transferee from the time of the transfer to its disposal and occupied throughout for the purposes of agriculture and;
(c) the replacement property was owned by the transferee from its acquisition to the relevant death and occupied throughout for the purposes of agriculture and;
(d) the replacement property is agricultural property immediately before the relevant death.

If the transferee disposes of the original property before the transferor's death and after that death, but still within twelve months of the disposal, reinvests the entire proceeds in replacement property conditions (a) and (c) above are disregarded and references to the time of acquisition are substituted for references to the time of the relevant death.[34]

4–18 Four particular problems arise with the replacement property provisions and are common to both business property relief and agricultural property relief. These are: **4–18**

(a) The *entire* proceeds of any disposal must be reinvested in the replacement property. In a falling market therefore a transferee who for sound commercial reasons wishes to acquire different business or agricultural property must either expand his operations (which may not make commercial sense or even be possible) or prejudice the entire relief and not just the proportion of the relief represented by that part of the proceeds which are not reinvested. In the present weak market for agricultural land this point may be of particular significance.
(b) The acquisition of the replacement property must occur within

[32] I.H.T.A. 1984, s.124A(5)
[33] I.H.T.A. 1984, s.124B
[34] I.H.T.A. 1984, s.124B(5)

twelve months *after* the disposal of the original property.[35] Even though it is contract dates which are relevant here a transferee may for commercial reasons need to acquire replacement property before disposing of the original property and this will prejudice the relief.

(c) The definitions of original and replacement property do not seem to allow more than one replacement. This may be a particularly acute problem for a transferee who has been given an asset qualifying for business property relief because it is used in a business or partnership within I.H.T.A. 1984, s.105(*d*) or (*e*) and would continue so to qualify in the transferee's hands. If the asset is one which by its nature will require frequent replacement the relief will be prejudiced.

(d) The legislation is far from clear as to how the various further conditions are to be satisfied at the time of the relevant death in the case of a transferee who is not an individual. The transferee for the purposes of both business and agricultural property relief is defined as "the person whose property the original property became on that chargeable transfer or, where on the transfer the original property became or remained settled property in which no qualifying interest in possession . . . subsists, the trustees of the settlement."[36] This does not cover the position where there was no qualifying interest in possession at the time of the transfer but subsequently a beneficiary has become entitled to the property absolutely or to an interest in possession in it. Similarly it does not deal specifically with the question of a transfer to a trust where a beneficiary has an interest in possession from the outset. In the latter case the Revenue will presumably follow the basic rule for inheritance tax that a beneficiary with an interest in possession is to be treated as if he were the absolute owner of the property.

In the case of beneficiaries who become entitled to the property or to an interest in possession in it after the original transfer it should, in the authors' view, be the beneficiary who then has to satisfy the various tests imposed on the transferee if any sense is to be made of the legislation. This could perhaps be achieved under a Revenue concession but it may well be that amending legislation will prove necessary.

Reduction in market value between transfer and death or earlier sale

4–19 Where the transferor dies within seven years of a transfer the basic rule **4–19**
is that the value transferred by the relevant PET or other chargeable lifetime transfer is to be calculated at the time of the transfer. Where the assets transferred have been sold at a lower value before the death or been retained and stand at a lower value at the time of death this could cause injustice and I.H.T.A. 1984, s.131 is designed to remedy this.

Where, because of the death of the transferor within seven years a PET becomes chargeable or additional tax becomes chargeable on any other

[35] *Cf.* the capital gains tax roll over relief under C.G.T.A. 1979, s.115 which refers to replacement acquisitions made 12 months before or three years after the disposal.

[36] I.H.T.A. 1984, s.113A(8)(*b*) & 124A(8)(*b*)

chargeable lifetime transfer the person paying the tax or additional tax may elect to substitute the lower market value at the time of sale or the transferor's death as appropriate for the market value at the date of the transfer.[37] In either case market value is adjusted to take account of any business property relief or agricultural property relief which may be in point.[38]

Example 9

A makes an absolute gift (a PET) of a Rembrandt painting to X on January 18, 1988. At that date the open market value of the painting would be £2 million. The art market suffers a severe recession and X (being an art dealer) falls on hard times and sells the painting during 1990 for its then open market value of £1.5 million. A dies in 1991 so that the PET becomes a chargeable transfer. X can elect for the tax to be calculated on a value of £1.5 million rather than £2 million.

If, however, X had not sold the painting and the art market had continued to decline so that at A's death the open market value of the painting had been only £1 million X could have elected that value rather than £2 million.

4–20 The election can only be made for market value at the date of the transferor's death if the asset is then still the property of the transferee or his spouse.[39] An election for market value at the time of sale can only be made if the asset was sold by the transferee or his spouse in "a qualifying sale."[40] A sale is a qualifying sale if [41]: 4–20

"(a) it is at arm's length for a price freely negotiated at the time of the sale and;
(b) no person concerned as vendor (or as having an interest in the proceeds of the sale) is the same as or connected with any person concerned as purchaser (or as having an interest in the purchase); and
(c) no provision is made, in or in connection with the agreement for the sale, that the vendor (or any person having an interest in the proceeds of sale) is to have any right to acquire some or all of the property sold or some interest in or created out of it."

The relief cannot be claimed for tangible moveable property which is a wasting asset. For these purposes, a wasting asset is one which at the time of the transfer has a predictable useful life not exceeding fifty years.

4–21 We have considered above the ways in which the death of the transferor within seven years of a transfer affects the tax due on that transfer. In passing, we have seen how this affects the transferor's personal representatives and the tax on the transferor's estate at death. Although this book is concerned with lifetime transactions it is necessary briefly to pull together those affects so as to understand the different total tax charges that can arise and the liability for those charges. Only then can ways be considered 4–21

[37] I.H.T.A. 1984, s.131(2)
[38] I.H.T.A. 1984, s.131(2A)
[39] I.H.T.A. 1984, s.131(*a*)
[40] I.H.T.A. 1984, s.131(*b*)
[41] I.H.T.A. 1984, s.131(3)

of providing for the tax or additional tax arising on a lifetime transfer which the transferor does not survive by seven years.

In summary, the main affects are:

(a) a PET which becomes chargeable is brought into account for the cumulative total applicable to any subsequent chargeable transfers including that deemed to be made on death;
(b) where business property relief or agricultural property relief is available at the time a PET is made but is subsequently restricted because further conditions considered at paragraphs 4–16 and 4–17 *supra* are not complied with, the cumulative total applicable to subsequent chargeable transfers including that deemed to be made on death is increased. The tax on the PET will be calculated without the benefit of the relief;
(c) where business property relief or agricultural property relief is available at the time of any other chargeable lifetime transfer but is subsequently restricted, the tax on the chargeable lifetime transfer will be recalculated without the benefit of the relief but this will not affect susequent cumulative totals;
(d) where an asset which is the subject of a PET or other chargeable lifetime transfer has decreased in value by the time of the transferor's death or earlier sale, tax or additional tax arising on the transferor's death within seven years can be calculated by reference to the lower value. This is only relevant to the tax or additional tax arising by reason of the death and does not serve to decrease subsequent cumulative totals;
(e) where tax or additional tax is chargeable on a PET or other chargeable lifetime transfer by reason of the death of the transferor within seven years, the tax or additional tax is primarily the liability of the transferee. If, however, it remains unpaid twelve months after the end of the month in which the transferor died his personal representatives will also become liable. If the personal representatives discharge the tax or additional tax which was primarily the liability of the transferee they are not given any right under the I.H.T.A. 1984 to recover from the transferee.

4–22 On this last point it may be that the personal representatives would have a right of recovery against the donee under the doctrine of contribution summarised in the First Edition of *Leake on Contracts* as quoted by Cockburn C.J. in *Moule* v. *Garrett*[42]: 4–22

"Where the Plaintiff has been compelled by law to pay, or being compellable by law, has paid money which the defendant was ultimately liable to pay, so that the latter obtains the benefit of the payment by the discharge of his liability; under such circumstances the defendant is held indebted to the plaintiff in the amount."

Of particular relevance in this regard is the case of *Brook's Wharf and Bull Wharf Limited* v. *Goodman Brothers*.[43] In that case *Moule* v. *Garrett*[44]

[42] (1872) L.R.7 Ex. 101
[43] [1937] 1 K.B. 534
[44] (1872) L.R.7 Ex. 101

was applied where the operators of a bonded warehouse were obliged under the relevant statute to discharge Customs duties which were primarily the liability of the importer. In holding that the warehousemen had a right of contribution as against the importer Lord Wright M.R., giving the judgment of the Court of Appeal, said; "The payment relieved the importer of his obligation. The plaintiff's were no doubt liable to pay the Customs, but, as between themselves and the defendants, the primary liability rested on the defendants. The liability of the plaintiffs as warehousemen was analogous to that of a surety."

Applying *Brook's Wharf and Bull Wharf Limited* v. *Goodman Brothers*[45] Atkinson J. in *Receiver for the Metropolitan Police* v. *Tatum*[46] summarised the principle thus; "Where A is compelled to pay money which B is legally liable to pay, A can recover from B, on whom the real liability rests."

4–23 The cases suggest that for the doctrine to apply therefore it is "the real liability" or "the primary liability" which must be ascertained. In the case of the further inheritance tax charge on the death of a donor within seven years of his gift it is not clear that the donee can be said to have the primary liability and for the personal representatives thus to be in a position "analogous to that of a surety." Once the liability of the personal representatives arises because of the failure of the donee to pay the tax then they fall within I.H.T.A. 1984 s.205 which provides that "where under this Act two or more persons are liable for the same tax, each of them shall be liable for the whole of it." It will be necessary for the courts to accept that the liability thus imposed on the personal representatives is merely part of the machinery for collecting the tax as was the case with the warehousemen's liability for the Customs duties in *Brook's Wharf and Bull Wharf Limited* v. *Goodman Brothers*[47] and that the primary liability rests at all times with the donee. **4–23**

4–24 With these points in mind an example will serve to illustrate the possible variations in the total tax charge depending on when the transferor dies, the nature of the property gifted and the way in which the transferee deals with it. **4–24**

Example 10

A (who has made no previous chargeable transfers) makes a gift to X (a PET) of £90,000 in cash on January 18, 1988. On September 5, 1988 he makes a further gift to X (a PET) of agricultural property with an agricultural value of £500,000 qualifying for Agricultural Property Relief at 50 per cent. Assuming that Finance Act 1987 rates apply throughout:

If A lives seven years or more from the date of the second PET (until September 5, 1995) no tax will be payable on that PET. If A dies before then, however, the tax payable will be as follows:

(a) If A dies between September 5, 1988 and September 4, 1991: Assuming X still owns the agricultural property and has been occupying it for agricultural purposes tax will be charged on £250,000

[45] [1937] K..B. 543
[46] [1948] 2 K.B. 68
[47] [1937] 1 K.B. 534

(£500,000 after 50 per cent. Agricultural Property Relief) at full rates assuming a previous chargeable transfer of £90,000 (the first PET having also become chargeable). Tax will be £108,000. If X had sold the property before A died so that Agricultural Property Relief was not available, the tax would be £258,000.

(b) If A dies between September 5, 1991 and September 4, 1992:
The first PET will still form part of the cumulative total but taper relief will reduce the rate of charge to 80 per cent.[48] of the full rates. If X has retained the property until A's death the tax will be £86,400. If he has not the tax will be £206,400.

(c) If A dies between September 5, 1992 and September 4, 1993:
Taper relief will increase and the charge will only be at 60 per cent[49] of the full rates. If X has retained the property until A's death the tax will be £64,800. If he has not the tax will be £154,800.

(d) If A dies between September 5, 1993 and September 4, 1994:
Taper relief now means the charge will be at 40 per cent[50] of the full rates. If X has retained the property until A's death tax will be £43,200. If he has not the tax will be £103,200.

(e) If A dies between September 5, 1994 and January 17, 1995:
Taper relief has now reduced the charge to 20 per cent.[51] of the full rates but the first PET still forms part of the cumulative total. If X has retained the property until A's death tax will be £21,600. If he has not the tax will be £51,600.

(f) If A dies between January 18, 1995 and September 4, 1995:
The first PET having now been more than seven years before the death it falls out of account. Taper relief still reduces the charge to 20 per cent.[52] of full rates. If X has retained the property until A's death tax will be £12,400. If he has not the tax will be £40,800.
Summarising this in tabular form:

A's death between	Tax if property retained	Tax if property sold
September 5, 1987 – September 4, 1990	108,000	258,000
September 5, 1990 – September 4, 1991	86,400	206,400
September 5, 1991 – September 4, 1992	64,800	154,800
September 5, 1992 – September 4, 1993	43,200	103,200
September 5, 1993 – January, 17, 1994	21,600	51,600
January 18, 1994 – September 4, 1994	12,400	40,800

Any property remaining in A's estate on his death between September 5, 1988 and January 17, 1995 will be taxed at 60 per cent whether or not agricultural property relief is available because both PETS will become chargeable and the lower rate bands will have been exhausted. On death between January 18, 1995 and September 4, 1995 however part of the lower rate

[48] I.H.T.A. 1984, s.7(4)(*a*)
[49] I.H.T.A. 1984, s.7(4)(*b*)
[50] I.H.T.A. 1984, s.7(4)(*c*)
[51] I.H.T.A. 1984, s.7(4)(*d*)
[52] I.H.T.A. 1984, s.7(4)(*d*)

bands will still be available if (but only if) agricultural property relief can be utilised.

4–25 As this example shows it is often impossible at the time the lifetime transfer, be it a PET or other chargeable transfer, is made to determine the total tax or additional tax which will arise on the transfer itself and on the transferor's remaining estate at death if he should die within seven years. Nonetheless it will always be sensible when a lifetime transfer is made to consider making provision for all or some of this potential tax liability by taking out seven year term insurance on the transferor's life. This area is considered in detail in the next chapter. 4–25

Chapter 5

Planning with Life Insurance

I. Introduction

5–01 The introduction of inheritance tax has naturally focused attention on the opportunities for making lifetime gifts in the form of PETS completely free of any charge to inheritance tax. It is essential however to remember that the death charge remains, that it becomes chargeable at 30 per cent., on an estate valued in excess of £90,000 and reaches 60 per cent., after £330,000. Whatever lifetime gifts are made the death charge will bite on the assets retained and on assets given away within seven years of death. 5–01

The use of insurance to cover additional tax on death within seven years of a gift has already been mentioned at para. 4–25 *supra*. Insurance is also useful in providing funds to pay the main death charge and as a means of increasing the overall capital assets available to one's heirs by way of savings out of income with the advantage of a capital sum payable whenever death occurs.

The use of life insurance in these areas is particularly attractive because of the favourable tax treatment afforded to life policies. The use of trusts to hold the policies and thereby reduce or eliminate the inheritance tax liability is considered below. The proceeds of life assurance policies are exempt from capital gains tax[1] and, subject to certain conditions, from income tax.[2]

This chapter looks at the three main types of life insurance used in inheritance tax planning these being term, whole life and endowment insurance and goes on to consider the mechanics of their use. There is also a brief section on the use of pension scheme policies in inheritance tax planning.

[1] C.G.T.A. 1979, s.143
[2] I.C.T.A. 1970, s.394

II. TYPES OF POLICY

Term insurance

5–02 Term insurance provides for the payment of a specified sum on the death of the life assured before a specified date. If the life assured survives beyond that date no payment will be made and, usually, no premiums returned. The sum payable on death within the term can be level or fluctuating. 5–02

This type of policy has two main uses in inheritance tax planning being:

(a) to protect a donee or the estate of a donor against an increased inheritance tax bill on the death of the donor within seven years of making the gift;

(b) to provide funds for payment of the inheritance tax charge on the premature death of the life assured or simply to provide immediate liquid funds on such premature death.

Taking these in turn:

(a) *"The Seven Year Policy"*

5–03 As has been seen in Chapter 4 the taper relief available to the donee where the donor dies within seven years of the gift does not necessarily produce a straight line decrease in the extra tax payable throughout the seven year period. The extra tax may vary further because of potential loss of Business Property Relief and Agricultural Property Relief. As taper relief does not apply to the value transferered it does not reduce at all the extra tax payable on the donor's estate because of cumulation of the gift within the period. In most cases it is unlikely that insurance companies will issue policies tailored to individual circumstances and either a compromise figure should be adopted or cover taken for the highest liability on a level term basis over the full seven years with any funds in excess of the actual liability being available as extra capital to the heirs. This assumes that the same policy is being used to cover both the extra tax on the gift and on the estate. It is possible that the donee may cover his own risk and the donor may not cover his estate at all. Whatever combination of cover is taken it is recommended that control of the proceeds is with trustees and not the donee for the reasons considered below. 5–03

As the policy will only run for seven years it must not have a surrender value greater than return of premiums if the proceeds are to be exempt from income tax.[3] In practice such policies will rarely have any surrender value.

(b) *"Premature death cover"*

5–04 This is perhaps life insurance in its purest form. It is useful where either: 5–04

(i) the life assured's assets are expected to remain in an illiquid form for a number of years and a forced sale to cover inheritance tax on death could be disadvantageous, or

[3] I.C.T.A. 1970, s.394 and Sched. 1 para. 1(4)

(ii) a young family is dependent largely on earned income from the life assured who has not as yet been able to establish any substantial capital assets to provide for that young family in the event of premature death.

The length of the term will depend on individual circumstances. Ten years is a normal minimum with the maximum depending on the age of the life assured at the commencement of the policy. Where there is doubt as to the term required covertible cover should be considered. For slightly higher annual premiums this offers an option throughout the term to convert the policy to a whole life or possibly a longer term policy at the company's then prevailing premium rates without further medical examination. In other words, a further policy is guaranteed regardless of the state of the life assured's health at the time of conversion. Convertible cover is also useful for a young life assured who wants to establish the basis for a "portfolio" of whole life policies to provide permanent cover for the inheritance tax charge on death (see para. 5–05 *infra*), but is not yet in a position to afford the full premiums on such policies.

Whole life assurance

5–05 This type of cover continues throughout the life of the assured subject to payment of premiums. On death the policy pays either a fixed sum, a fixed sum "plus bonuses" or "with profits" or an index-linked sum. Premiums may be payable throughout the life of the assured or according to an agreed schedule. Whole life insurance provides permanent cover for the inheritance tax charge on death on the assets remaining within the estate and can also provide liquid assets on the death of the assured. 5–05

It is not unusual between husband and wife for the majority of assets to pass on the first death to the survivor. The only substantial charge to inheritance tax is thus postponed until the second death. In these circumstances, whole life cover can be effected on a joint life basis, that is to say the policy proceeds will only be paid on the second death. With two lives assured the anticipated date of payment on the policy is postponed and annual premiums will therefore be lower. Consideration should be given to the funding of premiums after the first death and it is possible to effect a joint life policy whereby premiums cease on the first death. This will mean higher premiums than if they were to be paid until the second death but they will still be lower than on a single life policy as the anticipated date of payment is still to be delayed.

Whole life policies are usually "plus bonuses" or "with profits." This means there is annual participation in the general investment profits of the insurance company. The declared bonuses or profits are added to the sum assured and cannot be taken away. An alternative is a unit-linked policy where each premium buys a limited level of guaranteed cover and a number of units in an investment fund. The level of cover is then the guaranteed cover plus the value of those units from time to time (or in some policies the higher of the two).

5–06 As whole life insurance is normally taken out to provide *guaranteed* 5–06
cover for the inheritance tax charge on death the investment element of unit-linked plans may be considered inappropriate and should rarely if ever

make up a substantial part or the whole of an insurance based portfolio for these purposes.

To take whole life cover of any form for the full amount of the anticipated inheritance tax charge on death will be expensive and because of the accruing bonuses or, hopefully, good investment record, provide more cover than needed if the assured survives any length of time. A combination of whole life and decreasing term insurance has thus become one of the most popular tools in estate planning. An estimate of the rate at which bonuses will accrue is made and an initial sum assured taken which, with bonuses, will cover the full charge by, say, age 65. The shortfall up to age 65 is covered by a much cheaper decreasing term policy where the sum assured decreases at the same rate as bonuses are expected to accrue on the whole life policy.

To demonstrate this form of cover by a simple example:

Assume that A wishes to provide total cover in ten years time on a whole life basis of £10,000. Rather than take out an immediate whole life policy for £10,000 A could, assuming anticipated bonuses on the policy of five per cent compound per annum, take out a whole life policy for an initial sum assured of £6,139 with the balance being made up by a decreasing term policy over ten years. The actual figures for such an arrangement then work out as follows:

	Whole Life Cover	Term Cover	Combined Cover
Year 1	£6,139	£3,861	£10,000
Year 2	£6,446	£3,554	£10,000
Year 3	£6,768	£3,232	£10,000
Year 4	£7,106	£2,894	£10,000
Year 5	£7,461	£2,539	£10,000
Year 6	£7,834	£2,166	£10,000
Year 7	£8,226	£1,774	£10,000
Year 8	£8,637	£1,363	£10,000
Year 9	£9,060	£ 930	£10,000
Year 10	£9,522	£ 478	£10,000
Year 15	£12,763	Nil	£12,763

As will be seen from the extrapolation to Year 15, if the life assured survives beyond the term, bonuses will continue to accrue on the whole life policy so that the actual proceeds will exceed the anticipated liability providing further liquid assets.

5–06A The maximum cover under such a combined policy should be sufficient to meet the death charge assuming previous gifts have dropped out of cumulation. The extra tax if death occurs before the gifts have dropped out should be covered by term insurance as considered at para. 5–03 *supra*. **5–06A**

Endowment policies

5–07 An individual may wish to provide a capital sum for a child or dependant on attaining a specified age or on the individual's death before then. If assets are not available to be set aside in a suitable trust, an endowment **5–07**

policy might be considered. This will pay on the expiry of a specified term or the earlier death of the assured. The term is selected to expire on the person being provided for attaining the specified age. Such policies can include the possibility of capital growth by being of a unit linked or with profits nature.

The endowment policy is most common in mortgages and generally the investment record of insurance companies may not be considered sufficiently exciting to justify the use of an endowment policy for what are essentially investment purposes. Individuals may prefer to set aside regular sums for investment and effect a decreasing term policy to cover the possibility of premature death. Careful attention should however be given to existing endowment policies under mortgage arrangements where people move house or re-mortgage and obtain new endowment cover. The existing endowment policies may already have built up substantial claim values which in comparison to the premiums which remain to be paid represent excellent value. Rather than allow such policies to lapse it may be sensible to make lifetime gifts of them under the PET regime.

Mechanics of Planning

5–08 Once a policy has been selected how should it be held? Where any policy is being used in inheritance tax planning it must be transferred out of the donor's estate. If this is not done the proceeds of the policy will themselves form part of the donor's estate for inheritance tax purposes and if the proceeds are payable on death they will immediately be subject to a tax change so reducing the funds which were to be available to meet the death charge.[3a] 5–08

Annual and normal expenditure out of income exemptions

5–08A Before considering this matter in relation to specific circumstances reference must be made to the annual and normal expenditure out of income exemptions available under inheritance tax. These will often be available to exempt from tax premium payments by the donor on gifted policies. 5–08A

The annual exemption of £3,000 for transfers of value made by a transferor in any year[4] may often be sufficient. Where, however, premium payments exceed this or the annual exemption has been utilised in other ways consideration should always be given to the normal expenditure out of income exemption.[5] This provides that a transfer of value will be exempt if it can be shown:

"(a) that it was made as part of the normal expenditure of the transferor, and

(b) that (taking one year with another) it was made out of his income, and

[3a] I.H.T.A. 1984, s.171
[4] I.H.T.A. 1984, s.19
[5] I.H.T.A. 1984, s.21

(c) that, after allowing for all transfers of value forming part of his normal expenditure, the transferor was left with sufficient income to maintain his usual standard of living."

"Normal expenditure" appears to be taken by the Revenue as meaning habitual expenditure and in the case of policy premiums can apply to the first and subsequent premiums. There will be problems, however, if the first premium is paid before the policy is gifted. The Revenue then argue that the subject of the gift is the policy not the premium and the policy being an asset of a capital nature cannot be within the exemption. In such cases the Revenue only consider the exemption in relation to subsequent premiums paid by the transferor.

The expenditure must be out of income "taking one year with another" so that it is not possible to rely on the exemption where exceptional income was available in one year but thereafter the expenditure could only be supported out of capital. This will be a question of fact as will the final test that the transferor can maintain his usual standard of living with the remaining income available to him.

Planning with "the Seven Year Policy"

5–09 Ideally such a policy will be held in a way which ensures that the proceeds can be applied to meet the extra tax on the donee and/or the donor's estate if the donor should die within seven years of making a gift. Often the only method of ensuring this will be to transfer the policy to a discretionary trust as considered at para. 5–10 *infra*. 5–09

An individual donee effecting a policy to cover the possible extra charge on him and paying the premiums is likely to wish to retain the policy in his own name and this would not protect the donor's personal representatives against a claim for the additional tax if the donee failed to pay within 12 months of the donor's death (for the liability of personal representatives see para. 4–05 *supra*). Similar comments apply where the donor effects the policy and pays all premiums but assigns the policy to an individual donee absolutely. It should also be noted that in such a case although the assignment to the donee and payment of subsequent premiums will themselves be potentially exempt transfers they will all become chargeable on the donor's death during the term. To avoid the administrative problems this would cause for the personal representatives premiums should either utilise the annual or normal expenditure out of income exemptions.

Where the donee is a trust similar comments apply but if the trustees have been carefully selected the risk of them or their successors failing to pay any tax due is obviously less. Paras. 5–11 and 5–12 *infra*, explain how future premium payments need to be made in the case of a trust donee, and paras. 5–14 to 5–16 *infra*, consider the implications for the status of an interest in possession or accumulation and maintenance trust if the trustees pay the premiums.

5–10 In the case of a policy taken out to protect the donor's estate from increased tax through cumulation of gifts within seven years of death this should be held on trusts mirroring the assured's will. This might mean accumulation and maintenance trusts, life interest trusts or even absolute 5–10 assignments. None of these however cover the possibility of the assured changing his will.

To cover the various difficulties in each of these situations the policy or policies could be held in a discretionary trust giving the trustees power to appoint capital and income amongst a wide beneficial class and power to add to that class. Although the original transfer of the policy and subsequent premium payments will be chargeable transfers the annual or normal expenditure out of income exemptions should be available. There will be no possibility of an inheritance tax charge on the ten year anniversary of the settlement because the policy will either have expired or the proceeds been appointed before then. Such an appointment would be liable to an inheritance tax exit charge but provided the premiums are not extremely high and the settlor had no cumulative total when effecting the settlement of the policy (*i.e.* it should be effected before the main gift) such a charge should be at a nil rate. The calculation of the exit charge is considered in detail at paras. 3–06 to 3–15 *supra* and the valuation of the policy which will be required in the calculation is considered at para. 5–19 *infra*. The vital point for these purposes is that the higher the donor's cumulative total before making the discretionary trust the higher the potential exit charge. This is why the gift of the policy to a discretionary trust should take place before (or possibly on the same day as) the main gift.

5–11 The use of a discretionary trust provides the greatest possible flexibility for a policy covering both the donee and the donor's estate and ensures that the proceeds will be available where required. If however such a procedure is considered too complex or there is a real risk of an inheritance tax exit charge on an appointment of the policy proceeds separate policies should be taken for the donee and the donor's estate. The policy to cover the donee's extra tax, whether funded by the donee or by the donor, should in the case of a trust donee be held by the trust and in the case of an individual donee in trust for the donee for life with suitable capital remainders, the trustees being given power to advance capital and a specific power to apply capital by payment of tax assessed on beneficiaries. The inheritance tax treatment of such an arrangement depends on whether the donee or donor pays the premiums. If it is the donee the payments have no effect for inheritance tax purposes. If the donor is to pay the premiums they will usually be covered by the annual or normal expenditure out of income exemptions. If these exemptions are not likely to cover the premiums the donor should make a cash gift of the necessary amounts to the trustees of the policy who then apply it in payment of the premiums. This will ensure that the payment by the donor qualifies as a PET into an interest in possession trust. The extra stage is necessary because to qualify as PETS the value transferred by the payment of premiums by the donor must be attributable to property "which by virtue of the transfer, becomes settled property."[6] If the donor himself pays the premium the payment of money is presumably the value transferred and this money has not itself become settled property. It is not considered that payment by the donor can be a gift with reservation (see para. 6–09 *infra*). **5–11**

The policy taken to protect the estate of the donor should ideally be held

[6] I.H.T.A. 1984, s.3A(3)

on discretionary trusts as outlined above. If there is a possible inheritance tax exit charge on an appointment however the trust could mirror the expected provisions of the assured's will as to residue. Inheritance tax treatment of the premium payments will depend on the exact nature of the trusts but the payments should be covered by annual or normal expenditure out of income exemptions to ensure they do not have to be brought into account and recalculated if the assured dies within the term.

Finally as a general point under this heading it was noted above that an individual donee may choose to retain the policy in his own name where he is paying the premiums. This is unsatisfactory if full protection is to be provided to the donor's personal representatives if the donee fails to make payment of any additional tax. The donor should consider the influence which he may exercise over the donee by insisting that the policy is in place and assigned to a suitable trust before the gift is made. This does not ensure the donee will continue to make subsequent premium payments and where there is real concern on this score a single premium policy might be considered.

Planning with other policies

5–12 Policies effected to cover the main death charge on the free estate or provide additional liquid funds must be assigned to an individual or a trust in which the assured reserves no benefit to ensure that the proceeds are not themselves liable to inheritance tax as part of the assured's estate. **5–12**

If the proceeds are intended for a specific individual or such persons as may inherit from that individual a PET by way of an absolute assignment can be made.

Future premiums where the policy has been assigned absolutely to an individual will themselves constitute PETS if paid by the life assured. Annual or normal expenditure out of income exemptions should, however, be utilised wherever possible to avoid these PETS within seven years of the death being brought into charge (and see para. 6–09 *infra* as to why payment by the donor is not considered to be a gift with reservation). If the donee of the policy pays the premiums there are no inheritance tax consequences. The proceeds of the policy themselves will be exempt in the hands of the donee. If the donee predeceases the donor the value of the policy will form part of the donee's estate for inheritance tax purposes. Valuation of the policy for this and other inheritance tax purposes is covered in para. 5–19 *infra*.

Where the donor does not wish to make absolute assignments the policy can be assigned by way of a PET to an interest in possession or accumulation and maintenance trust. For the same reasons discussed at para. 5–11 *supra* in relation to interest in possession trusts the donor should transfer money to the trustees to allow them to pay the premiums to ensure that the payments are PETS.

5–13 If the donor has no suitable heirs as beneficiaries of an interest in possession or accumulation and maintenance settlement and does not wish to make absolute assignments of the policies to individuals a chargeable lifetime transfer to trust can be made usually with the benefit of annual or normal expenditure out of income exemptions. In these circumstances the **5–13**

wide form of discretionary trust considered above may again be suitable. Here, however, where a whole life policy or a term or endowment policy extending beyond ten years is in point the possibility either of a ten year anniversary charge or of a charge on an appointment of the policy or its proceeds after the first ten year anniversary of the settlement also has to be considered. Generally if an appointment is made within the first ten years the exit charge should be at a nil rate for the reasons outlined at para. 5–10 *supra*. Even if a charge does arise it should be of a low order and cannot exceed nine per cent. (see generally paras. 3–06 to 3–15 *supra*).

Assuming the policy does not mature before the first ten year anniversary the charge at that time will be calculated on the basis of the value of the policy after taking into account the cumulative total of the transferor at the time he made the settlement (see generally paras. 3–06 to 3–15 *supra* and, for valuation of the policy, para. 5–19 *infra*). Obviously if the policy is the only asset of the settlement and it is envisaged that a charge will arise on the first ten year anniversary but not on an appointment before then such an appointment should probably be made in advance of the aniversary. If the charge on the ten year anniversary is going to be nil however the settlement can safely be allowed to run for a further ten years as appointments in that period will be at a nil rate. The position should then be reviewed shortly before the next ten year anniversary and so on.

Payment of premiums by trustees

5–14 Where a policy is held in trust and the trustees pay premiums any income tax relief that would have been available to the donor in the case of policies written under I.C.T.A. 1970 s.226A (see para. 5–17 *infra*) will be lost. In the unusual case of pre-March 14, 1984 policies only now being assigned to trust life assurance premium relief under I.C.T.A. 1970 s.19 will also be lost if the premiums are paid by trustees. 5–14

Trustees can only pay premiums if they have power to do so under the trust instrument. Where this is drawn so as to give power to pay the premiums out of income difficult questions arise as to whether any such payment or, indeed, the mere existence of the power, can defeat an interest in possession in the settled property or prevent the trusts complying with I.H.T.A. 1984 s.71 as accumulation and maintenance trusts (see paras. 2–13 to 2–35 *supra* for a general discussion of such trusts).

The Revenue do not assert that the mere existence of such a power will normally negative the existence of an interest in possession but consider that its exercise may do.[7]

There are comments in *Pearson* v. *I.R.C.*[8] which strongly support the view that even the exercise of the power cannot prejudice an interest in possession. In that case both Viscount Dilhorne and Lord Keith of Kinkel asserted a distinction between dispositive and administrative powers, the latter type of power including a power to pay premiums out of income and not affecting the subsistence of an interest in possession. An interest in

[7] Dymond's Capital Taxes 1986, para. 16.466
[8] [1981] A.C. 253

possession was considered to be only a right to *net* income computed under the terms of the trust instrument.

The authors believe the dicta in *Pearson* provide a good defence to the suggestion that a power to pay premiums out of income or an exercise of that power defeats an existing interest in possession.

5–15 As regards accumulation and maintenance trusts there are two conditions which may be affected by the existence of a power to pay premiums out of income. These are the conditions set out in I.H.T.A. 1984 s.71(1) which (so far as material) states: 5–15

". . . this section applies to settled property if:

(a) one or more persons . . . will, on or before attaining a specified age not exceeding 25, become beneficially entitled to it or to an interest in possession in it, and
(b) no interest in possession subsists in it and the income from it is to be accumulated so far as not applied for the maintenance, education or benefit of a beneficiary."

The authors would again contend that the *Pearson* dicta mean the first condition is satisfied. The second condition, however, causes much greater problems as it refers specifically to income rather than an interest in possession. In *Carver* v. *Duncan*[9] the House of Lords held that in the absence of a direction to the contrary in the trust instrument life assurance premiums were to be paid out of capital. The House went on to hold that even where the trust instrument directed or permitted payment out of income the premiums remained a capital expense. Lord Templeman expanded on this thus, "If the income of a trust fund is only sufficient to pay the premiums on a ten year endowment policy, and income is directed by the settlor to be applied in payment of those premiums, the income beneficiaries are wholly deprived of any income during the ten year period and capital is augmented."

5–16 *Carver* v. *Duncan* suggests that it may be difficult to assert that "income" under the second condition in I.H.T.A. 1984 s.71(1) means net income as computed under the terms of the trust instrument. That being so it may be that payment of premiums out of income, or even the existence of a power to do so, may breach the second condition as the income applied is not being accumulated and the Revenue may not always accept that the application is for the benefit of a beneficiary. The Revenue seem to accept that premiums paid out of income on a policy to cover potential increased inheritance tax charges on the premature death of the donor will not affect an interest in possession. Such premiums "are regarded as costs or expenses of the trustees."[10] This would seem to support the view that such payments are an application of income for the benefit of a beneficiary and this may be the case also with other policies. Unfortunately it is not an area made clear by legislation or Revenue practice. 5–16

In view of these uncertainties the authors advise that either:

(a) the trustees are directed under the terms of the accumulation and maintenance settlement only to pay premiums out of capital or;

[9] [1985] A.C. 1082 at 1102
[10] Dymond's Capital Taxes 1986, para. 16.467

(b) where a full power to pay premiums out of capital or income is included the settlement also contains an express limitation on powers to the effect that they cannot be exercised in a way which would breach the conditions of I.H.T.A. 1984 s.71 (see para. 2–25 *supra*).

Although the latter alternative means that trustees will be uncertain as to whether or not they can validly pay premiums out of income it does ensure that if the point is later clarified in legislation or by the courts so that such a power is permissible in accumulation and maintenance settlements it will be available to the trustees.

Pension Benefits

5–17 A frequently neglected area in planning for inheritance tax is that of benefits payable on premature death under pension schemes or pension policies. In the case of a company pension scheme it is not unusual to find death in service cover, which is effectively term insurance, of four times annual salary. Under most modern schemes the benefit is held by the scheme trustees on discretionary trusts for the benefit of the employee's dependants and the trustees will take notice of any letter of nomination or letter of wishes provided by the employee. In practice the Inland Revenue do not attempt to charge inheritance tax in any way on these benefits. This being so the employee should consider nominating the benefits in favour of children or other heirs to whom legacies out of his free estate would normally be taxable. A surviving spouse can then be provided for out of the free estate (increased where necessary for younger families by way of term cover). No inheritance tax will be payable on the free estate because of the spouse exemption.[11] 5–17

Similarly where the self-employed effect term cover under I.C.T.A. 1970 s.226A (the premiums then being deductible, subject to certain limits, for income tax purposes) this should be assigned to trustees in much the same way as term policies generally and the same points made at paras. 5–09 to 5–11 *supra* apply.

5–18 Where a donor is in a position to effect term cover under I.C.T.A. 1970 s.226A this type of policy should be considered as a way of providing the seven year cover discussed at paras. 5–03 and 5–09 to 5–11 *supra*. This is because the premiums, provided they are to be paid by the donor, will attract income tax relief. 5–18

A self-employed pension policy under I.C.T.A. 1970 s.226 (where again the premiums, subject to certain limits, may be deducted for income tax purposes) provides two benefits. The first is the annuity or pension payable assuming the self-employed person lives to retirement age. The second is a death benefit payable on premature death, usually in the form of a return of premiums often with an increment for investment performance. The Inland Revenue in practice treat these benefits as severable so that it will be possible, without falling foul of the reservation of benefit rules, to effect a trust of the death benefit in favour of heirs and thus ensure it is outside the self-employed person's estate for inheritance tax purposes.

[11] I.H.T.A. 1984, s.18

Valuation

5–19 Various references have been made in this chapter to the valuation of policies for inheritance tax purposes. The general principle for policies is the same as for any other property, that is that the value is the price which the property might reasonably be expected to fetch if sold on the open market.[12] In arriving at this open market valuation it is not usually possible to assume that the market is aware of any confidential information bearing on the hypothetical sale (see *I.R.C.* v. *Lynall*)[13] although there is now an exception for sales of shares in unquoted companies.[14] In the case of a policy of life assurance the market valuation would fall to be made solely by reference to the terms of the policy and the age of the assured. A special rule does exist, however, which gives certain policies a minimum value regardless of market value.[15] This rule does not apply to most forms of term assurance.[16] For other types of policy the minimum value is either the total of premiums paid to the valuation date less sums received under the policy or, in the case of a unit linked policy, the lesser of the aggregate value of units at allocation and their aggregate value at the time in question. 5–19

[12] I.H.T.A. 1984, s.160
[13] [1972] A.C. 680
[14] I.H.T.A. 1984, s.168
[15] I.H.T.A. 1984, s.167
[16] I.H.T.A. 1984, s.167(3)

Chapter 6

Gifts with Reservation

I. Introduction

6–01 A gift with reservation carries with it the serious consequence that if the reservation of benefit continues until death, the property representing the gift at death will be included in the donor's estate. If the reservation ends before death, the donor will then be treated as making a PET. The idea is that if a donor continues to have the use or enjoyment of property which he has given away, he should be taxed as if he still owned the property. A crude example would be as follows: A owns a building which is let: he gives the freehold to S on the basis that S will pay over the rent (net of tax) to A. Here the freehold would be treated as remaining in A's estate. **6–01**

This is a coherent notion, but to give effect to it, a body of estate duty provisions has been exhumed which was notoriously arbitrary in its application: the well advised taxpayer could continue to enjoy the substance of his gift, while technically being "entirely excluded." This followed from a well settled distinction between a physical asset and limited interests in the asset. Thus, if A grants a lease to himself (via a nominee), and gives away the reversion, his continued occupation of the land is referable to his retained interest, not to the gift: in these circumstances, there is no reservation. The position is otherwise if the donee grants the lease to the donor.

It is interesting to compare the anti-reservation provisions in the rules concerning exempt gifts to charities, etc., which pre-date inheritance tax. Here it is provided that, for example, the exemption in question is not obtained if land is given "subject to an interest reserved or created by the donor": see para. 6–03.

Distinctions of the kind outlined above are hallowed by a long line of decisions of the House of Lords and Privy Council. Although not now binding, these decisions are of the highest persuasive authority, and, in the respectful opinion of the authors, are so clearly right that there is no question of the interpretations which they embody not being followed.

6–02 There is one difference between estate duty and inheritance tax which is liable to trap anyone simply putting into practice proposals that were known to be effective for estate duty. That is the the extension of the concept of benefits by associated operations, to include benefits by omissions, and where relevant, this innovation is stressed. Thus, if the gift comprises a freehold subject to a lease held by the donor, the lease having a rent review clause, it would not have signified for estate duty if the donee failed to exercise his rights to raise the rent: for inheritance tax this could well be a benefit to the donor by an omission. 6–02

Where there has been a gift with reservation, but the subject of the gift is disposed of by the donee before the donor's death, provision is made to trace the gift into other property: see para. 6–29 which also deals with accretions. The further implications of a death following a gift with reservation are dealt with at para. 6–34.

Gifts of money followed by a loan back to the donor present special opportunities for avoidance, and these are countered by the provisions considered at para. 6–27.

Benefits reserved to the spouse of the donor are not treated as benefits to the donor, but in the booklet "Inheritance Tax,"[1] it is pointed out that where a gift has been made which benefits the spouse of the donor:

> "there may be a need for clear evidence to show that the spouse has not used his or her benefits in a way which has directly or indirectly benefited the donor."

The Reservation Rules Have No Application To Gifts Made Before March 18, 1986.[1a] Premiums paid under pre inheritance tax policies of insurance are not counted as gifts, provided the policy is not varied post inheritance tax.[2]

[1] I.H.T. 1, para. 45. Issued by the Board of Inland Revenue, February 1987.
[1a] F.A. 1986, s.102(1).
[2] *Ibid* s.102(6)(7).

II. GIFTS TO SPOUSES AND OTHER EXEMPT TRANSFERS

6–03 The reservation rules do not apply to gifts to spouses or to the other exempt transfers listed below[3]: 6–03

small gifts
gifts in consideration of marriage
gifts to charities
gifts to political parties
gifts for national purposes
gifts for public benefit
maintenance funds for historic buildings
employee trusts.

See the suggestion at para. 3–24 for the exploitation of the intra-spouse gift.

Gifts to charities or political parties, and gifts for national purposes or public benefit, are subject to their own anti-reservation provisions, which, as mentioned previously, are more stringent than the general code. Thus, none of these exemptions applies to a gift of property if:

"(a) the property is land or a building and is given subject to an interest reserved or created by the donor which entitles him, his spouse or a person connected with him to possession of, or to occupy, the whole or any part of the land or building rent-free or at a rent less than might be expected to be obtained in a transaction at arm's length between persons not connected with each other; or

(b) the property is not land or a building and is given subject to an interest reserved or created by the donor other than:–

(i) an interest created by him for full consideration in money or money's worth; or

(ii) an interest which does not substantially affect the enjoyment of the property by the person or body to whom it is given."[3a]

For these purposes, any question whether property is given subject to an interest is determined as at 12 months after the transfer of value in question.

III. GIFTS AND TRANSFERS OF VALUE

6–04 As a preliminary it should be borne in mind that this subject is not limited to gifts that are potentially exempt transfers ("PETS"). As mentioned above the reservation rules do not apply to certain exempt transfers (*e.g.* a gift between husband and wife), but otherwise any gift is capable of being a gift with reservation. For example, the creation of a discretionary settlement is not a PET, but if the settlor was a discretionary object then (as will be seen: para. 6–40) it would be a gift with reservation, and as such the settled property would fall to be treated as part of the settlor's estate at 6–04

[3] *Ibid*. s.102(5).
[3a] I.H.T.A. 1984 ss.23(4), 24(3), 25(2), 26(7).

death. Provision is made[4] to avoid the double taxation that could otherwise occur in these circumstances, *i.e.* the charge on the creation of the settlement and the charge on death: see para. 6–34.

IV. MEANING OF "GIFT"

6–05 It will be recalled from para. 2–04 that, for the purpose of PETS, the key expression "gift to another individual" is a defined term. For present purposes, there is no definition of "gift." The dictionary definition of "gratuitous transfer of property" will suffice for most purposes, but it is possible to figure many fringe cases. For estate duty it was held (without discussion or elucidation) that "gift" included a transfer of property at an undervalue,[5] at least where the vendor intended to confer bounty, such intention being gathered from all the circumstances. Where there is no direct evidence of intent, then the existence of manifest undervalue is likely to be decisive.[6] In one part of the inheritance tax code, a distinction is drawn between "gift" and any other voluntary disposition "otherwise than for a consideration . . . not less than the value of the property. . . ."[7] It does not follow, however, that this shows "gift" to have a narrower meaning than that suggested above, because a disposition for less than full value might not be a "gift" through lack of intent to confer bounty. **6–05**

Difficult problems are posed where it is said that a covenant given by the donee represents full value for the disposition: in *A.G.* v. *Boden*[8] it was held that covenants by junior partners to work full time were full consideration for the acquisition of the senior partner's share in goodwill (he not being obliged to work full time). However, it was found as a fact that the value of the firm's goodwill was small, and no general conclusions can be drawn from the decision. Except where the parties are at arms' length, a court would be slow to infer an absence of bounty where assets of significant value are acquired in this way.

6–06 There is of course much in common between the mental element described above, and the "no gratuitous intent" escape provided by section 10 of the I.H.T.A., but the restrictions on the application of section 10 (*e.g.* only transactions as might be expected between unconnected persons) will make for discrepancies. **6–06**

Example

A owns 52 out of 100 issued shares in X Ltd. The value of four shares is £1000: 52 shares are worth £80000: 48 shares are worth £60000. A sells four shares to his son S for £1000.

Subject to the application of section 10, A makes a transfer of value of £19,000. He probably could not show that he would have sold the four shares to someone who was not connected, but it is considered that there would be no gift because of the absence of bounty in the transaction. But if

[4] F.A. 1986, s.104 and the Inheritance Tax (Double Charges Relief) Regulations reproduced in Appendix 2.

[5] *A.G.* v. *Johnson* (1903) 1 K.B. 617 and see *In Re Earl Fitzwilliam's Agreement* [1950] Ch. 448.

[6] *Letts* v. *I.R.C.* (1957) 1 W.L.R. 201 and *Crossman* v. *R.* (1886) 18 Q.B.D. 256.

[7] F.A. 1986, Sched. 20, para. 2(4).

[8] (1912) 1 K.B. 539. See also *A.G.* v. *Ralli* (1936) 15 A.T.C. 523.

A made the sale as one of a series whereby it was intended to pass a substantial part of his holding, it is thought that there would be no great difficulty in considering the bounty question in relation to the overall transaction. Accordingly, if A's intention was to sell all his shares to S for 13 × £1000, bounty would be present. Where the position would be obscure, is if A made a series of sales to different people, each sale by itself being at full value, yet the overall intent being to obtain far less than the value of the original holding. In cases like that, the absence of any concept of "gifts by associated operations" is likely to be significant.

A second area where there may be a transfer of value but no gift is where no property passes from the transferor to the transferee.

Example

A is the controlling shareholder of X Ltd.: S is allowed to subscribe for shares at par when a substantial premium would be justified. The notion of gift would have to be stretched beyond breaking point for it to be held that A had made a gift to S.[9]

Where property is acquired by reason of a disposition without property passing, *e.g.* the grant of a lease, then no doubt this can be fitted within the concept.

Interesting questions arise on the extent to which inheritance tax hypotheses are relevant in determining whether there has been a gift. Take the variation of the terms of a will pursuant to section 142 of the I.H.T.A. It seems plain that any element of gift in the variation falls to be disregarded for present purposes, because for all purposes of the I.H.T.A. the variation is treated as having been made by the deceased: *i.e.* the disposition in question (the instrument of variation) is deemed not to have been made. But what about the hypothesis that a person with an interest in possession in settled property is treated as the beneficial owner of that property? Suppose that A has a life interest in possession: he assigns his life interest for its full actuarial value: under the settled property rules, A is treated as making a transfer of value of the difference between the value of the settled property and the payment received for the assignment. But does he make a gift also? It is considered that he does not: the settled property rules do not treat A as making a disposition of the settled property upon the termination of his life interest, so that the only "disposition by way of gift" that A could make is the disposition of his life interest. On the assumed facts there is no gift because A receives the actuarial value of the interest, and, accordingly, if A remains in *de facto* possession of the settled property after the release, the reservation rules can have no application.

Treatment of partial consideration

6–07 It has been explained that there may be a gift, even though the donee makes some payment. For estate duty, the amount of the gift took into account the value paid to the donor, but for present purposes there is no corresponding provision and, accordingly, if the gift is with reservation, the 6–07

[9] Such a transaction would, of course, be a disposition under I.H.T.A. 1984, s.98.

property is liable to be included in the donor's estate *together* with the consideration received from the donee.

Sometimes it will be the partial consideration that represents the reservation. Thus, if the donor transfers property in consideration of an annuity that is on less favourable terms than could have been obtained in the market, there may be both a gift and a benefit reserved to the donor (the annuity) see para. 6–20. Had the annuity represented full value, there would have been no gift and so the question of reservation of benefit would not have arisen. An outright payment of partial consideration does not represent a reservation of benefit because it cannot be said to come out of the property received by the "donee": see para. 6–18.

V. DEFINITION OF GIFT WITH RESERVATION

6–08 There is a gift with reservation[10] where an individual disposes of any property by way of gift and: **6–08**

(a) possession and enjoyment of the property is not bona fide assumed by the donee at or before the beginning of the relevant period; or
(b) at any time in the relevant period the property is not enjoyed to the entire exclusion, or virtually to the entire exclusion, of the donor; or
(c) at any time in the relevant period the property is not enjoyed to the entire exclusion, or virtually to the entire exclusion, of any benefit to the donor by contract or otherwise: a benefit which the donor obtains by any associated operation is treated as a benefit to him by contract or otherwise[11]: "associated operation" includes an omission.[12]

These conditions reproduce the estate duty legislation on reservation of benefits, apart from:

(a) the introduction of the tolerance: "virtual exclusion";
(b) the extension of "associated operations to include omissions."

The "relevant period" means a period ending on the date of the donor's death and beginning seven years before that date or, if it is later, on the date of the gift. [13] Except where the gift is made within the seven years before death, the relevant period will be those seven years.

There is an exemption for the occupation of land, or the use of chattels for full consideration para. 6–15, and a further exemption for the occupation of land by infirm donors (see para. 6–14).

Any question whether any property comprised in a gift is at any time enjoyed to the entire exclusion, or virtually to the entire exclusion, of the donor and of any benefit to him is determined (so far as that question depends on the identity of the property) by reference to the property which is at that time identified under the tracing rules (see para. 6–29) as comprised in the gift.

[10] F.A. 1986, s.102(1)(2).
[11] *Ibid*. Sched. 20, para. 6(1)(*c*).
[12] I.H.T.A. 1984, s.268(1).
[13] F.A. 1986, s.102(1).

Possession by the donee

6–09 Conditions (b) and (c) represent the heart of this difficult subject: condition (a) is not very onerous and it is hard to envisage cases which fall to be treated as gifts with reservation by reason of (a) alone. All that condition (a) requires is that the donee should assume possession and enjoyment either at some time before the commencement of the relevant period, or at latest, at the beginning of that period: possession and enjoyment do not have to be continuous. 6–09

Example

Lord A has a picture on free loan to the National Gallery. He executes a deed giving the picture to S. Lord A dies more than seven years after the date of the deed. From the time of the gift to the date of death, the picture remains in the gallery. Condition (a) is infringed. If S had taken the picture home for a while at sometime between the gift and the commencement of the seven year period, condition (a) would not have been in point, and the gift would not have fallen within either of the other conditions. Further, the other conditions do not imply the continued enjoyment of the property by the donee, so that a subsequent gift of the property by the donee to a third party would be of no consequence of itself.

Condition (a) is not infringed merely because the donor makes a gift in settlement and the income is accumulated. The gift comprises the equitable interests of the beneficiaries, and they possess their interests "so far as the nature of the gift and the circumstances permit."[14] This benevolent view of the matter avoids a nonsensical result, but deprives the words of much of their meaning.

In the case of interests in land, the nature of the donee's possession and enjoyment will vary according to what other interests exist in the same land. Thus, although a freehold subject to a lease is spoken of as being "the reversion" to the lease, the donee of such a reversion assumes immediate "possession and enjoyment" by virtue of his right to receive the rent. In the case of chattels, there is no corresponding system of stratified ownership, though, of course, ownership may be joint, or there may be equitable interests. But in the picture example above, if at the time of the gift, the picture was subject to a hiring agreement with the Gallery, the gift would not carry with it the contractual right to the hire fee (compare the right to the rent of land which attaches to the landlord's estate and passes with that estate). If the right to the hire fee were to be assigned at the time of the gift of the picture, there would appear to be two distinct gifts:

(a) the picture;
(b) the right to the hire fee

—and whereas the donee would assume immediate possession and enjoyment of (b), this would not be true of (a) until such time as the hiring agreement ended. It would not appear to be possible to invoke the "enjoyment so far as the nature of the interest permits" doctrine, because this is

[14] *Controller of Stamp Duties, N.S.W.* v. *Perpetual Trustee Co.* [1943] A.C. 425.

limited to gifts of property which has inherent limitations on the manner in which it can be possessed and enjoyed, *e.g.*, a policy of life assurance.[15]

Where a donor contracts for a policy of assurance on his own life, gives away the policy and continues to pay the premiums, it is sometimes suggested that the payment of each premium represents a gift distinct from the policy, and that as the donee never assumes possession and enjoyment of the premium, the gift is with reservation. This point highlights the difference between "transfer of value" and "gift." It is considered that there is no gift where no property is acquired by the putative donee (there is, of course, no gift to the insurance company): "transfer of value" however is a defined term, *viz.* a disposition which reduces the value of the transferor's estate, and the payment of the premium as above would certainly fall within this definition.

VI. Exclusion of the Donor and any Benefit to Him

6–10 This part of this chapter is concerned with the two requirements that the property given to the donee must be enjoyed *both* "to the exclusion of the donor" *and* "to the exclusion of any benefit to him." 6–10

Each requirement is related to "the property" comprised in the gift, *i.e.* it is "the property" from which the donor must be entirely excluded, and it is "the property" which must be enjoyed free from any benefits to the donor. Accordingly, the first matter to be established is—what is "the property" for this purpose?

The Property

6–11 In considering whether the donor has been excluded from the property and whether it has been enjoyed free from any benefits to him, there is usually no difficulty in identifying the property, but cases where a single interest is fragmented by the gift require careful consideration. Take the following examples, the starting point in each case being that Dan is the sole owner of the fee simple in possession of Brookfield Farm: 6–11

(a) Dan partitions the farm into two parcels—Greater Brookfield and Lesser Brookfield: he gives Lesser Brookfield to his son Phil: Lesser Brookfield is the property from which Dan must be excluded;
(b) Dan gives Phil a one half undivided share: that share is the property;
(c) Dan grants a lease to himself and his wife Doris: he gives the reversion to Phil: the reversion is the property;
(d) Dan gives the fee simple to Phil on condition that Phil grants a lease back to Dan: the better view is that the property is the reversion but see below;
(e) Dan agrees to farm in partnership with Phil on terms that profits and capital are to be owned equally: Brookfield is declared by Dan to be partnership property: Phil's partnership share is the property;
(f) Dan settles Brookfield on himself for life, remainder to Phil: the property is Phil's interest in remainder;

[15] *Oakes* v. *Comm. of Stamp Duties N.S.W.* [1954] A.C. 57 at p. 78.

(g) Dan settles Brookfield on discretionary trusts, he being one of the discretionary objects: the property is the fee simple.

In (d) Dan's equitable right to the lease should be sufficient to make the reversion of the property, but this was doubted by the Court of Appeal in *Nichols* v. *I.R.C.*[16]: the authors respectfully consider the contrary view of Walton J. at first instance to be correct.[17]

6–12 Where the donor gives property subject to rights in his favour which fall short of a proprietary interest, the gift is not regarded as comprising the property minus the rights. Thus, in *Oakes*[18] the donor gave land upon trust for his children, the trusts including a right of the trustee to charge for management. The donor was the trustee, and his argument that the right to charge for management was something excluded from the gift failed because the right was not in the nature of a beneficial interest in the property. In the earlier case of *Munro*,[19] it was held that a gift of land subject to a lease or a licence to occupy exercisable by a partnership of which the donor was a member, was a gift of the property "shorn of the right which belonged to the partnership." 6–12

But the precise ambit of *Munro* is unclear so far as licences are concerned: the Privy Council said that if the interest of the partnership was not a lease, it was a "licence coupled with an interest." The interest referred to is a form of proprietary interest in land known as a profit à prendre (in this case, the right to farm the land). A licence coupled with such an interest has always been regarded as an interest in land, but it is unclear what other forms of licence fall to be so regarded, the law on this subject being in a state of development.[19a]

The subject of the retention of a severed interest is discussed in more detail below at para. 6–17.

Exclusion of donor

6–13 The requirement that the property be enjoyed "to the entire exclusion of the donor" has to be considered in relation to the subject of the gift. The simplest case is where the gift comprises the whole of the interest in a tangible asset. Suppose that A has for many years owned a holiday cottage. He tires of the location and gives the cottage to S, intending at that stage never to visit the cottage again. Some years later, he has a change of heart, and S allows A to stay there when S is not in occupation. Here the resumption of occupation by A means that the property is no longer enjoyed by S to the entire exclusion of A.[20] 6–13

Where the asset is income bearing (say the reversion to a lease), the donee's possession and enjoyment are represented by the receipt of the income, so that his possession and enjoyment are non-exclusive if he shares

[16] [1975] S.T.C. 278.
[17] [1973] S.T.C. 497.
[18] [1954] A.C. 57.
[19] [1934] A.C. 61.
[19a] See Megarry & Wade "*The Law of Real Property*" (5th ed. 1984), p. 808.
[20] *cf. Chick* v. *Commissioner of Stamp Duty for N.S.W.* [1958] A.C. 435.

the rent with the donor. In the case of a settled gift that confers no immediate right to income on anyone, the beneficiaries are collectively regarded as having possession and enjoyment (see para. 6–09), and accordingly, if the donor is included among them, there is non-exclusive possession and enjoyment, regardless of whether any income is actually paid to the donor.

As will have been inferred from the examples, the donor need have no enforceable right for the exclusion requirement to be infringed. As to rights of occupation, in *A.G.* v. *Seccombe*[21] it was held that for estate duty purposes, occupation as guest did not count, but this conclusion is not consistent with the approach of the Privy Council in later cases. In *Chick*,[22] the test applied was whether, on "the objective and outward facts," the donor was excluded. In *Chick*, the donor had in fact a legal right of occupation, but the decision does not appear to have turned on that. Moreover, *Seccombe* is a curious case where although the donor continued to reside in the house from the time of the gift until his death nine years later, the decision seems to have been based on a finding of fact that there was no "honourable understanding" that he should be allowed to remain indefinitely. One would have thought that *Seccombe* was a good example of exactly the type of case at which the reservation rules strike.

6–14 Part of the thinking behind the result in *Seccombe* was that some limit had to be placed on the concept of non-exclusion if even fleeting visits by the donor were not to infringe the requirement ("any other reading would drive the clause mad"). Were it not for *Chick*, it would be possible to avoid such a conclusion on the basis that the presence of the donor is relevant only where it is detrimental to the donee's rights of occupation. This doctrine of detriment to the donee is supported by authority in relation to benefits to the donor, but in *Chick* it was held to have no application to the question of whether he is excluded from the property. Inheritance tax has the concept (unknown to estate duty) of "virtual" exclusion.[23] It is possible that in one sense *Seccombe* is an example of virtual exclusion, in that the gift comprised not just a house, but a farm as well, and it may be that in the context of the whole gift, it is apt to say that the donor was virtually excluded, given that his presence extended to the house and farmyard only. It is clear, however, that the facts of *Seccombe* would not satisfy the requirements of the other inheritance tax innovation in this area, namely the special provision dealing with dependent relative donors who come back into occupation by reason of unforeseen changes in their circumstances. If in such unforeseen circumstances the donee is doing no more than making reasonable provision for the care and maintenance of the donor, the donor's non-exclusion is disregarded.[24] 6–14

The more usual case of virtual exclusion will be that of the gift of a house, which the donee uses as his residence: if the donor makes only the usual family visits to the house (staying for at most one or two weeks at a time), it is considered that the donor will be "virtually" excluded.

[21] [1911] 2 K.B. 688.
[22] *Supra.*
[23] F.A. 1986, s.102(1)(*b*).
[24] *Ibid.* Sched. 20 para. 6(1)(*b*). The donor may be a relative of the donee or the donee's spouse, but "relative" is not defined. Deliberate impoverishment does not count.

Occupation or use for full consideration

6–15 It has been explained that where a disposition is made for full consideration, there is no gift, and accordingly there is no scope for the application of the reservation rules. The provision now under consideration deals with a different case, namely where there has been a gift, and the donor comes back into occupation for full consideration. 6–15

Where the donor occupies land or enjoys rights over land for full consideration, he is treated as if excluded from the property. Likewise where he retains the use of a chattel for full consideration.[25] These apparently useful exceptions to the exclusion rule suffer from the defect that there is no mechanism for obtaining clearance that the consideration is "full." Particularly difficult problems are posed by agricultural tenancies. In relation to I.H.T.A., s.16 (grant of tenancy for full consideration not to be transfer of value), the Revenue view is that full consideration is the best rent that would be offered if the tenancy were put out to tender, as against the rent that would be fixed on a review under the Agricultural Holdings legislation. Whereas the latter can usually be predicted within narrow limits, at certain times at least, tender rents are highly unpredictable. In the booklet "Inheritance Tax," para. 42, the position is stated as follows:

> "[I]n the case of a lease, [the full consideration] condition may be satisfied where it is shown that both sides to the bargain have negotiated at arm's length and been separately advised and that the lease follows normal commercial criteria in force at the time it is negotiated":

However, the well advised donor will not need to rely on this provision, for he will make a gift only after having carved out for himself the interest he wishes to retain: see para. 6–17 below. Compare here the anti-reservation rule in relation to exempt gifts to charities etc., where any retained interest *created by the donor* must not be at a rent less than market rent: see para. 6–03.

Another example of occupation for consideration is where A gives a parcel of land to B, and A and B agree to farm that land in partnership, *together* with land retained by A. Here, A's rights over the land given to B are in consideration of B's rights over the land retained by A. The issue of how it is determined whether this type of consideration is "full" is considered below at para. 6–37.

The facts in *Macpherson* v. *I.R.C.*[25a] provide a useful illustration of what might amount to full consideration for the donor's retention of possession of chattels: in that case, it was agreed that an individual should pay trustees only £40 per annum for the enjoyment of certain valuable pictures whilst in his custody and should house, care for, repair and insure the pictures at his own expense. The Crown conceded that the agreement was not intended to confer any gratuitous benefit on the individual or anyone else, and that it was such a disposition as might be expected to be made in a transaction at arm's length between persons not connected with each other.[25b]

[25] *Ibid.* Sched. 20 para. 6(1)(*a*).
[25a] [1985] S.T.C. 471.
[25b] *Ibid.* at p. 476d. Not affected by decision of CA [1987] S.T.C. 73.

Changes in the property

6–16 The rules whereby property is traced through certain changes of form are discussed at para. 6–29 below in relation to the question of what property is treated as remaining in the donor's estate if the gift is a gift with reservation. The same rules apply so as to identify "the property" for the purpose of determining whether the donor has been excluded from it. For practical purposes, two points are of particular importance. First, the tracing rules do not apply to gifts of money. Second, there is no tracing after property has been sold for money. Thus, if A gives S a sum of cash which S uses to buy a house, no question arises of A not being excluded from the property, if he spends time there—though it will be appreciated that this leaves open the separate question of whether the visits comprise a "benefit": as to which see below at para. 6–18. The result is the same if A having given S a house S sells it and buys another: A can spend any amount of time in the new house without infringing the requirement now under consideration, but again, leaving aside the separate question of benefits. 6–16

Reference should be made to para. 6–30 for discussion of what amounts to a cash gift.

Exclusion of donor: fragmented interests

6–17 So far, examples of non-exclusion have been confined to cases where "the property" consists of the whole interest in a physical asset. Now consider cases where a limited interest is "the property." As explained at para. 6–11, where the donor fragments a single interest into different proprietary interests, it is only such interest as is given away that needs to be considered in relation to the question of whether the donor is excluded from the property: in such circumstances, the fact that the donor remains in occupation of the physical asset *in which the limited interest subsists* is not of itself determinative.[26] Thus, where the donor grants a lease to himself and his wife, and then gives away the freehold, the non-exclusion requirement is not infringed on account of the donor's continued occupation of the land pursuant to the lease. A corresponding point arises where the donor gives away an undivided share: the fact that he continues in occupation pursuant to his retained share does not amount to non-exclusion.[27] Likewise with the gift of a partnership share: continued use of the partnership assets is not material, because the partnership share is a distinct item of property in itself. Where the fragmentation is performed by the donee, who gives an interest back to the donor, then of course the position is different, and the donor is not excluded from "the property." In *Nichols*,[28] land was given subject to a condition that the donee should grant a lease back to the donor. The Court of Appeal inclined to think (without deciding the point) that the leaseback amounted to non-exclusion, even though the donor had an equitable right to the lease. The Court went on to say that the position would have been different if the donor had first obtained the lease 6–17

[26] *Munro* v. *Stamp Duties Comm.* (*N.S.W.*) [1934] A.C. 61.
[27] *Oakes* v. *Comm. of Stamp Duties* (*N.S.W.*) [1954] A.C. 57 at p. 71.
[28] [1975] S.T.C. 278.

under an "independent" transaction.[28a] The context of this remark makes it clear that "independent" here means "not dependent on some act by the donee": it does not mean that any lease obtained by the donor prior to the gift has to be obtained in circumstances in which the gift was not being contemplated. For example in *Oakes*,[29] the donor gave away a one-fifth undivided share in farmland to each of his four children, retaining a one-fifth interest for himself. He continued in residence, and on the footing that his continued residence did not go beyond his rights as co-owner (each co-owner being entitled to occupy jointly with the others), it was held that he was excluded from the property *i.e.* the four-fifths interest he had given away. In *Chick*,[30] the donor gave away the whole of the freehold interest and 17 months later came back into occupation pursuant to a partnership agreement with the donees. The opposite conclusion followed the different nature of "the property."

VII. EXCLUSION OF BENEFITS TO THE DONOR

6–18 The main body of section 102 speaks of benefits by "contract or otherwise." For the purposes of estate duty it had been held that this expression referred to legally enforceable benefits only, but the Schedule to section 102 extends the concept of relevant benefits to those "obtained by associated operations,"[31] and it is considered that this makes it unnecessary to examine further the estate duty interpretation of "contract or otherwise" (benefits by associated operations were introduced late into the life of estate duty, and received little judicial attention). 6–18

Estate duty learning remains authoritative on the relation that a benefit must have to the gift if the benefit is to be relevant. The relationship is expressed differently in different cases, but even on the formulation most favourable to the Crown the requirement that the gift must be enjoyed to the exclusion of any benefit, etc., is not infringed unless the benefit is "referable to" the gift.[32]

Two points may be made at this stage:

(a) where a single interest is fragmented and part is given away, benefits derived solely from the part retained are not "referable" to the gift: this proposition follows from the concepts discussed at para. 6–17;

(b) benefits arising out of the subject matter of the gift are "referable": this proposition covers not only the direct application of income arising from the gift to or for the benefit of the donor, but also;

   (i) benefits which arise out of obligations assumed by the donee as a consequence of the gift (*e.g.* landlord's repairing covenants);
   (ii) omissions to exercise rights which are conferred by the gift (e.g. the right to review rent); and
   (iii) benefits which, while provided out of the subject of the gift,

[28a] *Ibid.* at p. 285.
[29] *Supra.*
[30] *Supra.*
[31] F.A. 1986, Sched. 20, para. 6(2).
[32] *Nichols* v. *I.R.C.* [1975] S.T.C. 278, p. 284.

reach the donor by an indirect route (perhaps via a company: see para. 6–24).

(c) in some circumstances, benefits which cannot be traced to the gift in a literal sense, may nevertheless be regarded as referable to the gift: see para. 6–20 for a discussion of collateral benefits.

6–19 As will be seen, this classification of referable and non-referable benefits is not affected by the rules relating to benefits by associated operations (para. 6–22 below). **6–19**

The case of *Nichols*[33] provides examples of the types of benefit falling within (b) above. It will be recalled that there a father gave his son an estate on condition that the son granted a lease back to the father. The Court of Appeal inclined to think that the lease back was a reservation, but did not decide the point and considered the case on the footing that it was not. The estate included a residence which was occupied by the donor under the lease, and the lease contained a landlord's repairing covenant. It was held that the donee's obligation under the covenant was a benefit to the donor which—since it did not exist prior to the gift—could not be regarded as something not given within (i) above and, being an obligation which ran with the freehold interest, was clearly referable to the gift. At first instance it was also argued that the donee's failure to exercise his right to review the rent was also a referable benefit to the donor: this argument failed on the ground that omissions were not within the scope of the estate duty rules on benefits, but, as has been mentioned, omissions are expressly included in the definition of associated operations, and it seems clear that now such an omission would confer a referable benefit on the donor, regardless of whether the omission was part of an arrangement made at the time of the gift.

Collateral benefits

6–20 In *St Aubyn*,[34] it was doubted whether the reference to "exclusion" permitted the courts to look beyond benefits arising out of the subject matter of the gift. But these doubts did not encourage their Lordships to overrule *Worrall*,[35] and that case is clear authority for the proposition that some collateral benefits count: in *Worrall*, a father gave his son income bearing property and, in return, the son covenanted to pay the father an annuity (the annuity being less than full consideration). It was held that the son's enjoyment of the gift was not free of the benefit to the father of the annuity. Viscount Simonds said that the *Worrall* principle should not be extended, and Lord Radcliffe said that it did not follow from that case that all benefits are relevant "whether they are by way of reservation out of the subject-matter of the gift or not."[36] *Worrall* was there explained on the basis that the annuity payable to the father could only be regarded as paid out of the income received by the son in consequence of the gift, and it did not matter that the annuity was not charged on the gift. On this footing, the **6–20**

[33] *Ibid.*
[34] *St. Aubyn* v. *Att.-Gen.* [1952] A.C. 15. Applied in *Oakes supra.* at p. 75.
[35] *A.-G.* v. *Worrall* [1895] 1 Q.B. 99.
[36] [1952] A.C. 15 at pp. 25 and 48.

result in *Worrall* would have been different if the gift had been of a non-income bearing asset such as a picture. The point is that the aesthetic pleasure of the picture would not be diminished by the obligation to pay the annuity: see further para. 6–38.

Non beneficial benefits: non detrimental benefits

6–21 The first point to be considered here is the meaning of "benefit": if a donor gives full value for money, is what he receives a benefit? According to *Oakes*,[37] the answer is "yes." In that case, the donor settled property on his children, and the terms of the trust instrument entitled him to remuneration for managing the trust property. The management charge was held to be a benefit, even on the assumption that it was no more than was reasonable; but the authors wonder whether it really is apt to describe payments made in such circumstances as benefits. **6–21**

The second point also arises out of *Oakes*: the income from the settled property was spent on the maintenance of the children, thereby relieving the settlor of expense. On the question of whether this use of the income arising from the gift involved a benefit to the donor, the Privy Council said:

> "It is possible for a donee in the full and unrestrained enjoyment of his gift to use of spend it in a way that happens to produce some advantage to the donor without there being any loss or disadvantage to the donee . . . . [A]ny such advantage is not a benefit within the meaning of the section."[37a]

On this basis it was held that the maintenance payments involved no benefit, though it was indicated that the position might have been otherwise if there had been evidence that the payments had been motivated by self-interest (the settlor also being a trustee). The introduction of the notion of detriment to the donee seems an unwarranted gloss on the statute: all that appears to be required is concurrent benefit, of which one would have thought the maintenance payments were a good example, and in *Chick*,[38] the Privy Council left open this question of detriment. It is in any event unclear why in *Oakes*, the "no detriment" point was not discussed in relation to the management charges.

VIII. BENEFITS BY ASSOCIATED OPERATIONS

6–22 As associated operations are central to the following discussion, the definition needs to be set out in full: **6–22**

> " . . . 'Associated operations' means . . . any two or more operations of any kind, being:–
>
> (a) operations which affect the same property, or one of which affects some property and the other or others of which affect property which represents, whether directly or indirectly, that property, or income arising from that property, or any property representing accumulations of any such income, or

[37] [1954] A.C. 57.
[37a] *Oakes* [1954] A.C. 57 at 74.
[38] [1958] A.C. 435 at p. 449.

(b) any two operations of which one is effected with reference to the other, or with a view to enabling the other to be effected or facilitating its being effected, and any further operation having a like relation to any of those two, and so on,

whether those operations are effected by the same person or different persons, and whether or not the are simultaneous; and 'OPERATION' INCLUDES AN OMISSION."[39]

It is further provided that the grant of a lease for full consideration is not to be associated with any operation taking place more than three years after the grant.[40]

As previously mentioned, the concept of benefit by omission had no counterpart in estate duty, and the capital letters are intended to indicate the enormous importance of this change.

Sub-paragraph (a) above contains reference to property "representing" other property. This is not a reference to the tracing rules discussed at para. 6–29, but to a purely general idea of representation.

6–23 The way in which associated operations are incorporated into the reservation rules reflects the historical development of estate duty rather than the importance of such operations in this branch of the law. That is to say, the main body of section 102 refers to benefits reserved "by contract or otherwise." Associated operations are mentioned only in the schedule to that section. Because so much turns on identifying precisely the limit of the application of associated operations, it is necessary to look closely at the link between the schedule and section 102. Sched. 20 para. 6(1)(*c*) provides as follows:

"In determining whether any property which is disposed of by way of gift is enjoyed to the entire exclusion, or virtually to the entire exclusion, of the donor and of any benefit to him by contract or otherwise—

a benefit which the donor obtained by virtue of any associated operations . . . of which the disposal by way of gift is one shall be treated as a benefit to him by contract or otherwise."

Thus, in relation to the property which is disposed of by gift, associated operations occupy exactly the same place as benefits by contract or otherwise, *i.e.* it is only operations which in some way bear upon the "enjoyment" of "the property" that fall to be considered, so that there is no question of the concept of associated operations blurring the distinction between interests retained and interests given away. To achieve that result it would have been necessary to provide that:

"It shall be assumed that any property which is disposed of by way of gift is NOT enjoyed to the entire exclusion etc . . . where the donor obtains any benefit by associated operations."

It will be appreciated that this form of words is fundamentally different from the statutory "In determining whether." To illustrate, take the by-now familiar example of the donor granting a lease to himself and his wife,

[39] I.H.T.A. 1984, s.268(1).
[40] *Ibid*. sub. (2).

and then making a gift of the freehold. It will be seen from the definition of associated operations given above that the grant of the lease and the gift are within the definition: but the lease does not involve concurrent enjoyment of the donor and donee of "the property", because "the property" is the reversion only. Accordingly, "in determining whether the property is enjoyed to the entire exclusion of the donor" the benefit of the lease is not material. But the position alters if the rent is reviewable and the donee fails to exercise his rights when the time for review comes round: one feature of "the property" is the right to review the rent, and if the donee fails to exercise the right he is not enjoying the property to the full by reason of an omission which benefits the donor.

As confirmation of the view taken above on the place of associated operations in the scheme of relevant benefits, reference may be made to *Nichols* discussed at para. 6–19 above. There, although the estate duty associated operations provisions were invoked in argument, the case proceeded on the basis that the traditional distinction between interests given and interests retained held good, and it was not submitted that the grant of the lease back by the son to his father was *per se* a relevant benefit merely because it was an operation "associated" with the gift.

Further confirmation of the view taken above is to be found in a published exchange of correspondence with the Capital Taxes Office: the question was asked whether, if the owner of freehold property grants a lease to himself and his wife for twenty years at a peppercorn rent, and then gives the reversionary interest to his son, the lease would be a reserved benefit. The answer was no "if the true construction of the transaction is that the gift is of the reversionary interest only."[41–43]

Associated operations in perspective

6–24 It has been explained that the concept of benefits by associated operations does not lessen the importance of identifying "the property," and that benefits by associated operations are relevant only to the extent that they involve concurrent enjoyment by the donor and the donee of "the property." Further, although the definition includes operations carried out by different people, the only relevant recipient of benefits remains the donor. In view of these considerations, it appears to the authors that the associated operations provisions extend the range of material benefits in only three ways: 6–24

(a) by making it clear that benefits do not have to be legally enforceable by the donor;
(b) by introducing the concept of benefit by omission.
(c) by legislating for indirect benefits.

Two examples may help to show how these extensions might work in practice: A is the owner of land which is farmed by a company of which he is a director, the company having an annual tenancy. A gives the land to S, it being understood that S will not seek to raise the rent, as this would

[41–43] Law Society's Gazette, December 10, 1986 at pp. 3728/9.

reduce the company's ability to pay remuneration to A. The omission by S to raise the rent is an operation "effected with a view to facilitating" the payment of undiminished remuneration to A. These two events are therefore associated operations as defined: the remuneration is a benefit to A, and the provision of the benefit impairs the donee's enjoyment of the property. Accordingly, the gift to S is a gift with reservation.

The second example involves dividend waivers: A gives part of his shareholding in a company to S. With a view to maintaining A's dividend income from the company at its former level, S waives the dividend on the shares he has been given, thus enabling the company to pay a higher dividend on A's shares. Here, the waiver and the payment are associated operations, and the benefit to A is at the expense of the donee's enjoyment of the gift. Again therefore there is a gift with reservation.

See para. 6–39 and para. 6–40 for further discussion of indirect benefits, in the contexts of gifts of shares, and settlements where the settlor's spouse is a beneficiary, and reference may also be made to para. 45 of the booklet "Inheritance Tax" cited at para. 6–02 above.

Joint omissions

6–25 It is unclear to what extent, if at all, joint omissions count for present purposes. For example, suppose that A gives two one-third partnership shares to B and C, retaining the third share for himself. The terms of the partnership are such that it would be beneficial to B and C (and detrimental to A) for the partnership to be dissolved, but a dissolution can only be effected by a majority. The gifts were made on the understanding that B and C would not dissolve against A's wishes. There is no obvious reason why the joint omission of B and C should not be relevant, but the point is a novel one on which other views may be possible. 6–25

Changes in the property

6–26 This subject has been touched on in relation to the exclusion of the donor requirement at para. 6–16 above, and the same provisions apply for the purposes of identifying "the property": detailed discussion is to be found at para. 6–29 below. 6–26

IX. GIFTS AND LOANBACKS

6–27 The case where, following a gift, the donee makes a loan to the donor is subject to special rules because of the weakness of the tracing provisions so far as cash gifts are concerned. Thus, suppose that A gives B £10,000, which B lends back to A. Without special provision the position would be as follows: 6–27

(a) the gift would be a PET;
(b) the cash could not be traced, so that the gift would not be with reservation;
(c) the debt to B would be an allowable deduction in valuing A's estate,

so that he would continue to have the use of the money whilst at the same time he would have reduced his estate by £10,000.

Hence it is provided that, in the circumstances described above, the debt due to B is not deductible in valuing A's estate on death,[44] and if A repays the debt, he is then treated as having made a PET.[45] The provision in question—F. A. 1986, s.103—is not limited to simple transactions of this kind: in particular, the general rule is that the section is triggered by any gift at any time by the donor/debtor.[46] Accordingly, it is not possible to circumvent the section by having the loan precede the gift. Gifts via third parties are also caught.[47]

Regulations provide relief against the double-charges that could arise in these circumstances: see the examples to regulation 6 in Appendix 2.

X. TRANSACTIONS WITH POLICIES OF INSURANCE

6–28 Specific provision is made to cover certain types of insurance transaction which might otherwise escape the reservation code. First, section 103 mentioned above deals with deferred premiums under policies of life insurance which benefit third parties. If any premium under such a policy is outstanding at death, it is not an allowable deduction in valuing the assured's estate.[48] Second, any gift of a policy of life insurance on the life of the donor and/or the spouse of the donor is treated as a gift with reservation if the benefits payable on death vary according to benefits taken during life by the donor and/or the spouse of the donor.[49] 6–28

XI. TRACING THE PROPERTY

6–29 The tracing rules now to be considered have three applications in the present context: first, they identify "the property" for the purpose of determining whether the donor has been excluded from it and whether the donee's enjoyment of the property has been to the exclusion of any benefit to the donor.[50] Second, where there has been a reservation of benefit which lasts until the donor's death, the tracing rules determine what property is to be treated as being within his estate at death. Third, where the reserved benefit terminates before death, these provisions identify the subject matter of the notional transfer of value that then takes place.[51] Although at first sight the rules appear to form an elaborate code, in practice they are greatly simplified by the fact that property is not followed once it has been sold for cash (except in the case of settled gifts). 6–29

44 F.A. 1986, s.103(1).
45 *Ibid.* s.103(*b*).
46 *Ibid.* s.103(1)(*b*): but the application of the section is limited to the amount given by the donor/debtor for facilitating the loan: subs. (2).
47 *Ibid.* s.103(3)(4).
48 *Ibid.* s.103(7).
49 *Ibid.* Sched. 20 para. 7.
50 *Ibid.* Sched. 20 para. 6(2).
51 *Ibid.* Sched. 20 para. 2(1).

Cash gifts and sales for cash

6–30 The effect of the provisions concerning cash transactions (other than settlements of cash) is such as to make the other rules unimportant: 6–30

(a) a gift of cash is not subject to tracing,[52]
(b) the sale of property comprised in a non-cash gift puts a stop to further tracing.[53]

Accordingly, in these two cases, "the property" is, or becomes, the cash,[54] without regard to subsequent events.

In *Ralli Bros. Trustee Co.* v. *I.R.C.*[55] there is an interesting discussion of questions such as "if A contracts to buy Blackacre from B, and C, by way of gift, discharges the purchase price, is this a gift of cash or of Blackacre?" The suggested answer was that it is a gift of cash. In an earlier case[56] Lord Reid said that where a gift of money is subject to an obligation to buy some particular asset, this might well be viewed as a gift of the asset. It is considered that this kind of approach is more likely to be followed today and indeed, even where there is no binding obligation but merely an understanding, in some cases *Ramsay* could be invoked to import an obligation.

Where "the property" exists in a purely notional form because of the rules relating to cash transactions, it is considered that it is impossible to apply the reservation rules because, as has been explained, all questions of reservation of benefit turn on the donor's actual exclusion from the property and the donee's actual enjoyment of it free from any benefits to the donor. The legislation purports to keep this issue open by providing that[57]:

> "Any question whether any property comprised in a gift was at any time enjoyed to the entire exclusion, or virtually to the entire exclusion, of the donor and of any benefit to him shall (so far as that question depends upon the identity of the property) be determined by reference to the property which is at that time treated as property comprised in the gift."

However, in the absence of some provision which makes the question *not* depend upon the identity of "the property"—and it will be recalled that the associated operations rules do not have that effect—the "without prejudice" words in brackets achieve nothing.

Non-cash transactions

6–31 Where property other than cash is received in substitution for the property comprised in a gift, the gift is treated as having comprised the substituted property.[58] Accruals such as bonus shares are treated as being within 6–31

[52] *Ibid.* Sched. 20 para. 2(2)(*b*).
[53] *Ibid.* Sched. 20 para. 2(1) when read with para. 2(2)(*b*).
[54] Cash or "sum of money" of course includes cheques etc.: *Gresham Life Assurance Soc. Ltd.* v. *Bishop* [1902] A.C. 287.
[55] [1968] Ch. 215.
[56] *Sneddon* v. *Lord Advocate* [1954] A.C. 257 at p. 280.
[57] F.A. 1986, Sched. 20 para. 6(2).
[58] *Ibid.* para. 2(3).

the original gift (provision being made for rights issues, and similar transactions, so as to allow for expense incurred by the donee).[59]

Settled gifts

6–32 Property which is settled, whether by the donor or the donee, is represented by the settled property for the time being (including the proceeds of any loan made by the donor).[60] Accumulations of income are included.[61] Distributions of capital are treated as remaining in the settlement.[62] 6–32

Gifts by donee or death of donee

6–33 Settlements made by the donee of "the property" are considered above: in the case of other gifts, whether during life or on death, the property is followed as if the donee continued to own it.[63] 6–33

Merger

6–33A If the property received by way of gift merges with, or is otherwise extinguished in, property belonging to the donee, the donee is treated as continuing to own the extinguished property.[63a] For example, A owns a 50 year lease of Blackacre, and B owns the freehold. A gives the lease to B. By operation of law, the lease merges with the freehold, but for present purposes, it would be treated as continuing to exist, so that if A remained in occupation of Blackacre, he would not be excluded from "the property" (*i.e.* the lease). Accordingly, the lease would be treated as remaining in A's estate, though, of course, it would continue to waste. 6–33A

XII. CONSEQUENCES OF GIFT WITH RESERVATION

6–34 Where the reservation continues until death, the property in question is treated as being within the donor's estate at death.[64] Where the reservation ends within the seven years before death, the donor is then treated as making a PET of the property.[65] This last rule applies regardless of the form of 6–34

[59] *Ibid.* para. 2(3)(*c*), (6), (7) and para. 3.
[60] *Ibid.* para. 5(1)(3).
[61] As being "property comprised in the settlement" on "the material date," *i.e.* the death of the donor, or the time the reservation ceases: para. 1(1). Para. 5(5) (which purports to exclude certain accumulations) is otiose because it applies only to accumulations made "after the material date," and there is no basis on which such accumulations could, in any event, be taken into account.
[62] *Ibid.* para. 5(2): this provision may be wide enough to cover distributions of income from discretionary settlements.
[63] *Ibid.*, para. 2(4).
[63a] *Ibid.*, para. 2(4), (5)(*b*).
[64] *Ibid.* s.102(3).
[65] *Ibid.* s.102(4).

the original gift, so that the notional PET is treated as made, even where the original gift did not qualify as a PET.

It will be appreciated that the rules set out above are liable to create multiple charges in respect of the same gift. The main cases are as follows:

(a) the donor makes a PET within seven years of death, but reserves a benefit: in these circumstances, there will be a liability in respect of the PET, and either the property will be included in the estate at death or there will be a notional PET on the termination of the reservation;

(b) the donor makes a chargeable transfer at any time before death and reserves a benefit with the results as in (a).

Relief from double-charge is made by regulation.[66] The regulations contain helpful illustrations and notes, and these are reproduced as Appendix 2. See especially the examples to regulation 5.

Agricultural and Business Property Relief

6–35 The question of the application of these reliefs may arise: 6–35

(a) where "the property" is treated as remaining in the donor's estate at death;

(b) where the donor is treated as making a PET on the termination of a reserved benefit.

At any such time the appropriate relief is given to the donor, for which at that time *the donee* would have qualified, except that in determining whether shares qualify for 50 per cent., business property relief, the shares are treated as if they continued to belong to the *donor*.[67] As regards the rules concerning minimum periods of ownership or occupation, the donee is credited with:

(a) the donor's ownership prior to the donor's gift to the donee;

(b) the donor's occupation both prior to the gift and subsequent to the gift.[68]

There are special provisions concerning agricultural property companies.[69]

Where property is sold for cash, then, as has been explained, any reservation necessarily terminates with the sale (see para. 6–30). In these circumstances, there is a notional PET, but where there is a time lag between contract and completion, it appears that, in strictness, there can be no business or agricultural relief. The reason is as follows: under the tracing rules discussed at para. 6–29, the proceeds of sale are only substituted for the original property upon receipt. That then is the time at which the reservation ceases, but a transfer made by the donee/vendor at that time would

[66] *Ibid*. s.104 and the Inheritance Tax (Double Charges Relief) Regulations 1987 (S.I. 1987 No. 1130) reproduced in Appendix 2.

[67] *Ibid*. Sched. 20, para. 8 as amended.

[68] *Ibid*. Sched. 20 para. 8(2).

[69] *Ibid*. Sched. 20 para. 8(3).

not qualify for business property or agricultural relief because of the existence of the contract for sale.[70]

If the donee dies, and the reservation continues after his death, the above rules apply by reference to his personal representatives or the persons in whom the property is subsequently vested.[71]

XIII. THE RESERVATION RULES ILLUSTRATED

6–36 The object here is to show how the reservation rules will affect some transactions that are likely to be encountered in practice. The illustrations are grouped under five main heads: 6–36

(a) gifts of interests in land;
(b) gifts of partnership shares;
(c) gifts of shares in family companies.
(d) creation of settlements
(e) interests in private residences

Some of these subjects are also discussed in chapters 7 and 8.

Gifts of interests in land

6–37 At para. 6–11, examples are given of different types of "property" for the purposes of the reservation rules, the starting point in each case being the ownership of Brookfield Farm by Dan. Looking further at some of those examples: 6–37

1. Dan partitions Brookfield into Greater Brookfield and Lesser Brookfield: he gives Lesser Brookfield to Phil, and at the same time, Dan and Phil agree to farm the two properties in partnership (the land not being partnership property).

It will be appreciated at once that Dan's continued presence on Lesser Brookfield will infringe the exclusion of the donor requirement, unless the full consideration exemption applies (para. 6–15). On a simple view, this depends on whether Greater Brookfield has at least the same agricultural value as Lesser Brookfield. However, it is considered that the full consideration issue has to be examined in the light of the totality of the contract between the donor and the donee, so that, for example, if the two properties are of equal value, and the capital contribution of the partners is equal, but Dan is entitled to a greater share of the profits than Phil, even though his labour input is less, it is thought that the full consideration exemption would not apply. That is to say, if considered as a whole, the arrangement under which the donor occupies land that he has given away, contains an element of bounty in the donor's favour, it cannot be said that that his occupation is for "full consideration."

A separate point is this: at the time of the gift, Phil covenants to work full time in the business: is this covenant a benefit to the donor in the same way that the landlord's repairing covenant was held to be a benefit in *Nichols* (para. 6–19)? The answer is "no" because the benefit of the coven-

[70] I.H.T.A. 1984, ss.113 and 124.
[71] F.A. 1986 Sched. 20, para. 8(5).

ant does not arise out of the subject of the gift. But see para. 6–38 where the subject of the gift is a share in a partnership.

2. The same facts as above, but, prior to the gift, Dan and Phil were already farming the whole of Brookfield as partners.

Phil acquires Lesser Brookfield subject to the existing rights of the partners, which in the absence of a tenancy will be a licence (*cf. Munro*), and Dan's continued occupation in pursuance of those rights will not be a reservation.

The question of reservation can arise only to the extent that Phil has rights which he omits to exercise. If the "no detriment" argument is sound (see para. 6–21), then the omission to terminate would not be relevant if not detrimental to Phil. Alternatively, since the putative benefit would be Dan's continued occupation of Lesser Brookfield after the licence could have been terminated, the "full consideration" exemption would be available in the sense that there would be a mutual forebearance to terminate licences: but, of course, it would have to be demonstrated that, on the whole, Dan's omission was the "fair equivalent" of Phil's.

3. Dan gives Phil a one-half, undivided share in Brookfield, and they agree to farm in partnership.

When the Finance Bill 1986 was being considered in committee, the official view[72] of this type of case was that Dan's continued occupation was for full consideration because he "allows" Phil to occupy also. This answer shows an imperfect understanding of the rights of co-owners and, indeed, confuses the example now under consideration with that discussed at 1. above. One co-owner does not allow another to occupy, because he has no power to exclude: they each enjoy the right to occupy and neither can exclude the other, regardless of the relative sizes of their respective interests.[73]

The position immediately after the gift is that Dan simply continues to occupy in right of his retained interest (*cf. Oakes*), and there is no reservation. But suppose that Dan retained only a one-tenth undivided share yet enjoyed a half share of the profit? In these circumstances it would be necessary to consider Phil's rights (a) as partner, and (b) as co-owner. If Dan was enjoying a share of profits out of all proportion to his contribution to the partnership, then Phil's failure to dissolve the partnership would probably be a benefit to Dan by an associated omission. Alternatively, Dan's excess profit must be taken to come out of the nine-tenths share given to Phil, and on this basis would be a collateral benefit of the kind discussed in para. 6–20.

4. Dan grants a lease of Brookfield at a low rent to himself and Doris and gives the freehold to Phil: Dan and Doris farm in partnership thereafter.

Dan's continued occupation under the lease is not relevant because the lease is a retained interest. If the rent is reviewable periodically and Phil fails to exercise his rights to the full, there will be a benefit to Dan by an

[72] *Hansard*, June 10, 1986, col. 425.

[73] *Bull* v. *Bull* [1955] 1 Q.B. 234 and see generally, Megarry & Wade *The Law of Real Property* (5th ed., 1984), p. 441.

associated omission. If the lease contains landlord's repairing covenants, the covenants will represent relevant benefits (see para. 6–19 above).

Gifts of partnership shares

6–38 There is a well settled distinction between the assets of a partnership, and a partner's share in the partnership. Individual members have no beneficial interest in the assets during the continuation of the business, save for a future interest in the net assets following a dissolution.[74] 6–38

It follows from this that a gift of a share in a partnership is not the same as a gift of an interest in the underlying assets, the "property" for present purposes being the partnership share itself. Accordingly, if the partnership holds land, it is not material that the donor of a share in the business continues to occupy the land as partner.

As to covenants given by a donee partner (such as a covenant to work in the business), it appears to the authors that these are not capable of being referable benefits to the donor. The difference between such covenants, and the fatal, landlord's repairing covenant in *Nichols* (para. 6–19), is that the cost of the repairs could only be regarded as paid out of the rent, so as to make the benefit of the covenant come out of the subject of the gift in the sense explained at para. 6–20. By contrast a covenant to work full-time, although a benefit to the donor, in no relevant sense comes out of the subject of the gift. Of course, the new partner's covenants may be so valuable that the transaction is in any event not one of gift (*cf. Boden* para. 6–05).

Gifts of shares in companies

6–39 It is quite hard to figure cases of gifts of shares with reservation. The question that arises most frequently is whether the continued employment of the donor by the company, after the gift, could involve a referable benefit. In the ordinary case the answer will be "no," because the benefit of being remunerated does not arise out of the subject of the gift (see para. 6–18). Even where the shares given to the donee give him the power to procure the termination of the donor's employment, the failure of the donee to exercise that power will usually not involve a benefit by associated operations, because where the donor is merely paid at a commercial rate, it could not be said that the donee's failure to exercise his voting power to end the employment was an omission "effected with reference to" the payment of the remuneration: in such circumstances, it would not occur to the donee so to exercise his voting power, so there would be no nexus between the omission and the payment. Where, however, the donor is being over paid to such an extent that the company's ability to pay dividends is reduced, then it may well be that the failure of the donee to exercise his voting power so as to secure the lawful termination of the donor's employment would be a referable benefit to the donor by associated operations. 6–39

For a discussion of dividend waivers, see para. 6–24.

[74] *Marshall* v. *Maclure* (1885) 10 App.Cas. 325.

Creation of settlements

6–40 The issues of general interest here are as follows: 6–40

(a) is there any objection to the settlor being a trustee, or otherwise holding fiduciary powers?
(b) will a resulting trust to the settlor make the gift vulnerable?
(c) what are the consequences of;
  (i) the settlor being a discretionary object;
  (ii) the settlor's spouse being a discretionary object;
  (iii) the trustees having power to include the settlor as a discretionary object?

As to the settlor being a trustee or having fiduciary powers (for example, the power to veto the sale of trust property), it is clear that, in either case, there is no reservation.[75]

Where the settled property may return to the settlor under a resulting trust (say in the event of no beneficiary attaining 25), the settlor's equitable interest is something not included in the gift, so that it involves no reservation.[76]

Turning finally to discretionary trusts, as has been explained, the presence of the settlor among the class of discretionary objects means that the donees, as a class, do not enjoy the property to the exclusion of the settlor: it is immaterial whether any payment is made to the settlor because, collectively, the members of the class "possess and enjoy" the property together, even while the income is being accumulated (see para. 6–09).

Where the spouse of the settlor is included in the discretionary class, this will not of itself involve a reservation, but it is considered that, for example, distributions to the settlor's spouse for the purpose of providing for their joint maintenance would involve a benefit by associated operations (see para. 6–24).

Where the trustees merely have a power to include the settlor as a beneficiary, the position is obscure: the authors incline to think there is no reservation, but the official view is otherwise.[77]

Interests in private residences

6–41 If the donor gives away his entire interest but remains in occupation without paying full consideration, this will plainly be a gift with reservation. 6–41

If the donor grants to himself a fixed-term lease at a low rent, and gives away the reversion, the landlord having no repairing obligations, the donor's continued occupation under the lease will involve no reservation: see para. 6–17 and especially the discussion of "independent" transaction.

If the donor gives the donee an undivided share, but the donee does not take up residence as an occupier, this will be a gift with reservation on the ground that the donee does not bona fide assume possession and enjoy-

[75] *Oakes supra* at p. 72 and see the booklet "Inheritance Tax" at para. 44.
[76] See the booklet "Inheritance Tax" at para. 44.
[77] See Regulation 5: Example 1 in Appendix 2.

ment: see para. 6–09. If the donee does live in the property as occupier, then the continued occupation of the donor will not amount to a reservation, even if the donor's undivided share is smaller than the donee's. To avoid the question of whether the donee has the power to procure the sale of the property (the failure to exercise the power being a possible benefit to the donor by omission), it will be prudent to have an express trust for sale with a provision that the trustees shall not exercise their power of sale without the consent of the donor.

If, following a gift of an undivided share, the donor and donee share the expenses of maintenance, etc., it is considered that this does not involve a reservation, because any benefit to the donor does not come out of the subject matter of the gift: the gift is non-income bearing, whereas the "benefit" arises out of the expenditure of money (contrast *Nichols* where the donee/landlord's expenditure on repairs would have come out of the rent: para. 6–19). It is understood that the view of the C.T.O. is that common-purse arrangements are vulnerable only where the donee bears more than his fair share of the expenses.

CHAPTER 7

Shares in Family Companies

I. INTRODUCTION

7–01 The purpose of this chapter is to examine ways in which the members of a family company can plan its future ownership and control in the new inheritance tax climate. For this purpose "family company" is not a term of art and means quite simply a business carried on and owned by one or more families. 7–01

As has been said earlier, inheritance tax introduces into the old C.T.T. framework the "PET" coupled with the reintroduced concept of gifts with reservation. However, as will be seen, gifts with reservation are not a complex problem with family company shares; so, although the planning suggestions will discuss this issue, attention will also be given to other ideas to demonstrate solutions to non-tax problems flowing from a consideration of PETS and other gifts.

Thus, the chapter also considers why separate consideration should be given to the concepts of control and value of a company so as to concentrate the donor's mind on what it is he wishes to retain and what he wishes to give away.

Lastly, there is the issue of funding for I.H.T. where the donor does not survive the seven year period.

II. THE PET: GIFTS WITH RESERVATION

Basic principles

7–02 Let us examine a simple case. H owns 90 per cent. of Success Limited ("S Ltd.") (which has one class of shares only): his wife, W owns 10 per cent. They have one son, A aged 25, now employed in the business. H, W and A are all directors. S Ltd. is a trading company and has been thriving and building up value for some years. 7–02

H wishes to give A a direct interest in the business so as to mitigate the future impact of inheritance tax and also to ensure A's commitment, personally. He gives A 25 per cent. of the shares and then survives seven years. This is a PET provided H has not reserved a benefit.[1]

Reservation of benefits

7–03 To avoid a reserved benefit, clearly A should not give back to H any dividends on the gifted shares, either directly or indirectly. He could give them back to his mother, W even under a binding covenant as long as H does not benefit directly or indirectly from the payments to W.[2] In practice it is likely to be the taxpayer's executors who will find themselves having to argue the point and, although it will be for the Revenue to prove a reserved benefit, the executors will be in a difficult position if their principal witness has died! This arrangement is risky and should not be encouraged. 7–03

The donor's salary

7–04 In many cases where a person is contemplating a gift of shares in a family company, he is also a director of the company, drawing remuneration as such. His director's remuneration may indeed be his main source of income. The question arises as to whether there would be a reserved benefit if he remains a director of the company after making the gift and continues to draw remuneration as such. 7–04

In the authors' view there should normally be no danger of a reserved benefit, at least where the level of remuneration is justified by the director's services to the company. In this regard it is important to distinguish the decision in *Oakes*.[3] In *Oakes*, where there was a gift of grazing land in undivided shares, the donor was paid a fee for managing the property (which the Privy Council assumed was reasonable in relation to the services provided by him). This was held to be a reserved benefit. But the crucial point in *Oakes* was that the benefit to the donor was *coming directly from the subject matter of the gift*, namely the land. That is fundamentally different from the case where there is a gift of shares and the donor continues to receive a director's salary from the company. The salary does not come out of the subject matter of the gift because the subject of the gift is not the company's property but rather the shares in the company. In contrast to

[1] Thought should be given to ensuring A is not receiving the shares as a result of his employment.

[2] See para. 6–02 above.

[3] *Oakes* v. *Commissioner of Stamp Duties of New South Wales* [1954] A.C. 57; [1954] A.C. 57. See para. 6–12 above.

Oakes, therefore, there is no question of the remuneration being a benefit reserved out of the property given.

That is not quite an end to the matter because it is possible to have a collateral benefit not directly reserved out of the subject matter of the gift.[4] But if one accepts the principle that a collateral benefit is only relevant if it trenches upon the donee's enjoyment of the property given, there should be no difficulty with director's remuneration which is properly earned by service of the company. Such remuneration would not trench upon the enjoyment of the shares any more than the normal payment of remuneration to other directors and employees.

Even on the formulation of the test which is most favourable to the Revenue (*viz.* that the benefit is "referable to the gift"), the same result should follow. If the remuneration is properly earned, it is not referable to a gift of the shares; rather it is referable to the services provided by the director, in exactly the same way as remuneration paid to other directors or employees.[5]

7–05 It is possible that excessive remuneration which bears no relation to the services provided by the director could be held to be a reserved benefit, although this is by no means clear. In the authors' view, even excessive director's remuneration does not *necessarily* trench upon the enjoyment of the shares. Apart from the right to a return of capital in a winding up or otherwise (of which there is normally little prospect in the foreseeable future), the shareholder's main financial entitlement is to receive his share of such dividends as the company may decide lawfully to declare (if any); and the enjoyment of that right is not impaired, except possibly in the (fairly rare) case where it can actually be shown that the money would have been paid out by way of dividend had it not been paid out to the donor as director's remuneration. However, in the case of a salary which is disallowed for corporation tax purposes and which the Revenue treat as a distribution attracting ACT (an increasing problem), it can probably be said that the danger level has been reached.

One can figure extreme cases where the remuneration is so excessive as to cause a serious depletion in the net assets of the company and a substantial reduction in the value of the shares, which might be held to trench upon the donee's enjoyment (*cf.* the reference in *Oakes* to the benefit impairing or diminishing "the *value of the gift* to the [donees] or their enjoyment of it" (emphasis added)).

Moreover, if the wider "referability" test is applied, excessive remuneration which is voted to the donor as a result of the exercise (or possible even failure to exercise) of votes attaching to the shares given could be a reserved benefit, as being "referable" to the shares given.

In view of the possible application of the "referability" test, care should also be taken with any proposal to increase the level of the donor's

[4] See para. 6–20 above.

[5] It is understood that the Revenue do not regard a reserved benefit as arising where there is simply a continuation of reasonable commercial arrangements for the remuneration of the donor's ongoing services to the company entered into before the gift and which are in no way linked to or beneficially affected by the gift. The Revenue apply similar considerations where the gift is into a trust which empowers the trustees (including the settlor) to retain director's fees, etc.

remuneration at or about the same time as the gift. Such a proposal should be examined very carefully to see whether the proposed increase in remuneration could be said to be referable to the gift. To take an obvious case, an increase in the level of director's remuneration to make up for loss of dividend income on the shares to be given would be fatal on the "referability" test.

The benefits of a service contract

7–06 Where there is a risk that the donor/employee's director's remuneration could give rise to a reserved benefit it would be prudent, before any gift of shares is made, for the donor/employee to negotiate a suitable service contract with either fixed remuneration (including benefits) set out in it or at least a certain formula for calculating remuneration. The company must not have the ability to review the terms unilaterally. A service contract in favour of a director cannot run for more than five years (but a rolling five year term is acceptable) without the agreement of the shareholders in a general meeting by passing an Ordinary Resolution.[6] It is therefore possible with the agreement of the members to create a service contract that will take the donor up to retirement age but care should be taken over the problem that will be created if the contract is so beneficial to him that he has a significant right to compensation in the event of termination by the company. Large sums are paid now in such an event and failure by the donor to negotiate arms length compensation could constitute a chargeable transfer by him in the future. The donor may also be making a material reduction in the value of what he is giving away by reserving an overgenerous contract. **7–06**

Waiver of dividends

7–07 The donee should not waive his right to dividends that have been declared, for he would thereby be increasing the value of the donor's retained shareholding. As the right to a dividend is derived directly from the gifted shares this could be classified as a reserved benefit and should not be done. **7–07**

What does the donor wish to retain?

7–08 In view of what has been said above about long term service contracts, they are plainly not a wholly satisfactory answer, particularly in the case of a donor who wishes to retire in the foreseeable future; so the discussion has to be extended beyond questions of remuneration for the donor and his wife. **7–08**

Let us go back again to one of the basic principles that emerges from Chapter 6. You cannot reserve a benefit from property that has not been given away.

So before the donor gives anything away he should stop and think what it is that is important in the long term for him to retain. As a planning matter, this is dealt with later in more detail at paragraph 7–20 *et seq*.

[6] Companies Act 1985, s.319.

7–09 For now, let us assume that the donor has decided he wishes to retain: 7–09

(a) a directorship with reasonable remuneration until he retires;
(b) an income (in addition to any pension) beyond retirement;
(c) a say in major decisions;
(d) an equity stake in a future flotation or sale.

He starts off with all the above contained within his 90 per cent. shareholding. How does he achieve his objectives?

(a) His directorship he secures with a suitable service contract as discussed at para. 7–06. As long as the total remuneration package is reasonable this should present no problem. As has been said, the donor must agree the remuneration package (including benefits and pension arrangements within the terms of the contract) on or before the gift and should be advised that it will probably not be possible to review it upwards after the shares have been gifted.

(b) Income has to be provided by the creation of some form of preference shares with a cumulative or non-cumulative coupon. This is a most important arrangement in practice because, without it, it may not be possible to persuade the donor to retire at the correct time. Not only might this impede the natural progress of the company but also a stage may be reached at which the donor is being paid high remuneration and giving little or nothing in return which could create reservation of benefit problems (see para. 7–04). The coupon could be deferred for a time so as to tie in with the service contract and/or the donor's projected retirement date.

(c) A degree of control over important decisions can be attached to the preference shares.

(d) H keeps a small percentage of the ordinary shares for his equity stake. Alternatively, the preference shares could contain some conversion rights into ordinary shares at a future date or upon some future event.

The essence here is that those items which could create a reserved benefit, *viz.* salary as director or employee, dividends and some voting control, are first carved out into a newly created form of preference or other shares which are retained.

Only ordinary shares are then given away. The rights attaching to the preference shares are not reserved benefits because they are not derived from property that has been given away.

7–10 To create the correct balance in value between the preference shares and the ordinary shares is a delicate matter for discussion and design in each case. In the case of a company which is valued primarily on an earnings basis, if the ordinary shares carry all the usual rights other than weighted rights so as to give the preference shares a majority of votes on a sale or flotation and the preference shares only carry a modest coupon with all other rights to dividends left with the ordinary shares, this will leave most of the value and future growth in the company with the ordinary shares. With a company with high value underlying assets so that maximum value arises on a sale or break up, the allocation of voting rights may be different to keep value in the ordinary shares. In either case, if the donor then gives away a substantial portion of his ordinary shares and lives seven years, he 7–10 will have achieved a great deal in terms of long term inheritance tax planning.

Special attention has to be given to the coupon on the preference shares. If it is made cumulative with a high coupon so as to take some account of future inflation whilst recognising that the company may not be able to afford to pay it at the outset, this may store up cashflow problems for the company in the future and leave the donor with the prospect of paying income tax on income he has not received and his personal representatives paying inheritance tax on his death on an unpaid debt. It is also detracting from the long term value of the ordinary shares.

However, if the coupon is non-cumulative, it probably need only be set out at a low level to ensure that the company's business is not saddled with too much debt at the outset, but will this give the donor sufficient future income?

Perhaps the solution lies in some form of index linked coupon but, whatever the answer, the rights attaching to the preference shares must be determined prior to or at the time of the gift and not altered subsequently in favour of the donor.[7]

Incidentally, a restructuring in this way does not interfere with the donor's ability to claim business property relief on his new shares.[8]

III. GIFTS INTO TRUST: THE SETTLOR AS TRUSTEE

7–11 Having dealt with the straightforward type of gift between the donor and his son, assume now that the donor ("H"), minded to give away some part of the value of the company ("S Ltd"), is concerned because his son ("A") is not yet old enough to be given any degree of control. Indeed, perhaps A is one of three children under 25, any one of whom may come into the business, and it is too soon to make a decision about transferring shares to any one or more of them in particular. As to whether and how H is likely to favour a child who does come into the business—see below under General Planning. 7–11

Where H and his trustees still wish to be able to select the future path of devolution of the shares and his children are under 25, H is advised that he can create a PET by gifting the shares into an Accumulation and Maintenance Trust for his children.[9] If A's children are over 25, a gift into settlement with an immediate life interest to a life tenant over 25 is also now a PET, so H may choose to adopt this route rather than an outright gift.

In both cases, we need to consider the special problems that arise as a result of the decision to gift shares into settlement.

First named trustee

7–12 First of all it is important to dispel a fairy widely held misconception. It is often said that the settlor of a settlement should not be the first named trustee, as though being first named trustee has significance. The misconception probably arises from the fact that companies do not recognise trusts on 7–12

[7] *Nichols* v. *I.R.C.* [1975] 1 W.L.R. 534.
[8] I.H.T.A. 1984, s.107.
[9] Paras. 2–13 *et seq.*

their share registers as a matter of company law. They recognise joint shareholders but the company is not concerned to know whether they are nominees, beneficial joint holders or trustees. From the company's point of view only one shareholder can vote and it is the first named of joint shareholders who has this right. But if the joint shareholders are trustees, then in taking a decision on how to vote they must all be consulted and act unanimously unless they have otherwise and properly delegated such a decision to one of their number or to someone else. The first named trustee, in exercising the vote, is merely carrying out a joint decision so it matters not the order in which trustees are registered. The question is should the settlor be a trustee at all?

As to reservation of benefit, it is clear that, provided the settlor is not remunerated for being a trustee, the exercise of his fiduciary powers and duties is not material so far as the reservation rules are concerned.[10]

Trustees have duties and powers which are set out in the trust instrument and the framework of the general law. Trustees have a duty to manage the trust assets for the benefit of the beneficiaries as a whole in accordance with the terms of the trust subject to any powers set out in the trust instrument allowing them to deviate from this rule, such as a power to prefer one beneficiary over the others, which might then enable them to select particular investments to benefit that beneficiary.

But keeping to the general case, the courts have made it quite clear that trustees are presumed to have acted in accordance with their duties unless they can be proved to have acted otherwise.[11] In other words, if say they vote on a block of their shares, they are presumed to have voted in the interests of the beneficiaries as a whole and the Revenue would have to prove otherwise to establish that trustees had voted in breach of trust, *e.g.* to benefit the settlor if the settlor is not a beneficiary.

7–13 Given this analysis, there is no reason in principle why a settlor should not be a trustee. But now let us consider the position in practice. 7–13

Firstly, the settlor as donor and trustee will inevitably have a possible conflict of interests on votes of importance. To take an extreme example to illustrate the point, say the settlor has 70 per cent. of the votes and the trustees 30 per cent. A decision in principle has been taken by the settlor and the trustees to sell the company in two years or so when it is anticipated it will be able to show a good trading position. Meanwhile, the settlor runs into personal serious cashflow problems and finds a buyer for the company who offers a price for the settlor's 70 per cent. that will solve his immediate problems. However, the buyer will only purchase if he has 100 per cent. of the votes. The trustees take the view that by holding off another year or two as planned they could achieve a substantially better price for their shares. It is obvious what they should do but the settlor is a trustee and is trying to persuade his co-trustees to vote to sell.

Whatever the decision all will probably be well as long as the settlor properly consults his co-trustees, who perhaps should also take legal advice on the matter before making a decision. But the case of *Turner* v. *Turner*[12]

[10] *Law Society Gazette*.

[11] *Oakes* v. *Commissioner of Stamp Duties of New South Wales* [1954] A.C. 57.

[12] *Turner* v. *Turner* [1984] Ch. 100 at 107.

has to be remembered in which trustees signed deeds in front of them without any explanation (and making no enquiry about them) and it was held that the trustees were acting as no more than cyphers and the deeds were of no effect.

This emphasises the point so often glossed over when settlements are set up, *i.e.* the independence of the trustees. The trustees' independence and duties should always be spelt out to a settlor in detail with a summarised projection of what can happen when major decisions have to be taken with the trustees voting in the interests of the beneficiaries *as a whole* and not either to benefit the settlor or to benefit a particular beneficiary who is one of a class but whose livelihood may depend upon a decision such as whether or not to sell the company. If the trustees decide to exercise their voting power in some way which will benefit the life tenant they would be well advised to obtain a written request from the life tenant so to act. This would at least give the trustees some future protection under s.62 Trustee Act 1925 unless it is felt that such action is in itself evidence of a breach of trust.

Drafting the Trust Instrument

7–14 When it comes to drafting the trust instrument some thought should be given to any special terms that need to be incorporated because it is to receive family company shares as its sole or main asset. Reference should be made to the precedent in Appendix 1. However, the following points should be noted in this context all of which are relevant whether one is drafting an accumulation and maintenance trust or an interest in possession trust: 7–14

(a) specific authority to invest in the shares of the company or any substituted shares—although this will normally be covered in a modern wide investment power, that power still has to be exercised properly and the authors believe it is helpful to spell out specific authority to ensure the trustees cannot be criticised for retaining one single specified illiquid investment;
(b) unless the deed states otherwise, where the trustees have some material voting control, they are under a duty to exercise it actively. Whether such a duty should be allowed to stand or (as is often the case) be overridden is a decision to be taken in every case. Most trustees will not like to be burdened with this duty but there are occasions when they should be in the interests of the beneficiaries. However, even if the duty is left, it may be appropriate to absolve the trustees from liability for failure to exercise the duty under all circumstances. On the other hand, if they have a discretion whether or not to cast their vote they can avoid having to give reasons for their decision which could be a useful defence when the burden of proof on some issue is on the Revenue;
(c) the settlor may retain a power to veto any sale of the trust assets[13];
(d) if a trustee is or may be a director/employee, it is necessary to auth-

[13] In some circumstances this could create a reversed benefit.

orise trustees to be able to keep their fees/salary, otherwise they may be making an unauthorised profit from their office as trustee[14];

(e) there should always be included an express power to appoint non-resident trustees as often it is appropriate to take this action prior to a sale or flotation of the company.

IV. RELATIONSHIP BETWEEN VALUATION AND BUSINESS PROPERTY RELIEF ("BPR")

7–15 The relationship between valuation and BPR is not always properly appreciated when planning gifts of family company shares. The related property rules in I.H.T.A. 1984, s.161 apply *prima facie* only for valuation purposes. But when considering BPR, the relief in sections 104 and 105 applies to shares "which gave the transferor control." In section 269 will be found the definition of "control" and "control" extends to shares which are related property within section 161. **7–15**

We now have a new provision in the Finance Act 1987 which states, broadly, that in relation to quoted companies (which expression now includes companies quoted on the U.S.M.) business property relief is only available (at 50 per cent.) on shareholdings giving control whereas with unquoted companies, 50 per cent. BPR is also available on a holding of more that 25 per cent., and not more than 50 per cent. provided it *was* part of a controlling holding and has been held for at least two years.

7–16 For most practitioners, to come across a controlling holding in a quoted company will be a rarity but where it exists and the owner wishes to give all or part of it away, potentially there will be little purpose in him giving away only a small amount. 40 per cent. of a quoted company with *no* relief will almost certainly give rise to a much higher liability to tax than 51 per cent., with 50 per cent. BPR and no ability to pay by instalments. The solution is obvious. This new rule must now act as a disincentive to obtain a listing in a large number of cases. It is not difficult to imagine cases where the cash flow problems arising out of the death of a major (but not controlling) shareholder could seriously damage the fortunes of the company and its members as a whole. Plainly, much thought should be given to this problem prior to a flotation. **7–16**

7–17 In the case of an unquoted company, prior to the Finance Act 1987, it was of crucial importance to consider how many shares the donor ("H") and/or his wife ("W") should give away. Much depended on the basis of valuing the shares, but generally there was little point in making a transfer of value which just brought the holding from a little over 50 per cent. to a little under. **7–17**

Now this will be less of a problem. In theory, because of the "loss to donor" principle of valuation, it should not make a difference whether one is transferring 2 per cent. of a 51 per cent. holding followed later by a further 20 per cent., or 22 per cent., in one transfer. Both transfers will attract 50 per cent. BPR and the total by which the donor's estate is diminished is the same. Nevertheless, in practice, provided there is no link

[14] Where the settlor is a trustee, see footnote 5 above for the Revenue's views on reserved benefits.

between the two transfers, the former method may produce a more beneficial result depending on valuation. However, because in many companies there may be little difference in value between a holding of just over 25 per cent. and one just under, it remains of some importance to avoid making a transfer of value attracting 50 per cent. BPR which leaves the donor with just under 25 per cent. which, in turn, will only attract relief at 30 per cent. BPR. It would be preferable for the donor to give away more at that stage so that he can claim 50 per cent. relief as necessary on a higher proportion of his holding.

Shares owned by spouses: related property valuation

7–18 It should be borne in mind that shareholdings of spouses are subject to a special method of valuation which can have an important bearing on planning exercises. The rule is that where both spouses own shares in the same company, their respective holdings of the same class fall to be valued as a single unit, the share price of that unit then being applied to the separate holding.[15] Thus, if X Ltd. has 100 issued shares, of which 40 are held by H and 20 by W, their respective shares would be valued as if part of a 60 per cent. holding; and, accordingly, if on that basis the value per share is £60, H's shares will be valued at 40 × £60, and W's 20 × £60, even though their respective actual values might be £40 and £20. 7–18

A feature of the related property rules made even more relevant after the Finance (No. 2) Act 1987 is that a disposition by one spouse may cause a reduction in the value of the estate of the other, but *there is no mechanism for taxing this collateral loss*. Thus, if in the above example, W were to give away her 20 shares, the loss to her estate would be 20 × £60 = £1,200 (subject to business property relief at 50 per cent.). There would also be a loss to H's estate of £1,200 the difference between £2,400 and £1,200 but this would not be chargeable. However, under the new rules in F. (No. 2) A. 1987 the £1,200 would still attract BPR at 50 per cent.

This is because spouses are entitled to the 50 per cent. rate of relief if their aggregate shareholding gives control prior to the gift.[16]

Fragmentation of value: retention of de facto control through trusts

7–19 Where the donor is anxious to retain *de facto* control (see below), he will usually find his requirements met through a key shareholding in the hands of trustees. Thus, suppose that X Ltd. has 100 issued shares all held by A: he may think along the lines of gifts giving rise to the following structure: 7–19

A — 22
Mrs A — 26
Trustees — 30
Son 1 — 11
Son 2 — 11

Working on the assumption that the trustees (who could be Mr and Mrs A) will share the views of A on all questions concerning the company, A

[15] I.H.T.A. 1984, s.161(4) and (5).
[16] See Chapter 6.

will have retained *de facto* control of X Ltd. while, at the same time, having reduced his estate considerably, though as shown above the shares held by A and his spouse would be valued together under the related property rules.[17]

If the gift to the trustees is not a PET, because the settlement is discretionary (see below), the question has to be considered of whether the sequence of events is material:

Suppose that the order of events is first, gift to W; second, gifts to S1 and S2; third, gift in settlement. Some values will have to be assumed for the illustration to be clear:

(a) shares valued as part of a 100 per cent. holding are worth £100 each;
(b) shares valued as part of a holding 51–99 are worth £80 each;
(c) shares valued as part of a holding 26–49 are worth £60 each;
(d) shares valued as part of a holding 7–25 are worth £40 each.

Thus in A's estate, the 100 shares are worth £10,000 and following the gift to W, the 78 shares are worth 78 × £100 because of the related property rules.

The gifts to S1 and S2 are PET'S so that no calculations need to be made in relation to them if A survives for seven years. Immediately before the gift in settlement, the shares in A's estate when valued with those of Mrs A are worth 52 × £80, *i.e.* £4,160; after the gift in settlement, his 22 shares are worth 22 × £60, *i.e.* £1,320; therefore, the transfer of value equals £2,840 which after BPR at 50 per cent., becomes £1,420. If A had made the gift in settlement first, his transfer of value would have been:

Initial value	100 × £100 = £10,000
Less gift into settlement	30 × £100 = £ 3,000
Value of shares after gift	70 × £ 80 = £ 5,600

So the transfer of value equals £4,400 which, after BPR at 50 per cent., equals £2,200.

It is not suggested that general conclusions can be drawn from this example: the point is that the sequence of events *may* make a difference, and that the possibility should be investigated.

V. GENERAL PLANNING

7–20 Let us now try and pull the points in this chapter together by turning our attention to the general planning conclusions that can be drawn from what has been said above. It is commonly the case that an entrepreneur puts so much energy into building up a business that, by the time he comes to plan for the long term future, the company has already acquired a significant value even though legally it may still only be a £100 company with two shares issued! Let us now extend the illustration in para. 7–02 above to assume that the donor, H, the entrepreneur, has two children, one of **7–20**

[17] See Chapter 6.

whom comes into the business, "A," and one of whom pursues a career outside the business, "B." If not already in existence, it is assumed that both sons will produce children of their own.

Before planning any gift of shares, H will have to ask himself the following questions amongst others:

(a) Has he created a business for the benefit of himself alone or for the benefit of himself and his family? In other words, does he plan to sell it?
(b) Has he created a business which he would like to be associated with his family in the future for intangible reasons (such as those more akin to the devolution of the traditional landed estate) or has he simply created value?
(c) To what extent are other members of the family dependent on the business for employment, income, and capital cash?
(d) Could the business prosper in the event of his untimely death, or will the value in that event be better protected by an immediate sale?
(e) If the business is retained after his death, how important is it to ensure that his successor in the business has control over major decisions as opposed to value? Should control be spread around the family or only value spread around?
(f) How is provision to be made for H's widow?
(g) What impact will a future flotation have on capital tax planning?

The answers to most of the above questions revolve around H giving detailed consideration to the difference between control and value. Perhaps there is no problem and H is happy for control and value to devolve equally amongst his descendants, and this is what frequently happens, but often unwittingly. However, in cases where control and value become widely dispersed after two or three generations of devolution, the interests of different shareholders become diverse. Pressures build up for dividends from those not employed in the business whilst those trying to manage (who may be distant cousins) resent depletion of cash resources required for new capital investment and can feel that those with no direct input in the business should be grateful for what they get. It could be said that such a company has the disadvantages of a public company in terms of remoteness between management and proprietors without the advantages of unhappy minority shareholders being able to market their shares freely. Loss of control can mean loss of momentum for the business. In many cases more careful thought will lead to the conclusion that the two concepts of control and value should be segregated. It may be that H is happy for A to inherit control and value, but then B will have to be provided for in other ways and H may not have other suitable assets. So H may wish A to have control and some value, with other value passing to B and to A's and B's respective descendants. In the latter case, one way or another, control and value will have to be segregated.

7–21 Valuation can make or break any planned transfer of shares in a family company. The valuation of private company shares is notoriously difficult and unpredictable. With the best will in the world and the most expert advice it is usually not possible to advise a client in advance of a transfer 7–21 what value will be agreed with the Shares Valuation Division of the Inland Revenue and thus what the tax consequences will be. At best, one has to work out a bracket of values and plan for the worst. At worst, a serious error would cripple the business. This is so in relation to a straightforward one share class company. The problem is significantly more difficult with different classes of shares. This can be turned to advantage because the Shares Valuation Division find valuation as difficult as those advising the shareholder and to create a slightly unusual class of shares can open up new avenues for negotiations. If the shares are the subject of a PET it may be thought that the valuation problem will evaporate, but it will be imprudent when making a PET to ignore the consequences of death within seven years and the problem is brought sharply into focus when one tries to decide the level to which to insure the donor's life against this risk. Moreover, the Revenue may insist on a value being agreed if an election is made for capital gains tax purposes for a chargeable gain to be held over; they are entitled to insist but in practice do not always do so.

However many shares are given away, the loss to donor principle discussed above must not be forgotten. However, it should also be remembered that it does not apply to interest in possession settlements.[18] Thus, if some shares are already in an interest in possession settlement with some owned absolutely by the life tenant and if the overall plan is to give away most if not all the shares, the settled shares should be transferred first as they will not be aggregated with the absolute shares for valuation purposes; but the reverse would not be true. This is even more pertinent now that the termination of an interest in possession is a PET, so there may always be some advantage in holding some shares in such a settlement. If the decision in the Court of Appeal in *Craven* v. *White*[19] is upheld on appeal, this will add even more force to the argument. The question of the inter-relationship of 50 per cent. and 30 per cent. BPR explained above at paras. 7–15 *et seq*. will also have to be carefully considered.

Reverting to the common case of H who quite simply owns most or all of the shares absolutely, how does he deal with the answers to the questions in paragraph 7–20?

Future sale of the company

7–22 If the donor plans to sell the company at some future date he should not necessarily wait until he does sell to decide whether or not he would wish to give some of the proceeds to other members of his family. This is because once he has sold he is only likely to have cash or other assets not attracting relief to give away. However, if he gives away shares now which qualify for relief, the relief can be claimed provided the sale takes place after the seven year period from the gift has elapsed.[20] A course of action along these lines will make the discussion below about the donor retaining control most pertinent.

7–22

[18] I.H.T.A. 1984, s.52(1).
[19] *Craven* v. *White, The Times* March 26, 1987 C.A.
[20] I.H.T.A. 1984, s.113A.

Retention of the company for the donor's family

7–23 Next, let us assume the donor feels that having created a business he hopes it will stay in the family. But being a successful businessman he only wants to see those members of his family employed in the business who are capable. Furthermore, although in the short term he considers he should retain the ultimate control over major decisions such as sale or flotation, such decisions should devolve in due course to the next senior member of the family, "A." But to do so will simply store up more inheritance tax problems for A in the future; so, much of the value should be earmarked for A's present or future children and still further value earmarked for A's brother "B" and his family. It is presumed that the value element will probably have to produce income so as to pay the inheritance tax on the gifts (or at least be in a position to do so in the event of the donor's death within seven years)[21] and, in the case of his grandchildren, pay maintenance and school fees for the beneficiaries. These decisions should all be tied in with the questions raised at para. 7–09 when the reservation of benefit problems were considered. 7–23

The simple company law route

7–24 To solve the problems posed in para. 7–20, the donor could consider the following type of structure. Having secured his own service contract and pension arrangements to avoid any reservation of benefit problems, he then resolves to restructure the company so as to create two or perhaps three different classes of shares: 7–24

(i) *Class A*
These shares contain controlling voting rights on those issues important to the donor such as sale, flotation or whatever. They are intended to devolve to A but not necessarily immediately; they may devolve under the donor's will. Alternatively, he may put these shares into a voluntary trust (*i.e.* with himself as life tenant) as a means of determining their devolution to A (so as to act as an incentive to A in the business). Alternatively, he may give A a right of pre-emption tied in with other shares or he can have an option to buy; but these latter two courses are to be avoided if possible because, assuming the shares have value, the exercise of a right of pre-emption or an option will forfeit the ability to pay the inheritance tax by instalments. These shares will have no rights to dividends or on a winding-up.

(ii) *Class B*
These are the shares intended to contain most of the value because they will have the rights to dividends and a prior charge on assets on a winding-up. Company lawyers will make the rights much more sophisticated than this but it is the essence of the matter. These

[21] See paras. 4–02 *et seq.*

shares will probably be given to A and B and some on accumulation and maintenance trusts for the donor's grandchildren and remoter issue.

(iii) *Class C*
As an optional third class of shares there can also be preference shares carrying a coupon which is cumulative or non-cumulative, immediate or deferred. They are designed to provide continuing income for the donor after retirement and he will very likely leave them to his widow for life in his will with remainder over to his grandchildren. They are unlikely to carry votes.

It is not the purpose of this book to examine the company law aspects in detail but in the experience of the authors the above type of structure can be fairly readily devised. Other tax problems will arise such as value shifting for capital gains tax but they are generally surmountable.

The simple trust law route

7–25 There will be cases where it is not convenient to restructure the constitution of the company. There may be uncooperative minority shareholders; indeed, the company may be a public company but with more than 50 per cent. still under the donor's control. The creation of different classes of shares may be perceived as adding further difficulties on a future sale or flotation (although these can be overcome by a prior collapse of the different classes of shares back into one and the only problem will be the valuation question as between the different classes). In the case of an asset based company such as a property business, control in itself may have too high a value to make the company law route worthwhile, although in such a case particular attention has to be given to which class of shares has the right to wind up the company.

In these cases it may be more appropriate for the donor to achieve his objectives using a trust or series of trusts as discussed above at paras. 7–11 *et seq*.

We have to consider first, value and then, control. Value is transferred by a simple transfer of shares. This can be from the donor to A but again, to avoid A's future inheritance tax problems, shares can be put into an accumulation and maintenance trust for the donor's grandchildren. A transfer of shares to B may have to be subject to an option to repurchase. The donor may then give the benefit of this option to the trustees for his grandchildren which might prudently be coupled with insurance on B's life so as to ensure the trustees will have funds to exercise the option.

When it comes to control, in order to take maximum advantage of the 50 per cent. BPR, the donor decides to transfer most of his shares leaving him with no direct control at all. The maintenance of control comes from retaining various powers under the terms of the interest in possession or accumulation and maintenance trust. With careful drafting by the trust lawyer, the donor reserves the power of veto over certain decisions such as a sale of trust assets together with positive powers such as a power to vote at least on certain issues (watch the reservation of benefit problem but this should be acceptable if the power is reserved at the outset). There is also a provision in the trust instrument for the donor to nominate who should succeed to these fiduciary powers, failing which devolution in favour of A is made to be automatic, although ultimately the powers will probably devolve on the trustees.

The widow's position is more difficult under the trust route and it may be necessary to make greater provision for her through pensions but some shares could be settled on her for life with remainder over on trusts for the donor's grandchildren and the donor reserving similar powers in his wife's trust.

The confluence of company and trust law: value freezing

7–26 There will be many cases where either the company or family structure is not as simple as those discussed hitherto and when the problems are often best solved in a meeting of the company lawyer and the trust lawyer. 7–26

It is not possible in any book concerned with tax planning in such a complex area to do more than suggest possible avenues which may be fruitful in some cases, but to illustrate how company and trust law can work together let us go back to the outline share structures in para. 7–24 but instead assume that the heir, "A" is as yet unmarried with no children and his younger brother, "B" is married but does not yet have children. Devolution of the Class A shares is still clear but what should happen to the Class B shares? One solution is for the donor to make a declaration of trust in relation to some of the Class B shares to the effect that their current value is held for A absolutely but any increase in value is held on discretionary trusts for the donor's descendants. The B shares can attract business property relief, if appropriate, because an entire interest in them is being given away; but the donor is giving A an absolute interest in the shares as tenant in common (which is still therefore a PET because section 3A(2)(*a*) I.H.T.A. 1984 will not apply) and, provided the value of the interest in the shares settled on the discretionary trusts as tenant in common is nil, or at least within the donor's unused nil rate band, the beneficial rules for discretionary trusts in the first 10 years of their life set out in chapter 3 will apply. As a consequence if A or B have children within the next 10 years, the future increase in value can be appointed to the donor's grandchildren at no additional tax cost.

This requires very careful document drafting to ensure a nil or low value of the settled portion of the Class B shares, but it can be done.

One word of warning: as a result of such a manoeuvre, what A now has is an equitable interest in the B shares and not an interest in the shares themselves so he will not be able to claim business property relief on a transfer of value by him *at any time* until two years after the shares have been appropriated to his interest as tenant in common. This risk can probably only be covered with insurance or assurance written in trust. The trustees will be in a similar position.

A further advantage of always considering how trusts can help in restructuring companies is the greater ease with which settled property can be exported as opposed to property owned absolutely where the owner himself has to become non-resident. A simultaneous or near simultaneous gift in settlement and export will always be open to attack under *Furniss* v.

Dawson[22] so consideration should be given to holding all material shareholdings in a company which are likely to increase substantially in value in trust action which has even more relevance now that the Finance (No. 2) Act 1987 extending PETS to interest in possession settlements has passed into law.

7–27 It should be emphasised that if the share capital of an unquoted close company is altered to create a new class of shares which are to be vested in a donee or the trustees of an accumulation and maintenance settlement, careful consideration should be given to the mechanics of implementing the arrangement. 7–27

If the donee or trustees subscribes directly for the new shares in the company and the effect is to reduce the value of the holdings of the existing shareholders, there would be a *chargeable transfer* by the existing shareholders (*not* a potentially exempt transfer). This is because the alteration of the share capital would be deemed to be a disposition by the existing shareholders under I.H.T.A. 1984, s.98 (alteration of a close company's share capital). Any resulting reduction in the value of the existing shareholders' estates would therefore be a transfer of value; and it is specifically provided that such a transfer of value is not a potentially exempt transfer.

In such circumstances the better course would be to issue the new shares to the existing shareholders first, by way of a bonus issue. That will avoid any deemed chargeable transfer under section 98 (because there is no reduction in the value of their estates). They can then simply give away the new shares in the normal way as a potentially exempt transfer.

If the existing shares would qualify for business property relief, the relief should also be given on the new shares in the event of the gift becoming a chargeable transfer by reason of the donor's death within the following seven years, notwithstanding that the new shares were not owned by the donor for the two year minimum period. The new shares would be regarded as "replacement property" under section 107 I.H.T.A. 1984. Technically there is some doubt about this in the case of 50 per cent. relief for controlling shareholdings. There the operative provision is section 107(1)(*a*) which refers to the new property "replacing" other property. The word "replace" does not seem apposite in relation to a bonus issue where the new shares are an addition to, rather than a replacement of, the old shares (although doubtless the value of the new shares will replace the loss of value on the old shares). However, in practice the bonus issue will be regarded by the Revenue as replacement property within section 107(1)(*a*). The point does not arise in the case of 50 per cent. or 30 per cent. relief for minority holdings where the relevant provision[23] simply requires that the new shares be identified with the old shares for capital gains tax purposes as a reorganisation.

It will be apparent that the authors consider many inheritance tax problems can be solved through the use of differing classes of shares but such solutions motivated by tax considerations alone often are unsatisfactory without a simultaneous review of the concept of the family company in the context of the proprietors and their relatives both now and in the future.

[22] *Furniss* v. *Dawson* [1984] A.C. 474.
[23] I.H.T.A. 1984, s.107(4).

Those large companies which are still private have usually only managed to stay so because the devolution problem was properly addressed early on. Otherwise success often leads in due course either to sale or flotation leading to loss of control and probable loss of business property relief particularly now that under the Finance Act 1987 such relief no longer applies to shares quoted on the USM.

VI. FUNDING THE TAX ON A CHARGEABLE TRANSFER

7–28 As with most illiquid assets, it is crucially important when a PET of family company shares is made to consider at that time how the tax is to be funded if the donor should die within the relevant period. 7–28

This can be done in several ways of which the following are examples:

(a) Insurance.[24]
(b) Ensure that the company has adequate reserves (or at least a borrowing capability) to buy in the shares from the donee.[25]
(c) Structure the company pension fund trust to be able to buy shares off the donee/taxpayer.
(d) Structure the company prior to gift so as to allow a dividend or coupon to be paid on the gifted shares/stock so as to generate cash in the hands of the donee.
(e) Death in service benefit.

7–29 Taking these points in turn: 7–29

(a)—Insurance is fully discussed in Chapter 5 but every care should be taken to see that where policies are written in trust the policy proceeds can either be given to the donee or the trustees can pay the donee's tax bills for him. This may not be straightforward when the donee is an accumulation and maintenance trust.

In the case of a company where the surviving shareholders will be obliged to exercise an option or right of pre-emption on the death of a shareholder, make sure the survivors will have adequate funds to do this. They may have to take out insurance. This problem is explored in relation to partnerships in Chapter 8 and similar comments may apply to companies. If two businessmen X and Y come together to form a "50/50" company and Mr X dies, they are likely to want Y either to buy the shares off X's PRs on death or at least to have a material say in what happens to them. X will want Y to buy the shares so that his widow is provided for but this means losing the instalment option and, possibly more importantly, it means negotiating an arm's length value for the shares. So why don't X and Y ensure that under the constitution of the company X and Y can bequeath their shares to each other (subject to inheritance tax) and provide for their respective widows with insurance? This would preserve not only the business property relief but also the instalment option.

7–30 (b) and (c) above also both have the disadvantages of inducing a sale with similar undesirable consequences. 7–30

Firstly, from the inheritance tax point of view, the option to pay the tax by instalments is lost. Provided the cash is available to buy the shares this

[24] See generally Chapter 5.
[25] Companies Act 1985, s.162 and Finance Act 1982, s.53 and Schedule 9.

does not present a cashflow problem but again it is not sensible to give up an interest free loan from the government!

Secondly, from the C.G.T. point of view, the sale will constitute a disposal giving rise to a chargeable gain with no reliefs. Assuming the gain on the original PET has been held over the chargeable gain will be computed using the deceased's own base value. On a PET by virtue of a gift in settlement, it may be possible to postpone the charge to capital gains tax by exporting the trust in the fiscal year prior to the disposal so as to bring the chargeable gain since the shares were first transferred to the trust within the provision of section 80 F.A. 1981, but this will trigger a chargeable gain on the original held over gain payable by the deceased's PRs but not deductible in his estate for inheritance tax. This may or may not be desirable. If such a plan has been thought through too carefully in advance then beware *Furniss* v. *Dawson* (and see the comments of Scott J. in *Cholmondeley and another* v. *I.R.C.*).[26]

Furthermore, on a purchase the vendor and purchaser have to agree a price which may be difficult enough in itself but being connected persons, whatever the price agreed, the Revenue may substitute their own version of full market value with obvious difficult consequences.[27]

7–31 (d) has its own problems. Unless of a substantial size and with a wide diversity of shareholders, most family companies try to avoid paying dividends. There are many reasons for this which include: 7–31

(a) accelerated ACT;
(b) at present, accumulation within a company is subject to a lower rate of tax than the highest rates of income tax;
(c) it is disadvantageous for share valuation;
(d) cashflow for the business.

At first sight, the problem is not made easier by reason of the fact that the tax bill is intended to be funded by a dividend that may never be declared. However, the imaginative company lawyer or accountant should be able to devise some form of non-cumulative preferred dividend or coupon which is only paid when necessary.

7–32 (e) has a lot of attractions. Inheritance tax has not altered the principle accepted by the Revenue that, if the trustees of the pension fund have a discretion as to the allocation of the death in service benefit, such allocation other than to the surviving spouse will not be a chargeable transfer. It is therefore important to ensure first of all that the donee of the shares (particularly the trustees of any trust to which shares have been given) is a beneficiary of the trust and that the letter of wishes to the trustees covers the wish for the trustees to assist the donee with the tax bill. 7–32

This assumes that the donor is and will remain an employee (see above on reservation of benefit). The Revenue limit in such arrangements is four times the relevant salary. Apart from the obvious problem that it may be necessary (if possible) to pay the donor a high salary to achieve the desired level of term insurance, there is the added question of committing a high proportion of the donor's salary (and therefore the company's cash) to a

26 [1986] S.T.C. 384.
27 C.G.T.A. 1979, s.62.

pension contribution for a considerable time, possibly to no purpose if the donor survives seven years. However, the principle is straightforward and frequently provides a solution.

It may be necessary to pay a salary for pension purposes in excess of that actually required by the employee/donor. The undrawn salary, franked with income tax, can obviously be left in the company as a loan account which can be beneficial for the company's cash flow whilst at the same time allowing access to cash at a later date without accelerated ACT or additional income tax. However, the reader will no doubt already have spotted that this can be expensive in national insurance contributions and such an asset does not attract business asset relief in the employee's estate.

CHAPTER 8

Farming and Farming Companies

I. INTRODUCTION

8–01 Farming is perhaps one of the most difficult and complex areas in the field of inheritance tax planning, raising many difficult questions of valuation, the effect of granting agricultural tenancies, the availability of agricultural or business property relief, and if so at what rate, whether any proposed transactions will affect the relief, and now further complications caused by the reintroduction of the estate duty reservation of benefits rules which can be particularly troublesome in the area of the unincorporated farm. **8–01**

There is no single course of action which can be recommended over all others as being the best for inheritance tax purposes because the circumstances and the requirements of the individuals concerned will vary so much from case to case. In any given case there will probably be a number of possible courses of action which can be taken to mitigate inheritance tax, none of which will be perfect. It is always a question of weighing up the various possibilities and deciding which one is likely to produce the best overall result consistently with the long term interests of the family and the business.

In this chapter all the authors can hope to do is examine the possible courses of action which might be taken in any given case, describing their likely overall effect, and what they may achieve, indicating the problems and pitfalls which may be encountered, and try to give guidance as to the circumstances in which a particular course of action might be more suitable than others.

II. UNINCORPORATED FARMS

8–02 Suppose A owns a farm Blackacre and has farmed it for many years as a sole trader. He has a son, S, who has been working on the farm for a number of years as an employee, and whom A hopes will take over the farm sooner or later, on A's death, if not before. A wishes to make a gift of all or part of the farm now to his son, with a view to reducing the inheritance tax prospectively payable on his death. What are the possibilities? 8–02

(1) Gift of the whole of the farm

8–03 Consider first the simple case of an outright gift of the whole of the farm. 8–03

A may be happy to retire completely from farming. He might not need any income from the farming business, having sufficient income from other sources (retirement annuities, investment income, etc.) to provide for himself (and his wife after his death). His son may be sufficiently experienced now to be able to take over the farm completely. In such circumstances, A might well consider giving away the entire farm (both the land and the business) to his son absolutely.

Such a gift is probably the simplest and potentially the most effective for inheritance tax purposes. There should be no reservation of benefit problems if it is a gift with no strings attached, and A has no more involvement in the business or the land (the farm house being excepted from the gift, see para. 8–13 below). The gift itself will be a potentially exempt transfer, free of all inheritance tax if A survives for seven years. End result: if A survives for seven years, the whole of the value of the farm (apart from the farmhouse) and the business escapes inheritance tax.

If A dies within the seven year period, the potentially exempt transfer will retrospectively become a chargeable transfer (although the tax on that chargeable transfer is only due six months after the end of the month in which the donor died). Tax will be charged at the death rates, subject to taper relief if A survives the gift by more than three years. The charge would be on the value of the land and the business at the date of the gift. Fifty per cent. agricultural relief should be available, assuming that the land is still owned by S at the date of A's death. (If S sells the land before the donor's death, see paras. 4–14 *et seq.* above for the possible withdrawal of agricultural relief under the Inheritance Tax Act 1984 (ss.124A and 124B). If the land has development value, the agricultural relief will be limited to the agricultural value of the land, but the excess should qualify for business property relief at 50 per cent.[1] The tax can be paid by S in interest free instalments over 10 years, so long as he retains the farm (para. 4–05 above).

(2) Gift of a share in the farm

8–04 The circumstances last envisaged where A can contemplate giving away the whole of the farm are perhaps somewhat unusual in practice. More commonly A is not ready or willing to retire completely from farming or, even 8–04

[1] I.H.T.A. 1984, s.105(1)(*a*) (property consisting of a business or interest in a business). A's share in the other assets of the business will of course also qualify for 50 per cent. business property relief under this section.

if he wants to retire, will continue to require all or some of the income from the farming business. He may therefore not be prepared or willing to contemplate a gift of the whole of the farm "with no strings attached," but might be prepared to give away a share of the farm to his son.

Suppose he gives away a one half undivided share in the land and other assets of the farming business to his son, the land thereafter being farmed by A and S in partnership in equal shares (whether pursuant to a formal partnership agreement or not). The gift of the half share in such circumstances would not *per se* be a gift with reservation, A's continuing occupation of the farm and entitlement to half the profits being attributable to the half share in the land and other assets which he has retained.[2]

The gift would be a potentially exempt transfer, which would be free of inheritance tax if A survives for seven years. That would leave an undivided half share of the farm comprised in A's estate which, if no further steps are taken, would be a chargeable asset of his estate on death. 50 per cent. agricultural relief (or business property relief in so far as the land has development value) would be available so long as there is no binding contract for the sale of the deceased partner's share in the partnership agreement or otherwise at the time of death.[3] The tax may also be paid by interest free instalments, although not if the deceased partner's share is to be sold or to be satisfied by a payment under the partnership agreement.[4] (To preserve the right to pay the tax by interest free instalments, a bequest of the business interest will often be preferable so care should be taken in drafting the partnership agreement to see that this is possible.)

If A dies within the seven years, tax will also be charged on the gift of the half share (the potentially exempt transfer having become a chargeable transfer) at death rates, subject to taper relief if A survived for more than three years. Again 50 per cent. agricultural relief (or business property relief in so far as there is development value) will be available, assuming S retains his half share until A's death; also, S's right to pay the tax by interest-free instalments will continue so long as he retains the share given to him.

8–04A This strategy should not be relied upon if A wishes to retain some benefit over and above his share of profits and rights of occupation which are attributable to the undivided share retained by him. If, for example, he takes 75 per cent. of the profits when he has retained only a 50 per cent. share in the land and other assets, there would probably be a gift with reservation. Similarly, if A was entitled to a first slice of the profit (*e.g.* the first £10,000) on his own, only the excess being distributed between the partners, again there would very likely be a gift with reservation (*cf.* the donor's entitlement in *Oakes*[5] to a salary for managing the property which *was* held to be a benefit reserved). Care should also be taken with covenants under the partnership agreement which might be collateral benefits to A, *e.g.* if S is required to devote all his time and attention to the business,

[2] *Cf. Oakes* v. *Commissioners of Stamp Duties of New South Wales* [1954] A.C. 57 and para. 6–17 above.
[3] I.H.T.A. 1984, ss.124 and 113.
[4] I.H.T.A. 1984, ss.227(4)–(6).
[5] [1954] A.C. 57.

A being under no such obligation.[6] Even a provision that the partnership will discharge (or indemnify A for) the liabilities of the business prior to the formation of the partnership could be a collateral benefit. The correct relationship between A and S should be maintained on all matters such as drawings and contributions to losses.

Provided that care is taken on these points, however, this strategy can be a simple and effective means of getting part of the value of the farm out of the donor's estate for inheritance tax purposes while still enabling him to farm the land (although now in partnership) and share in the profits. However, if one accepts the principle that the donor's share of profits must not exceed his share in the land and other assets retained by him to avoid a gift with reservation, the potential tax saving which can be achieved by this strategy in any given case will depend upon what share of profits the donor requires for the future. If, for example, he only requires one quarter of the profits for the future, this strategy can be used to give away three quarters of the value of the land and other assets, which should be a worthwhile exercise. If, however, he requires three-quarters of the profits for the future, then this strategy can only be used to remove one quarter of the value of the assets from his estate, which may not be enough. In such circumstances, to get more out of his estate for inheritance tax purposes, a rather different approach may be called for as discussed below.

(3) A gives freehold to S, S leases the land back to A and S in partnership, the lease back being for full consideration

8–05 Although in principle this is a possible course of action, it is very difficult to work successfully in practice. The problem is that to avoid a gift with reservation, the lease back of the land must be for full consideration[7] and in most cases it will be difficult to fix the amount of rent and other terms of the lease back so as clearly to satisfy this requirement (see paragraph 6–15 above). This area of valuation has become much more difficult since estate duty days. The problem is particularly difficult because the Revenue will only express a view if and when a potential tax charge arises (normally on the donor's death), by which time it will be too late to do anything about it if the rent has been set too low. Moreover, even if the rent turns out to be only slightly too low, the consequences will be quite disastrous because the whole of the land comprised in the gift will still be deemed to be comprised in the donor's estate; there is no scaling down for partial consideration. However, there will be cases, where the land agents for the landlord and tenant are confident they can agree a rent which will be accepted by the District Valuer as a full rent for an incoming tenant, when this strategy will be feasible.

In the current days of fairly static if not falling rents, it may be more palatable to risk "over-egging" rent to err on the side of caution, the tenant knowing that at a review in three years time his rent may come down but still be regarded as full consideration. This would probably be a bold move

[6] It is arguable that even an *unenforceable* arrangement or understanding between the parties that S (alone) would work full time on the farm could be a collateral benefit.

[7] F.A. 1986, Sched. 20, para. 6(1)(*a*).

but at least there is a good prospect of the rent remaining static which could be acceptable.

Nevertheless the authors concede that because of the uncertainties and risks involved in this strategy, most tax-payers will look at the alternative plans available on which the remainder of this chapter concentrates.

In particular where it is thought that the proposed lease back would probably be for full consideration but there is some doubt in that regard, consideration should be given to the alternative strategy (described below)[8] of granting the lease first and then giving away the freehold subject to the lease. This will avoid a gift with reservation even if it should turn out that the lease was not for full consideration.

This alternative strategy of creating the lease first may be preferable even where it is fairly certain that the lease will be for full consideration, because the grant of the lease will reduce the value of the freehold to a tenanted basis of valuation without any transfer of value.[9] If the donor then gives away the freehold reversion and dies within the following seven years, tax would be charged only on the tenanted value of the freehold reversion (albeit with agricultural relief probably at 30 per cent. only rather than 50 per cent.: see paragraph 8–07A below).

(4) Creation of partnership; lease to partnership for a fixed period at low rent; gift of freehold reversion

8–06 Suppose A enters into partnership with S and possibly also Mrs A and Mrs S; he grants a lease to the partnership and subsequently gives the freehold reversion to S. 8–06

As will shortly be seen this course of action raises complex and technical questions which the gift of an undivided share at (2) above by and large avoids. Its big advantage, however, is that it can remove most of the value of the land from the donor's estate for inheritance tax purposes whilst still leaving it open to him to keep a substantial share of the profits as a partner (contrast the gift of the undivided share where his share of profits cannot exceed his share of the land and other assets retained by him). But see paragraph 8–12 below for the C.G.T. implications, which can be serious.

Under this procedure, the lease in favour of the partnership is created before the gift of the freehold reversion (compare (3) above). The gift of the freehold is thus made subject to a pre-existing right to occupy the property pursuant to the lease to the partnership and this is not a gift with reservation, even if the lease is for a nominal rent.[10] Care should be taken, however, to avoid landlord's repairing and other onerous covenants which

[8] Para. 8–09 below.

[9] See I.H.T.A. 1984, section 16 (grants of agricultural tenancies for full consideration).

[10] *Munro* v. *Stamp Duties Commissioner for New South Wales* [1934] A.C. 61 and paragraph 6–17 above. The *Munro* principle may also apply if a licence is granted to the partnership rather than a lease. (In *Munro* the rights of the partnership to occupy the land were described as either a lease or a licence *coupled with an interest.*) However, if a licence is to be used, care would have to be taken to ensure that the licence will be fully binding on the donee and that he cannot terminate it after the gift of the freehold. In the authors' view the lease is much the safer route.

might independently give rise to a reserved benefit even if the lease is created first.[11]

8–07 If the lease is for less than full consideration, it must not be a "lease for life" within the Inheritance Tax Act 1984, s.43(3). Otherwise the land will be settled property in which the partners as tenants will have an interest in possession, so that at least part of the property will still be deemed to be comprised in A's estate as settled property. "Lease for life" is widely defined and includes, *inter alia*, a lease which is for a period ascertainable only by reference to a death or which is terminable only on or at a date ascertainable only by reference to a death. In that regard, a lease which is terminable on the death of one or more of the partners would be fatal; and a lease for the duration of the partnership which in turn is terminable on the death of a partner is probably also best avoided. There is, however, no objection to a lease for a fixed period equal to A's life expectancy (or possibly the life expectancy of the survivor of A and Mrs A if she is also a partner). If the lease is still in existence on the expiry of the fixed term, the partners will have security of tenure under the Agricultural Holdings Act 1948, although the rent will, of course, be reviewed. (If A is still a partner at that time, S, the owner of the freehold reversion, *must* take the appropriate steps to review the rent; otherwise there could be a reserved benefit to A by associated operations, see paragraph 6–23 above). 8–07

The grant of the lease to the partnership could itself result in a substantial transfer of value by A (unless for full consideration, see paragraph 8–05 above) because the freehold (at that point still owned by A) would thereafter be valued on a tenanted basis rather than with vacant possession. It is unclear to what extent this transfer of value would be a potentially exempt transfer within the Inheritance Tax Act 1984 s.3A(2)(*a*) as being attributable to property which by virtue of the transfer becomes comprised in the estate of another individual. The transfer of value (*viz.* the reduction in the value of the freehold) is attributable to the grant of the lease, but the lease does not become comprised in the estate of "another individual," *viz.* the donee. The most one can say is that the lease has become comprised *partly* in the estate of the donee, he being entitled at most to an undivided share in the lease[12] (the balance being comprised in the donor's estate). Insofar as the transfer of value is attributable to the lost "marriage value" between the lease and the freehold reversion, the wording of section 3A(2)(*a*) may not be entirely apt, even on the wide construction accepted by the Revenue (paragraph 2–05 above).[13]

If it is desired to avoid this point, the better course may be for A to grant the lease to a nominee in favour of himself (rather than to the partnership) and then give away the freehold reversion. The transfer of value on the gift of the freehold would then be the full vacant possession value of the land, less the value of the lease retained by A. This would clearly be a PET. A could then simply retain the lease as an asset of estate, allowing the part-

[11] *Nichols* v. *I.R.C.* [1975] S.T.C. 278 and paragraph 6–19 above.

[12] and perhaps not even that: see paragraph 6–38 above.

[13] The other limb of s.3A(2), *viz.* that the transfer of value is exempt to the extent that the estate of the other individual is increased is unlikely to be of any assistance in this regard (see paragraph 2–06 above).

nership to farm the land pursuant to a licence or even sub-lease from him as (head) tenant.

8–07A Whether the lease is granted directly to the partnership or to a nominee in favour of A, agricultural relief on the gift of the freehold reversion would probably be at the lower rate of 30 per cent. only. 8–07A

The 50 per cent. relief is only available if "the interest of the transferor in the property immediately before the transfer carries the right to vacant possession, or the right to obtain it within the next twelve months."[14] It is unclear how this provision applies where immediately before the transfer the transferor has two interests in the property, one of which carries the right of vacant possession (the lease or a share in the lease) and the other of which does not (the freehold reversion); but it is thought that the provision probably would not apply in such a case, at any rate where the transfer of value is wholly attributable to the interest which does not carry the right to vacant possession. On that basis, only 30 per cent. relief would be available as "any other case."[15] If that view is correct, then this strategy does suffer a disadvantage if the donor dies within the following seven years, namely that a substantial part of the total value transferred will only attract 30 per cent. relief rather than the full 50 per cent. relief which would have been available on the whole value if nothing had been done. How serious a drawback it is in any given case will depend upon how likely it is that the donor will survive the seven years (in which case it will turn out to be no disadvantage at all) or even for more than three years when it will be compensated to a greater or lesser extent by taper relief.[16]

In each case, the tax can be paid by interest-free instalments by the donees so long as the property is not sold (paragraph 4–05 above).

8–08 The authors consider it desirable to avoid the position whereby the tenancy vests in S alone on A's death and merges in the freehold reversion. If the lease is granted to the partnership, it is preferable to include another individual or individuals as partners (*e.g.* Mrs A and/or Mrs S) who can continue to farm the land in partnership under the tenancy after A's death. The surviving partners can subsequently dissolve the partnership and terminate the tenancy if desired. 8–08

Including Mrs A as a partner (possibly with a small share of profits during A's lifetime but with power for him to nominate her as the successor to his share on his death) may also be desirable anyway as a convenient means of providing her with an income after his death.

The lease (or A's share in the lease) will be an asset comprised in his estate which, if nothing further is done, will become chargeable on his death (or on the death of his wife if it accrues to her on his death). This may be a valuable asset in its own right, particularly if the lease was for a nominal rent for a fixed period which is not yet expired. Even where it has expired, and significant rent is being paid under the Agricultural Holdings Act 1948, it may still have an inherent value on the basis that the arbitration rent would be lower than a tender rent (paragraph 6–15 above), and

[14] I.H.T.A. 1984, s.116(2)(*a*).
[15] *Ibid.*, s.116(2).
[16] But note that taper relief only reduces the *rate of charge*, leaving the amount of the chargeable transfer unaffected (paragraph 1–02 above). Contrast agricultural relief which reduces the amount of the chargeable transfer.

possibly also on the ground that in any event the freeholder would pay a sum for the surrender of the tenancy to restore the freehold to vacant possession. In the authors' view that depends upon a pure question of fact, namely how anxious the freeholder is to recover vacant possession, and how much he would be prepared to pay to get it. But it is understood that this view is not shared by the Revenue, who will argue that the lease has substantial value on this account irrespective of whether the owner of the freehold actually wishes to recover vacant possession. In fact recent evidence from land agents shows that this "premium," where it exists, is falling but the Revenue still take the point. It is particularly relevant now with dairy farms where significant value can be attributable to the "tenant's share" of the value of the milk quota.

If it is provided (whether in the partnership agreement or otherwise) that the deceased partner's share of the lease should pass to the surviving partners without payment, this restriction will not affect the value of the share of the lease for inheritance tax purposes except to the extent that there was consideration for that restriction.[17] A *Boden* type of arrangement under which S was obliged to work full time in the business (A being under no such obligation) might represent consideration justifying no payment being made for A's share of the lease, so that section 163 would not apply and the value of his share of the lease would be nil. The danger in that is that if the partnership agreement taken as a whole includes an element of bounty, and is thus a gift, a provision that S is to work full time in the business without a corresponding obligation on A might be a reserved benefit to A. The result of that would be that the whole of the lease (and not just his share of it) would be deemed to be comprised in A's estate on his death under the Finance Act 1986, s.102 (gifts with reservation), although not, of course, the freehold reversion which is kept outside the partnership and is the subject of a separate gift.

50 per cent. business property relief would be available in any case provided there is no binding contract for sale (paragraph 4–12 above), and the tax can be paid by interest-free instalments provided there is no sale or payment under the partnership agreement in satisfaction of the deceased's share (paragraph 8–04 above).

(5) As in 4. but the lease is for full consideration

8–09 As explained in (3) there is a major difficulty in fixing the rent so as to be confident of showing that it is full consideration. In contrast to (3), however, the risks of getting it wrong under this strategy (where the lease is granted prior to the gift) are not nearly so great, because there should be no reservation of benefit in any event. (The lease having been granted *before* the gift of the freehold, there should be no necessity to rely upon the statutory exception for full consideration.) As will be seen later this strategy may be particularly useful where there are a number of intended donees, one or more of whom will not be involved in the business (whether as partners or otherwise): see paragraph 8–11 below.

[17] I.H.T.A. 1984, s.163 (restriction on freedom to dispose, *etc.*)

There are a number of advantages for inheritance tax purposes in this strategy over (4) (lease for nominal rent), the main one being that if one can show that the lease was for full consideration, the grant of the lease would not be a transfer of value, although it may depreciate the value of the freehold reversion.[18] If A dies within the following seven years, there would only be one chargeable transfer, namely the gift of the freehold reversion valued on a tenanted basis.

Additional advantages are that it avoids any problem of a lease for life (leases for full consideration being expressly excepted from section 43(3)); and it avoids the risk of the donor having a share of the "fag" end of an obviously valuable lease at a nominal rent comprised in his estate on death (although even a lease at a commercial rent may be valuable as already explained).

As against that, a lease for full consideration can be disadvantageous for income tax purposes. In practice, the consideration will have to be in the form of rent (a premium could give rise to an income tax charge under the lease premium provisions).[19] The rent would reduce the profits of the partnership which are earned income in the hands of the partners (other than sleeping partners), creating a corresponding amount of unearned income in the hands of the freehold reversioner. That may not be very serious at the moment, but could prove very expensive in the long term if the unearned income surcharge is ever re-introduced. The reduction of the trading income would also restrict the amount which the partners could contribute to retirement annuity schemes qualifying for tax relief, *etc.* Moreover, if the payment of rent results in the partnership trading at a loss, one would have to make sure that the loss can be used against other income. If the partnership is consistently showing losses, there may be difficulty in setting off the losses against other income.[20]

Quite apart from the income tax position, the donor would have to be prepared to see the partnership profits (and correspondingly his share of them) reduced at the expense of the rent going to the donee of the freehold reversion. If the whole object of the exercise is to get the capital value of the farm out of his estate for inheritance tax purposes whilst preserving his income or most of it, a lease at a rack rent will probably have to be ruled out.

Sometimes, however, a lease at a commercial rent can be attractive, particularly where all or part of the freehold reversion is to be given to someone who is not working in the business, *e.g.* one of the children who has no interest in farming or the trustees of an accumulation and maintenance settlement for young children or grandchildren; the rent under the lease may be a convenient way of providing the donee or trustees with a desired source of income. It may even be advantageous for income tax purposes if the donee's marginal rates of tax (or as the case may be the trustees' rates of tax) are lower than the partners' marginal rates. (See further paragraph 8–11 below.)

[18] *Ibid.*, s.16 (grants of tenancies of agricultural property for full consideration, *etc.*).
[19] Income and Corporation Taxes Act 1970, ss.80 *et seq.*
[20] *Ibid.*, section 180 (restrictions on set off of farming losses against general income).

(6) Gift of part of the farm to S; S and A farm the whole in partnership sharing profits equally

8–10 Under this strategy, A would give the entire freehold in part of the land 8–10 to S, and A and S would agree to farm the whole of the land in partnership, sharing profits equally (the land not being partnership property).

If the value of the land given to S does not exceed the value of the land retained by A, then the continued occupation by A of S's land under the partnership should not be a reserved benefit, being for full consideration (namely S's corresponding occupation under the partnership agreement of the land retained by A).[21] However, if the partnership agreement is made at the same time, care should be taken to ensure that there is no collateral benefit to A under the partnership agreement which would not be covered by the statutory exception for full consideration (see paragraph 6–37 above).

The gift of part of the land to S would be a PET. If A should die within the following seven years, agricultural relief would be available on the chargeable transfer at the rate of 50 per cent., provided the land is still owned by S at A's death (paragraph 4–14 above). Agricultural relief would also be available at the rate of 50 per cent. in respect of the land retained by A.

(7) Donees not engaged in the business

8–11 So far, we have been assuming that the donee is actively engaged in the 8–11 farming business. But suppose the donee is not at all involved in the business, or suppose there are a number of donees, one or more of whom are involved in the business (*e.g.* the farmer's eldest son) but others of whom are not (youngest son, daughter, or perhaps the trustees of an accumulation and maintenance settlement for grandchildren); what then?

Most of the courses of action examined above can be adapted to meet these cases where the donees include one or more persons who are not involved in the business, although some may be more suitable than others.

For example, the gift of an undivided share in the farm ((2) above) will probably (although not necessarily) involve the donee or donees farming the land in partnership. If one or more of the donees is not to be actively involved in the business, this may not be a very suitable arrangement. One solution might be to bring the non-farmers (or the trustees of an accumulation and maintenance or interest in possession settlement) in as limited partners, having no part to play in the management of the business.

However, their presence even as sleeping partners may be considered undesirable in the long term interests of the family and the business. In that event, if some but not all of the donees are involved in the business, the solution is likely to be along the lines of (4) or (5), *i.e.* a lease to a nominee for the donor or at a rack rent to a partnership consisting of the donor and those donees to be involved in the business, and a gift of the freehold reversion (in undivided shares) to all the donees. The lease to the partnership at a rack rent may be preferred if it is desired that those who are not

[21] I.H.T.A. 1984, Sched. 20, para. 6(1)(*a*).

involved in the business should have some income straight away. The former method (lease at a nominal rent for a fixed period) would leave those not involved in the business without income until the fixed period expired and a rent became payable under the Agricultural Holdings Act 1948.

Where none of the donor's children or grandchildren is interested in farming, and the donor nevertheless wants to make a gift of the land while still continuing to farm it, the most practical course is likely to be creating a lease in favour of himself (and/or his spouse) via a nominee and dispose of the freehold reversion. If he does not want to pay any rent, the lease could be at a nominal rent for fixed period equal to his life expectancy. Should he survive the fixed period, he would have security of tenure under the Agricultural Holdings Act 1948, although at that point he would have to pay a proper rent as determined in accordance with the statute.

The freehold reversion can be given away by way of a PET which will be free of tax if the donor survives for seven years. If he dies within the seven years, tax will be charged at the death rates, subject to taper relief where appropriate and with agricultural relief (although possibly only at 30 per cent. rather than 50 per cent.; see paragraph 8–07A above).

That would leave just the lease comprised in the donor's estate, which is a wasting asset. If he dies before the end of the fixed period while the lease is still at a nominal rent, the "fag" end of the lease will be an asset with some value, which will be chargeable subject to 50 per cent. agricultural relief.[21a] If he dies after the fixed period when he is holding over under the Agricultural Holdings Act 1948, the Revenue may still contend that the lease was in existence immediately before A's death, and thus should be brought into charge as an asset comprised in his estate immediately before death.[22] In the authors' view any claim for tax in such circumstances should be resisted. Even if the lease was still in existence immediately before A's death, it is strongly arguable that A's imminent death would be foreseeable immediately before his death, so that the value of the lease is minimal.

(8) C.G.T. disadvantages of lease at nominal rent

8–12 One disadvantage in the last strategy[23] is the loss of part of the existing C.G.T. base cost for the land. The gift of the freehold reversion would be a part disposal for C.G.T. purposes, requiring an apportionment between the part given away (the freehold reversion) and the part retained.[24] Under "hold-over" relief the donees would inherit that part of the donor's base cost which is attributable to the reversion.[25] The rest of the base cost which is attributable to the lease would be written off with the passing of time, the lease being a wasting asset.[25a] 8–12

The result is that if the land is ever sold, the donees could face an unduly

[21a] The donor should not leave the "fag" end of the lease by will to the donee of the freehold reversion: see I.H.T.A. 1984, s.268(3) (transfers of value by associated operations). The best course may be to leave it as an exempt gift to his widow, and allow it to expire in the course of time in her estate.

[22] *Ibid.*, s.4(1).

[23] and any other strategies involving a lease at a nominal rent: see, *e.g.* (4) above.

[24] C.G.T.A. 1979, s.35.

[25] F.A. 1980, s.79(1)(*b*).

[25a] C.G.T.A. 1979, Sched. 3, para. 1.

large charge to C.G.T. That would be particularly serious where one or more of the donees is not engaged in the business and thus has no opportunity to roll over the gain.[26] Where the existing base cost of the land is high, this can be very serious and must be carefully weighed against the prospective inheritance tax saving if a sale of the land is a realistic possibility in the future.

(9) The Farmhouse

8–13 One difficult question in practice is whether the farmhouse can safely be included in any of the arrangements proposed to be made in respect of the farm as a whole without a reserved benefit arising. **8–13**

Suppose for example the donor is giving away an undivided share in the land (paragraphs 8–04 and 8–04A above). Can he also give away at the same time a corresponding undivided share in the house without a reserved benefit?

In the authors' view, he can if the donee is also living in the house. Being in occupation of the house, the donee will bona fide assume possession and enjoyment of the interest in the house given to him[27]; and the donor's continuing occupation of the house would be attributable not to the share of the house which he had given away, but to the share which he had retained (paragraph 6–37 above). On that basis there would be no reservation of benefit. (See further paragraph 6–41 above.)

If, however, the donee is not living in the house (and is not receiving any rent) it is hard to see how he can be said to have assumed possession and enjoyment of the interest in the house given to him.[28] In such circumstances the authors consider it advisable to exclude the house from the gift.[29] It may be possible to make a separate arrangement for a lease of the farmhouse and a gift of the freehold reversion along the lines suggested in paragraph 8–06 above; but this may have a long term C.G.T. disadvantage because the donee's base cost will be the market value of the freehold subject to the lease, rather than the full value of the house with vacant possession.[30]

More generally, if a lease arrangement is adopted for a gift of the farmland (*e.g.* paragraph 8–06 above), the arrangements can normally cover the house as well. Whether the donee is living in the house or not, he will assume possession and enjoyment of the interest given (the freehold reversion subject to the lease) by receipt of the rent (if any) payable under the

[26] Under C.G.T.A. 1979, s.115 (replacement of business assets).

[27] F.A. 1986, s.102(1)(*a*).

[28] *Ibid.*

[29] It is considered that the farmhouse would probably still qualify for agricultural relief in the donor's estate notwithstanding that he has given away an undivided share in the adjoining farmland. There is no requirement in the legislation that the donor's interest in the farmhouse must be the same as his interest in the farmland. The test is simply whether the farmhouse is of "a character appropriate to the property" (*i.e.* the land): I.H.T.A. 1984, s.115(2).

[30] C.G.T.A. 1979, s.29A (acquisitions otherwise than by way of bargain at arm's length). It should not be necessary to claim hold-over relief, as the chargeable gain accruing to the donor should be covered by the private residence exemption (C.G.T.A. 1979, s.101 *et seq.*).

lease. If the donee is also given a share of the lease, he may not assume possession and enjoyment as regards that gift if he is not in occupation of the house. But that should not affect the separate gift of the freehold reversion.

III. FARMING COMPANIES

8–14 Farming companies can be classified into two main types for present purposes: 8–14

1. those companies which own the land; and
2. those companies which do not own the land, instead farming the land under some form of licence or tenancy from the owner of the freehold, who is often also a majority shareholder in the company.

Companies falling within the first category give rise to very much the same sort of planning considerations and techniques as family trading companies in general, and the reader is referred to the separate chapter dealing with family companies. Here it will merely be noted that where the transferor's shareholding (together with his spouse's, if any) gives control of the company, then insofar as the value of the shares is attributable to the value of the agricultural property inside the company, it will qualify for agricultural relief rather than business property relief.[30a] The rate of agricultural relief will be the same, however, *i.e.* 50 per cent., so long as the company's interest in the land carries the right to vacant possession, or the right to obtain it within the next 12 months. Insofar as the value of the shares is attributable to other assets in the company (or to development value in the land) it will qualify for 50 per cent. business property relief in the normal way under section 105(1)(*b*) (controlling shareholdings). For shareholdings which do not give control of the company (even taking account of a spouse's shareholding), there is no agricultural relief, but there will normally be business property relief at 30 per cent. (or in some cases 50 per cent.: see para. 7–15 above).

8–15 What we are mainly concerned with in this section is the second class of farming company, namely, where the land is kept outside the company and farmed by the company pursuant to a tenancy or licence from the land owner. 8–15

Take the following fairly simple case: A owns the freehold of Blackacre. Blackacre is farmed by X Limited pursuant to a tenancy which is protected under the Agricultural Holdings Act 1948. A owns 75 per cent. of the issued share capital of X Limited. Assume that Blackacre is worth £1,000,000 with vacant possession, and £500,000 on a tenanted basis. The net asset value of X Limited (disregarding the lease) is, say £100,000.

This fairly common set of circumstances raises a number of difficult valuation questions, the most important of which is the value of the freehold interest in Blackacre. At first sight, its value would appear to be the value on a tenanted basis, *i.e.* £500,000. Not so, say the Revenue. In their view the land must be valued together with a shareholding in the company as a single unit of valuation, on the basis that a purchaser of the land and the

[30a] I.H.T.A. 1984, s.122.

shares together would pay a price which reflected the full vacant possession value of the land; having bought the two together, he could then wind up the company, terminating the lease and restoring the freehold to full vacant possession value.

8–16 It is not entirely clear whether the Revenue's approach is correct. Inheritance tax is charged on the total value of an individual's entire estate on death (or, in the case of an *inter vivos* chargeable transfer, the value of his estate before the transfer less the value of his estate immediately after the transfer). One is therefore essentially valuing the entire estate rather than individual assets (compare capital gains tax, where one normally simply values the asset disposed of).[30b] In valuing the estate for inheritance tax purposes, the estate must be divided or grouped into "natural units" of valuation as a matter of common sense.[31] So, a block of ordinary shares and a block of preference shares would be valued together as a single unit of valuation if they would fetch a better price if sold together.[32] So also with farms which may be easily aggregated or sub-divided so as to fetch a better overall price.[33] What is not clear is whether one can aggregate *different* types of property (*e.g.* land and shares in a company) as a natural unit of valuation. The decided cases (which are few in number) concern only grouping assets *of the same type*. It is therefore open to argument that land and shares in the company cannot be aggregated to produce a higher overall value as suggested by the Revenue. That said, it may well be that properties of a different type can be aggregated for valuation purposes if it is practical to do so and any reasonably prudent man would do so to obtain a more favourable price.

On that basis there is at least a substantial risk that most of the full vacant possession value of Blackacre would be included in A's estate. This would be getting the worst of all possible worlds because, although the vacant possession value of the land would be included in A's estate, the land would still only qualify for 30 per cent. relief because the *interest in the land* does not carry the right to vacant possession, or the right to obtain it within the next 12 months.[33a] For that purpose it is irrelevant that the *shares* can be used to restore the land to vacant possession.

The Revenue would take the same view if A's shareholding was 51 per cent. and not 75 per cent., on the basis that although the shareholding would not give the right to wind up the company, it would give control over the company and consequently the ability to force the company to surrender the lease (unless the articles of the company state the contrary). This is a much more arguable case because, as a matter of company law, the company would have to be paid a proper price for the surrender of the lease if minority shareholders are not to be prejudiced. The capital gains tax liability of the company on the surrender of the lease would also have to be taken into account, subject to the possibility of "rolling-over" the gain under the Capital Gains Tax Act 1979, s.115 (replacement of business

[30b] *Henderson* v. *Karmel's Executors* [1984] S.T.C. 572.
[31] *Duke of Buccleuch* v. *I.R.C.* [1967] 1 A.C. 506.
[32] *A.-G. for Ceylon* v. *Mackie* [1952] 2 All E.R. 775.
[33] *Duke of Buccleuch*, *supra*.
[33a] I.H.T.A. 1984, s.116(2)(*a*).

assets).[34] Such an arrangement would be much less straightforward and not nearly so attractive to a prospective purchaser, who, if he is interested at all, would probably require a heavy discount for his trouble. (This would also tend to cast further doubt on whether the aggregation of the land and the shares is a natural unit of valuation).

8–17 From a practical point of view, the risks are far too great and something should be done about it. The obvious course would be for A to give away the freehold by way of a PET. A could of course retain all his shares in the company, receive dividends on his shares and draw director's remuneration as before, without any danger of a reserved benefit over the land. So, from an income point of view, all he would lose would be the rent under the lease. 8–17

If he survives for seven years the PET would be free of inheritance tax and the whole (or virtually the whole) of the value of the land would escape inheritance tax, leaving only the value of the shares in the company comprised in his estate (see below). If he dies within the seven years, the PET would become a chargeable transfer taxable at death rates, subject to taper relief where appropriate. The amount of the transfer of value, on the Revenue's view, would be as follows:

Value of freehold with vacant possession (£1,000,000) plus the value of the shares (75 per cent. of the net asset value of the company) (£75,000) = £1.075m.
Less the value of the shares (75 per cent. of the net asset value of the company after the transfer) (£0.075m)
= £1,000,000.

In fact, the net asset value of the company would be regarded by the Revenue as rather more than £100,000 on account of the company's agricultural tenancy (see below). On that basis A's shareholding after the transfer would be valued in excess of £75,000, with a corresponding reduction in the transfer of value. Agricultural relief would be available, assuming the land is retained by the donee, at 30 per cent. (not 50 per cent., see paragraph 8–16 above).

That would leave just the value of the shares comprised in A's estate. There would still be a difficult valuation question left, namely whether the value of the company as a whole is increased on account of its agricultural tenancy, and the value of the shares correspondingly increased by a proportionate fraction. The Revenue will argue that it is, possibly by a large amount. (It is not unusual for the Revenue to attribute to the lease a value equal to one half the difference between the value of the freehold with vacant possession and its value on a tenanted basis). If that is correct, then A's retention of his 75 per cent. shareholding in the company will still leave a very valuable asset comprised in his estate (although obviously not nearly as valuable as the land itself).

Whether the Revenue's approach is correct is another matter.

The authors would like to stress one very important if basic point in this regard. What one is valuing for inheritance tax purposes is the asset com-

[34] See C.L.A. circular 3/81 for the Revenue's views on what account can be taken of tax in respect of chargeable gains within a company when valuing shares in the company.

prised in the individual's estate, namely the shares in the company, *not* the lease inside the company. Many misconceptions stem from a failure to grasp that basic point.

8–18 In the authors' view, the question of whether the value of the shares is to be increased on account of the company's agricultural tenancy, and if so by how much, largely depends upon a pure question of fact, namely whether a prospective purchaser of the shares would pay more for them because of the company's agricultural tenancy, and if so how much. In the case of a 100 per cent. shareholding, a purchaser may well be prepared to pay a hefty premium for the shares because he will in effect be buying a perpetual agricultural tenancy which he could not otherwise get (or not without paying an even larger premium), although he will probably want some discount for a company which is not or may not be "clean." Where he is buying less than 100 per cent. of the shares, however, the situation may be entirely different. Because a man will pay a substantial amount for a 100 per cent. shareholding in a company to get in effect a perpetual agricultural tenancy, it cannot simply be assumed by analogy that he would pay a proportionate amount for a 75 per cent. holding. The latter is an entirely different proposition; he would not in substance be buying a perpetual agricultural tenancy on his own because there would be other people interested in the tenancy as shareholders in the company, albeit as minority shareholders only. It is possible that he might pay a substantial sum for a 75 per cent. holding; but it is a question of fact and no assumptions can be made in that regard. 8–18

It is also possible that a purchaser may pay extra for the shares on the basis that the company can turn the lease to account. Again, in the authors' view it is a pure question of fact. It is often said in that regard that even if the lease is non-assignable, one has to assume that it could be assigned in accordance with the principle in *Crossman*.[35] That is a misconception. The *Crossman* principle is that where a non-assignable asset has to be valued at the price it would fetch if sold in the open market, one must assume (contrary to fact) that it is assignable, because that is what the legislation requires you to do. However, the *Crossman* principle only applies to *the asset being valued*, which in this case is not the lease itself but the shares in the company. In valuing the ***shares***, it cannot be assumed that the *lease* is assignable if it is not in fact assignable.

It is of course always possible for the company to surrender the lease to the owner of the freehold. But whether the freeholder would be prepared to pay for the surrender, and if so how much, is again a question of fact and depends *inter alia* upon whether the particular freeholder in question is anxious to recover vacant possession. Many owners of freehold agricultural land would not wish to do so if there is a satisfactory tenant. It certainly cannot automatically be assumed that the freeholder will be anxious to take a surrender of the lease, or that he would pay a substantial sum to do so.

8–19 To conclude this discussion, it may be that the value of the shares is greater on account of the company's agricultural tenancy. In the author's view it will depend upon the facts which may be very difficult to determine. 8–19

[35] *I.R.C.* v. *Crossman* [1937] A.C. 26.

The Revenue will certainly argue that the value of the shares should be substantially increased on account of the company's tenancy. In the circumstances consideration should be given to an additional gift of some of the shares by way of a PET to reduce the potential value left in A's estate. In that connection the discussion in the general chapter on Family Companies will be relevant, particularly the donor's continuing to draw director's fees, retention of some shares, business property relief, etc. (See also para. 8–14 above as to agricultural relief on controlling shareholdings so far as the value of the shares is attributable to the agricultural property inside the company.)

APPENDIX 1

Precedents

The two precedents provided in A and B establish accumulation and maintenance trusts in the following forms.
Precedent A—this is a basic form for a single class of beneficiaries who become absolutely and equally entitled on attaining the Specified Age.
Precedent B—again this is intended for a single class of beneficiaries but with the trustees having power to vary the shares in which those beneficiaries will take. On attaining the Specified Age a beneficiary will only take a life interest in his share, the remainder being to his or her children with power for the beneficiary to appoint an income interest to a surviving spouse. The detailed trusts for beneficiaries over the Specified Age are set out in Clause 6. Where a beneficiary dies under the Specified Age leaving children, those children will inherit his or her share.

As will be see from the definition of the beneficiaries in clause 1(b) both precedents are intended for a class satisfying the "common grandparent" test, being children or grandchildren of the settlor born before the first of them attains the Specified Age. Precedent 2 could in fact be used for a "mixed" class with the power of appointment in clause 4 and the power to accelerate interests in possession in clause 5(e) being exercised as required to ensure the 25 year rule is not broken. In such circumstances it may, however, be better to amend the precedent so that it automatically provides for interests in possession to arise after 25 years unless the trustees exercise an overriding power to the contrary.

Apart from the power of appointment and engrafted trusts for a beneficiary's share contained in precedent 2, the two precedents take the same form and most of the clauses are self explanatory. The following are, however, worthy of particular comment:

(a) Trusts for beneficiaries under the Specified Age (clause 5 in both precedents):
This clause ensures that the provisions of section 71(1)(*b*) are complied with but in a flexible way. In particular income can be distributed to any of the beneficiaries under the Specified Age. Once the Specified Age has been reached, the beneficiary has an interest in possession in his Share of the Trust Fund.

(b) Ultimate default trusts (clause 6 in precedent 1, clause 7 in precedent 2)
If no beneficiary has previously attained the Specified Age and no beneficiary is for the time being in existence, sub-clause (a) provides that income is to be accumulated so long as further beneficiaries may come into existence and the accumulation period is running. This maintains the accumulation and maintenance status of the

trusts for as long as possible and vesting under the default trusts of sub-cluase (b) will only occur at the expiry of the accumulation period or when the possibility of further beneficiaries is exhausted.

The description of the default beneficiaries to be inserted in sub-clause (b) will obviously depend on the wishes of individual settlors but the precedents are drafted on the basis that both the settlor and the settlor's spouse will be completely excluded. However, as regards reservation of benefit, there is no objection to a resulting trust in favour of the Settlor (see para. 6–40) and such trusts will not have income tax repercussions if they are designed to comply with I.C.T.A. 1970 ss.447(2)(*a*)(iv) and 457(6)(*d*).

(c) Administrative powers (clause 7 in precedent 1, clause 8 in precedent 2 and the first schedule)
A wide variety of administrative powers are incorporated to ensure ease of administration in unforeseen future circumstances. The powers, although wide, must be exercised in accordance with the beneficial provisions of the settlement.

Precedent A

Basic form – absolute trusts*

Index to clauses

A–01 THIS SETTLEMENT is made the day of One thousand nine hundred and A–01

* This precedent is adapted from Practical Trust Precedents published by Longman Group Plc, 21–27 Lamb's Conduit Street, London WC1 3NS and is reproduced with the kind permission of the Publishers.

BETWEEN

(1) ('the Settlor')
(2) ('the Trustees' which expression shall where the context so admits include the trustees or trustee for the time being of this Settlement)

WHEREAS

(A) THE Settlor wishes to make this Settlement and has transferred or delivered to the Trustees or otherwise placed under their control the property specified in the Second Schedule and from time to time further monies investments or other property may be paid or transferred to the Trustees by way of addition
(B) IT is intended that this Settlement shall be irrevocable

NOW THIS DEED IRREVOCABLY WITNESSES as follows

A–02 **1 Definitions** A–02

IN this deed where the context so admits

(a) 'the Trust Fund' shall mean
  (i) the property specified in the Second Schedule and
  (ii) all money investments or other property paid or transferred by any person or persons to or so as to be under the control of and (in either case) accepted by the Trustees as additions and
  (iii) all accumulations (if any) of income directed to be held as an accretion to capital and
  (iv) the money investments and property from time to time representing the said money investments property additions and accumulations
(b) 'the Beneficiaries' shall mean
  (i) the existing [grand] children of the Settlor namely:
  who was born on 19
  who was born on 19
  who was born on 19
  who was born on 19
  (ii) every other [grand] child of the Settlor born after the date of this Settlement but before the first [grand] child to attain the Specified Age shall do so
(c) 'the Trust Period' shall mean the period ending on the earlier of
  (i) the last day of the period of 80 years from the date of this Settlement which period (and no other) shall be the applicable perpetuity period or
  (ii) such date as the Trustees shall by deed specify (not being a date earlier than the date of execution of such deed)

(d) 'the Accumulation Period' shall mean the period of 21 years from the date of this Settlement or the Trust Period if shorter
(e) 'interest in possession' shall have the meaning it has for the purposes

of section 71 of the Inheritance Tax Act 1984 or any statutory modification or re-enactment of such section

(f) "the Specified Age" in respect of any Beneficiary shall mean during the Accumulation Period the age of 25 years and at the termination of the Accumulation Period shall mean such lesser age (not being less than 18 years) as the Beneficiary shall by then have attained and otherwise during the Trust Period shall mean the age of 18 years.

A–03 2 Trust for sale A–03

THE Trustees shall hold the Trust Fund upon trust as to investments or property other than money in their absolute discretion to sell call in or convert into money all or any of such investments or property but with power to postpone such sale calling in or conversion and to permit the same to remain as invested and upon trust as to money with the like discretion to invest the same in their names or under their control in any of the investments authorised by this Settlement or by law with power at the like discretion from time to time to vary or transpose any such investments for others so authorised.

A–04 3 Trusts of added property A–04

THE Trustees shall hold the Trust Fund upon with and subject to the trusts powers and provisions of this Settlement and the Trustees shall have the right at any time during the Trust Period to accept such additional money investments or other property as may be paid or transferred to them upon these trusts by the Settlor or any other person either personally or by testamentary act or disposition (including property of an onerous nature the acceptance of which the Trustees consider to be beneficial)

A–05 4 Trusts of capital and income A–05

(a) THE capital and income of the Trust Fund shall be held upon trust for such of the Beneficiaries as attain the Specified Age before the end of the Trust Period or are living and under that age at the end of the Trust Period and if more than one in equal shares absolutely

(b) The provisions of Clause 5 below shall apply to the presumptive share or entitlement in or to the Trust Fund of any of the Beneficiaries such presumptive share or entitlement being in that clause called 'the Share' and that one of the Beneficiaries who is primarily interested in the Share being called 'the Primary Beneficiary'

A–06 5 Trusts for beneficiaries under the Specified Age A–06

THE following provisions shall apply to the Share during the Trust Period while the Primary Beneficiary is living and under the Specified Age

(a) The Trustees may pay or apply any income of the Share for or towards the maintenance or education or otherwise for the benefit of the

Primary Beneficiary or any other or others of the Beneficiaries who are for the time being living and under the Specified Age

(b) The Trustees may also pay or apply any capital of the Share for or towards the maintenance or education or otherwise for the benefit of the Primary Beneficiary providing that capital shall not be so applied in a way which would or might prevent the Primary Beneficiary from becoming entitled to or to an interest in possession in the capital so applied on or before attaining the Specified Age nor in such a way that the income of the Share might in the meantime be dealt with except by being applied for the maintenance education or otherwise for the benefit of one or more of the Beneficiaries for the time being living and under the Specified Age or by being accumulated

(c) Subject as above during the Accumulation Period the income of the Share shall be accumulated as an accretion to the capital of the Share

(d) Subject as above section 31 of the Trustee Act 1925 (as modified below) shall apply to the income of the Share

(e) Notwithstanding subclauses (a) (c) and (d) above the Trustees may at any time or times by deed or deed revocable during the Trust Period or irrevocable and executed during the Trust Period direct in relation to all or any part of the Share that from the date of such deed or on the attainment by the Primary Beneficiary of an age less than the Specified Age or on the occurrence of any other event (not being earlier than the date of the deed) prior to the Primary Beneficiary attaining the Specified Age the income of the Share or the relevant part of the Share shall be paid to the Primary Beneficiary

A–07 **6 Ultimate default trusts** A–07

(a) SUBJECT as above during the Accumulation Period (no Beneficiary having previously attained the Specified Age) and so long as a further Beneficiary or further Beneficiaries may come into existence the income of the Trust Fund shall be accumulated

(b) Subject as above and if and so far as not wholly disposed of for any reason whatever by the above provisions the capital and income of the Trust Fund shall be held in trust for [such of the Beneficiaries as are living at the date of this Settlement in equal shares] absolutely

A–08 **7 Administrative powers** A–08

THE Trustees shall in addition and without prejudice to all statutory powers have the powers and immunities set out in the First Schedule provided that the Trustees shall not exercise any of their powers so as to conflict with the beneficial provisions of this Settlement

A–09 **8 Extended power of maintenance** A–09

SECTION 31 of the Trustee Act 1925 shall be deemed to apply as if the words 'may in all the circumstances be reasonable' had been omitted from paragraph (i) of subsection (1) and in substitution there had been inserted the words 'the Trustees may think fit' and as if the proviso at the end of subsection (1) had been omitted

A–10 9 Extended power of advancement

SECTION 32 of the Trustee Act 1925 shall be deemed to apply as if the proviso (a) of subsection (1) had been omitted

A–11 10 Restrictions on certain powers

DURING such period as these trusts qualify as accumulation and maintenance trusts in that they comply with the provisions of section 71 of the Inheritance Tax Act 1984 or any statutory modification or re-enactment of such section or would so qualify but for the existence of the powers conferred on the Trustees by Clauses 7 to 9 inclusive and Clause 14 such powers shall not be exercised in such a way that would or might prevent a Beneficiary who is under the Specified Age and has not become entitled to or to an interest in possession in all or part of the Trust Fund from becoming entitled to such an interest on or before attaining the Specified Age or in such a way that the income of all or part of the Trust Fund might in the meantime be dealt with except by being applied for the maintenance education or otherwise for the benefit of one or more of the Beneficiaries for the time being living and under the Specified Age or by being accumulated

A–12 11 Trustee charging clause

(a) ANY trustee which shall be a trust corporation or company authorised to undertake trust business shall be entitled in addition to reimbursement of its proper expenses to remuneration for its services in accordance with its published terms and conditions for trust business in force from time to time and in the absence of any such published terms and conditions in accordance with terms and conditions as may from time to time be agreed between such trustee and the Settlor or (if the Settlor is unfit unable or unwilling to act) the person or persons by whom the power of appointing new trustees is for the time being exercisable

(b) Any trustee who is a solicitor or other person engaged in a profession or business shall be entitled to charge and be paid all normal professional or other charges for business done services rendered or time spent personally or by such trustee's firm in the administration of these trusts including acts which a trustee not engaged in any profession or business could have done personally

A–13 12 Appointment of new trustees

(a) DURING the lifetime of the Settlor the power of appointing new trustees shall be vested in the Settlor

(b) A person may be appointed to be a trustee notwithstanding that such person is not resident in the United Kingdom and remaining out of the United Kingdom for more than 12 months shall not be a ground for the removal of a trustee

A–14 13 Clause headings A–14

THE clause headings are included for reference only and do not affect the interpretation of this Settlement

A–15 14 Proper law forum and place of administration A–15

(a) THE proper law of this Settlement shall be that of England and Wales and all rights under this Settlement and its construction and effect shall be subject to the jurisdiction of and construed according to the laws of England and Wales

(b) The courts of England and Wales shall be the forum for the administration of these trusts

(c) Notwithstanding the provisions of subclauses (a) and (b)

- (i) The Trustees shall have power (subject to the application (if any) of the rule against perpetuities) to carry on the general administration of these trusts in any jurisdiction in the world whether or not such jurisdiction is for the time being the proper law of this Settlement or the courts of such jurisdiction are for the time being the forum for the administration of these trusts and whether or not the Trustees or any of them are for the time being resident or domiciled in or otherwise connected with such jurisdiction
- (ii) The Trustees may at any time declare in writing that from the date of such declaration the proper law of this Settlement shall be that of any specified jurisdiction (not being a jurisdiction under the law of which this Settlement would be capable of revocation) and that all rights under this Settlement and its construction and effect shall be subject to and construed according to the laws of that jurisdiction
- (iii) The Trustees may at any time declare in writing that from the date of such declaration the forum for the administration of these trusts shall be the courts of any specified jurisdiction

A–16 15 Exclusion of settlor and spouse A–16

(a) NO discretion or power by this Settlement or by law conferred on the Trustees or any other person shall be exercised and no provision of this Settlement shall operate directly or indirectly so as to cause or permit any part of the capital or income of the Trust Fund to become in any way payable to or applicable for the benefit of the Settlor or any person or persons who shall previously have added property to the Trust Fund or the spouse for the time being of the Settlor or any such person or persons

(b) The prohibition in this clause shall apply notwithstanding anything else contained or implied in this Settlement

16 Stamp duty certificate

THE Settlor hereby certifies that this instrument falls within category L in the Schedule to the Stamp Duty (exempt Instruments) Regulations 1987

IN WITNESS whereof the parties hereto have hereunto set their hands and seals the day and year first above written

A–17 THE FIRST SCHEDULE

[*Administrative powers*]

[*See* A1–19 to A1–41]

A–18 THE SECOND SCHEDULE

[*The initial trust fund*]

SIGNED SEALED and DELIVERED etc

ADMINISTRATIVE POWERS

Index to clauses

The First Schedule

A–19 **1 Power of investment** A–19

(a) SUBJECT as provided below any monies requiring investment may be invested in or upon any investments of whatever nature and wherever situate whether producing income or not (including the purchase of any immovable or movable property or any interest in such property and including purchases made for the purpose of enabling all or any or more of the Beneficiaries to have the occupation use or enjoyment in specie of the asset purchased or other purposes which the Trustees consider to be in the interests of any one or more of the Beneficiaries) as the Trustees shall in their absolute discretion think fit so that the Trustees shall have the same full and unrestricted powers of making and changing investments of such monies as if they were absolutely and beneficially entitled to such monies and without prejudice to the generality of the above the Trustees shall not be under any obligation to diversify their investment of such monies

(b) The acquisition of any reversionary interest or any policy of insurance or assurance sinking fund policy or other policy of whatever nature or any annuity or securities or other investments not producing income or of a wasting nature or for any other reason not within the meaning of the word "investment" strictly construed shall be deemed to be an authorised investment of trust monies if the Trustees shall consider the same to be for the benefit of any one or more of the Beneficiaries

(c) Where any such reversionary interest policy security or investment as is described in subclause (b) is comprised in the Trust Fund or where any other security or investment is sold with the right to receive the dividend or interest accrued or accruing no part of any accretion to the value or of any premium or bonus or other sum (whether in respect of arrears of or prospective dividend or interest or income or otherwise) which accrues or is payable when the same falls into possession or is redeemed or matures or on repayment of the capital monies so secured or when any sale or disposal is made shall be apportionable to or be treated as income

(d) The Trustees shall have the power to exchange property for other property of a like or different nature and for such consideration and on such conditions as they in their absolute discretion think fit

A–20 **2 Power to lend and to give guarantees** A–20

(a) THE Trustees shall have power to lend money or property to any one or more of the Beneficiaries either free of interest or on such terms as to payment of interest and generally as the Trustees shall in their absolute discretion think fit

(b) The Trustees shall have power to guarantee the payment of money and the performance of obligations in respect of any existing or future borrowings by any one or more of the Beneficiaries from third parties or guarantees indemnities or other commitments of like nature given to third parties by any one or more of the Beneficiaries including without prejudice to the generality of the above the power to pledge the whole or part of the assets comprising the Trust Fund in support of any such guarantee given as above by the Trustees and to enter into such indemnities as they shall in their absolute discretion think fit in connection with any such guarantee

A–21 **3 Power to permit occupation of property and enjoyment of chattels** A–21

THE Trustees shall have power to permit any one or more of the Beneficiaries to occupy or reside in or upon any real or immovable property or to have the enjoyment and use of chattels or other movable property for the time being held upon these trusts on such terms as to payment of rent rates taxes and other expenses and outgoings and as to insurance repair and decoration and generally upon such terms as the Trustees shall in their absolute discretion think fit

A–22 **4 Power to borrow** A–22

THE Trustees shall have power to borrow and raise money on the security of the Trust Fund for any purpose (including the investment of the monies so raised as part of the Trust Fund) and to mortgage charge or pledge any part of the Trust Fund as security for any monies so raised and to guarantee the payment of money and the performance of obligations in respect of borrowings by any company fully or partly owned by the Trustees and in connection with such guarantees to enter into such indemnities as the Trustees shall in their absolute discretion think fit.

A–23 **5 Powers in relation to real property** A–23

WHERE the Trust Fund for the time being includes any real or immovable property (in this clause referred to as 'the land')

(a) The Trustees may lease all or any part of the land for any purpose and whether involving waste or not and for any term and either wholly or partly in consideration of a rent (whether fixed or variable) or fine or premium or the erection improvement or repair or any agreement to erect improve or repair buildings or other structures on the land and may accept (with or without consideration) surrender of any lease of all or any part of the land

(b) The Trustees may in executing any trust or power of sale sell all or any part of the land either wholly or partly in consideration of an annual sum payable either in perpetuity or for any term (whether definite or indefinite) and being either reserved out of the land sold or secured in such other manner as the Trustees shall in their absolute discretion think fit

(c) The Trustees may in executing any trust or power of sale or leasing

(i) sell or lease all or any part of the land whether the division is horizontal or vertical or made in any other way

(ii) sell or lease or reserve any easement or right or privilege over all or any part of the land

(iii) sell or lease or except or reserve any timber or mines or minerals on or in or under all or any part of the land together with any easements rights or privileges of cutting or working and carrying away the same or otherwise incidental to or connected with forestry or mining purposes

(iv) impose and make binding for the benefit of all or any part of the land sold or leased any restrictions or stipulations as to user or otherwise affecting any part of the land retained

(v) accept in exchange for all or any part of the land to be sold or leased (either with or without any money paid or received for equality of exchange) any other real or immovable property or any lease

(vi) enter into any contract or grant any option for the sale or leasing of all or any part of the land or otherwise for the exercise by the Trustees of any of their above powers

(d) The Trustees shall not be bound to see nor be liable or accountable for omitting or neglecting to see to the repair or insurance of any buildings or other structures on the land or to the payment of any outgoings or otherwise as to the maintenance of the land or any buildings or other structures on the land but may maintain repair or insure the same in such manner and to such extent as they shall in their absolute discretion think fit

(e) The Trustees may from time to time expend monies altering or improving the land or any buildings or other structures on the land (including erecting demolishing or rebuilding the same) to such extent and in such manner as they shall in their absolute discretion think fit and any certificate in writing of any architect or surveyor employed by the Trustees to the effect that any work specified in such certificate is or includes an alteration or an improvement to the land or any such building or other structure shall be conclusive as between the Trustees and the Beneficiaries that any money expended on such work was properly expended in exercise of this power

A–24 6 Powers in relation to chattels A–24

WHERE the Trust Fund for the time being includes any chattels (in this clause referred to as 'the chattels')

(a) The Trustees may sell lease hire deposit store or otherwise deal with the chattels upon such terms as they shall in their absolute discretion think fit

(b) The Trustees shall not be bound to see nor be liable or accountable for omitting or neglecting to see to the repair or insurance of the chattels but may repair and insure the chattels in such manner and to such extent as they shall in their absolute discretion think fit

A–25 7 Power to trade A–25

(a) THE Trustees shall have power to trade or take part in any venture in the nature of trade whether solely or jointly with any other person and whether or not by way of partnership (limited or general) and for these purposes make such arrangements as they shall in their absolute discretion think fit and may delegate any exercise of this power to any one or more of their number or to a company or partnership formed for this purpose

(b) Any power vested in the Trustees under this Settlement shall (where applicable) extend to any arrangements in connection with any such trade or venture and in particular but without prejudice to the generality of the above the Trustees' powers of borrowing and charging shall extend to any borrowing arrangements made in connection with such trade or venture and whether made severally or jointly with others or with unequal liability and the Trustees shall be entitled to be fully indemnified out of the Trust Fund against all personal liability to which they may become in any manner subject in connection with any such trade or venture

A–26 **8 Power to give indemnities** A–26

(a) THE Trustees shall have power to enter into any indemnity in favour of any former trustee or any other person in respect of any fiscal imposition or other liability of any nature prospectively payable in respect of the Trust Fund or otherwise in connection with this Settlement and to charge or deposit the whole or any part of the Trust Fund as security for any such indemnity in such manner in all respects as they shall in their absolute discretion think fit

(b) The Trustees shall have power to give or enter into any indemnity warranty guarantee undertaking or covenant or enter into any type of agreement that they shall in their absolute discretion think fit relating to the transfer or sale of a business or private company shareholding held or owned for the time being by the Trustees whether relating to the business or company itself its assets liabilities shares or employees or any other aspect of the business or company in favour of any transferee purchaser or other relevant party and including any limitation or restriction on value or otherwise as the Trustees shall in their absolute discretion think fit

A–27 **9 Exclusion of apportionment** A–27

THE statutory and equitable rules of apportionment shall not apply to this Settlement and the Trustees shall be permitted to treat all dividends and other payments in the nature of income received by them as income at the date of receipt irrespective of the period for which the dividend or other income is payable

A–28 **10 Power to deal with insurance policies** A–28

THE Trustees shall in addition and without prejudice to all statutory and other powers conferred upon them have the following powers in relation to any insurance policy ('the policy') from time to time comprised in the Trust Fund

(a) To borrow on the security of the policy for any purpose

(b) To convert the policy into a fully paid-up policy for a reduced sum assured free from payment of future premiums

(c) To surrender the policy wholly or any part or any bonus attaching to the policy for its cash surrender value

(d) To sell the policy or any substituted policy on such terms as the Trustees shall in their absolute discretion think fit

(e) To exercise any of the powers conferred by the policy or with the consent of the insurer to alter the amount or occasion of the payment of the sum assured or to increase or decrease the amount of the periodic premiums (if any) payable under the policy or to alter the period during which the premiums are payable and to do any of these things notwithstanding that the sum assured may be reduced subject always to production of evidence of insurability satisfactory to the insurer

11 Power to vary administrative provisions A–29

THE Trustees shall have power at any time or times during the Trust Period by deed or deeds to revoke or vary any of the administrative provisions of this Settlement or to add any further administrative provisions as the Trustees may consider expedient for the purposes of this Settlement and without prejudice to the generality of the above for ensuring that at all times there should be a trustee of this Settlement and that the Trust Fund shall be fully and effectively vested in or under the control of such trustee and that the trusts of this Settlement shall be enforceable by the Beneficiaries provided always that the powers conferred by this clause shall only be exercisable if the Trustees shall be advised in writing by a lawyer of at least ten years' standing qualified in the law of the jurisdiction which for the time being is the proper law of this Settlement that it would be expedient for the purposes of this Settlement that the administrative provisions be revoked varied or added to in the manner specified in such written advice and such power shall be exercisable only by the Trustees executing a deed in a form appropriate to carry such advice into effect

12 Release of powers A–30

THE Trustees may by deed or deeds and so as to bind their successors as trustees release or restrict the future exercise of all or any of the powers by this Settlement or by law conferred on their either wholly or to the extent specified in and such deed or deeds notwithstanding the fiduciary nature of any such powers

13 Power of appropriation A–31

THE Trustees shall have power in their absolute discretion to appropriate any part of the Trust Fund in its then actual condition or state of investment in or towards satisfaction of any interest or share in the Trust Fund as may in all the circumstances appear to them to be just and reasonable and for the above purposes from time to time to place such value on any or all investments or other property as they shall in their absolute discretion think fit

14 Power to vote and to employ nominees and custodians A–32

IN respect of any property comprised in the Trust Fund the Trustees shall have power

(a) To vote upon or in respect of any shares securities bonds notes or other evidence of interest in or obligation of any corporation trust association or concern whether or not affecting the security or the apparent security of the Trust Fund or the purchase or sale or lease of the assets of any such corporation trust association or concern

(b) To deposit any such shares securities or property in any voting trust or with any depositary designated under such a voting trust

(c) To give proxies or powers of attorney with or without power of substitution for voting or acting on behalf of the Trustees as the owners of any such property

(d) To hold any or all securities or other property in bearer form or in the names of the Trustees or any one or more of them or in the name of some other person or partnership or in the name or names of nominees without disclosing the fiduciary relationship created by this Settlement and to deposit the said securities and any title deeds or other documents belonging or relating to the Trust Fund in any part of the world with any bank firm trust company or other company that undertakes the safe custody of securities as part of its business without being responsible for the default of such bank firm trust company or other company or for any consequent loss

A–33 15 Power to delegate management of investments

(a) THE Trustees shall have power to engage the services of such investment adviser or advisers as the Trustees may from time to time think fit ('the investment adviser') to advise the Trustees in respect of the investment and reinvestment of the Trust Fund with power for the Trustees without being liable for any consequent loss to delegate to the investment adviser discretion to manage all or part of the Trust Fund within the limits and for the period stipulated by the Trustees and the Trustees shall settle the terms and conditions for the remuneration of the investment adviser and the reimbursement of the investment adviser's expenses as the Trustees shall in their absolute discretion think fit and such remuneration and expenses shall be paid by the Trustees from the Trust Fund

(b) The Trustees shall not be bound to enquire into nor be in any manner responsible for any changes in the legal status of the investment adviser

(c) The Trustees shall incur no liability for any action taken pursuant to or for otherwise following the advice of the investment adviser however communicated

A–34 16 Power to receive remuneration

NO trustee shall be liable to account for any remuneration or other profit received by such trustee in consequence of such trustee acting as or being appointed to be a director or other officer or servant of any company notwithstanding that such appointment was procured by an exercise by such trustee or by the Trustees of voting rights attached to securities comprised in the Trust Fund

A–35 17 Power to promote companies

THE Trustees may (without prejudice to the generality of their powers of investment) promote or join with any other person or persons in promoting or incorporating any company in any part of the world or subscribe for or acquire any of the shares or stock or debentures or debenture stock or loan capital of any company with a view to or in consideration of

(i) the establishment and carrying on by such company of a business of any kind which the Trustees are for the time being authorised to carry on themselves and the acquisition of any of the assets comprised in the Trust Fund which may be required for the purposes of such business
(ii) the acquisition of the assets and undertaking of any business being carried on by the Trustees under the above power
(iii) the acquisition of all or any of the assets comprised in the Trust Fund to be held as investments of the company acquiring the same

–36 18 Trustees not bound to interfere in business of company in which the settlement is interested A–36

THE Trustees shall not be bound or required to interfere in the management or conduct of the business of any company wherever resident or incorporated in which the Settlement shall be interested although holding the whole or a majority of the shares carrying the control of the company but so long as the Trustees shall have no notice of any act of dishonesty or misappropriation of monies on the part of the directors having the management of such company the Trustees shall be at liberty to leave the conduct of its business (including the payment or non-payment of dividends) wholly to the directors and the Beneficiaries shall not be entitled to require the distribution of any dividend by any such company or require the Trustees to exercise any powers they may have of compelling any such distribution

–37 19 Power to insure property A–37

THE Trustees shall have power to ensure against any loss or damage from any peril any property for the time being comprised in the Trust Fund for any amount and to pay the premiums out of the Trust Fund

–38 20 Power to appoint agents A–38

THE Trustees shall have power instead of acting personally to employ and pay at the expense of the Trust Fund any agent in any part of the world whether attorneys solicitors accountants brokers banks trust companies or other agents without being responsible for the default of any agent if employed in good faith to transact any business or act as nominee or do any act in the execution of these trusts including without prejudice to the generality of the above the receipt and payment of monies and the execution of documents

–39 21 Power to permit self-dealing A–39

THE Trustees shall have power to enter into any transaction concerning the Trust Fund notwithstanding that one or more of the Trustees may be interested in the transaction other than as one of the Trustees

A–40 **22 Indemnity**

IN the execution of these trusts no trustee shall be liable for any loss to the Trust Fund arising by reason of any improper investment made in good faith or for the negligence or fraud of any agent employed by such trustee or by any of the Trustees although the employment of such agent was not strictly necessary or expedient or by reason of any mistake or omission made in good faith by such trustee or by any of the Trustees or by reason of any other matter or think except wilful and individual fraud or dishonesty on the part of the trustee who is sought to be made liable

A–41 **23 Delegation of powers**

(a) THE Trustees may delegate to any one or more of their number the operation of any bank account in their names

(b) Any trustee shall have power at any time (notwithstanding any rule of law to the contrary) by deed or deeds revocable during the Trust Period or irrevocable and executed during the Trust Period to delegate to any person (including in cases where there is more than one trustee to any other or others of the Trustees) the exercise of all or any powers conferred on such trustee notwithstanding the fiduciary nature of such power or powers

Precedent B

Basic form—trusts engrafted*

Index to clauses

* This precedent is adapted from Practical Trust Precedents published by Longman Group Plc, 21–27 Lamb's Conduit Street, London WC1 3NS and is reproduced with the kind permission of the Publishers.

B–01 THIS SETTLEMENT is made the day of One thousand nine hundred and B–01

BETWEEN

(1) ('the Settlor')
(2) ('the Trustees' which expression shall where the context so admits include the trustees or trustee for the time being of this Settlement)

WHEREAS

(A) THE Settlor wishes to make this Settlement and has transferred or delivered to the Trustees or otherwise placed under their control the property specified in the Second Schedule and from time to time further monies investments or other property may be paid or transferred to the Trustees by way of addition
(B) IT is intended that this Settlement shall be irrevocable

NOW THIS DEED IRREVOCABLY WITNESSES as follows

B–02 **1 Definitions** B–02

IN this deed where the context so admits

(a) 'the Trust Fund' shall mean
  (i) the property specified in the Second Schedule and
  (ii) all money investments or other property paid or transferred by any person or persons to or so as to be under the control of and (in either case) accepted by the Trustees as additions and
  (iii) all accumulations (if any) of income directed to be held as an accretion to capital and
  (iv) the money investments and property from time to time representing the said money investments property additions and accumulations
(b) 'the Beneficiaries' shall mean
  (i) the existing [grand] children of the Settlor namely:
  who was born on 19
  who was born on 19
  who was born on 19
  who was born on 19
  (ii) every other [grand] child of the Settlor born after the date of this Settlement but before the first [grand] child to attain the Specified Age shall do so
(c) 'the Trust Period' shall mean the period ending on the earlier of
  (i) the last day of the period of 80 years from the date of this Settlement which period (and no other) shall be the applicable perpetuity period or

(ii) such date as the Trustees shall by deed specify (not being a date earlier than the date of execution of such deed)

(d) 'the Accumulation Period' shall mean the period of 21 years from the date of this Settlement or the Trust Period if shorter

(e) 'interest in possession' shall have the meaning it has for the purposes of section 71 of the Inheritance Tax Act 1984 or any statutory modification or re-enactment of such section

(f) "the Specified Age" in respect of any Beneficiary shall mean during the Accumulation Period the age of 25 years and at the termination of the Accumulation Period shall mean such lesser age (not being less than 18 years) as the Beneficiary shall by then have attained and otherwise during the Trust Period shall mean the age of 18 years

B–03 **2 Trust for sale**

THE Trustees shall hold the Trust Fund upon trust as to investments or property other than money in their absolute discretion to sell call in or convert into money all or any of such investments or property but with power to postpone such sale calling in or conversion and to permit the same to remain as invested and upon trust as to money with the like discretion to invest the same in their names or under their control in any of the investments authorised by this Settlement or by law with power at the like discretion from time to time to vary or transpose any such investments for others so authorised

B–04 **3 Trusts of added property**

THE Trustees shall hold the Trust Fund upon with and subject to the trusts powers and provisions of this Settlement and the Trustees shall have the right at any time or times during the Trust Period to accept such additional money investments or other property as may be paid or transferred to them upon these trusts by the Settlor or any other person either personally or by testamentary act or disposition (including property of an onerous nature the acceptance of which the Trustees consider to be beneficial)

B–05 **4 Trusts of capital and income**

THE capital and income of the Trust Fund shall be held upon trust for such of the Beneficiaries as attain the Specified Age before the end of the Trust Period or are living and under that age at the end of the Trust Period or die under that age and before the end of the Trust Period leaving a child or children surviving and if more than one in such shares as the Trustees by deed or deeds revocable during the Trust Period or irrevocable and executed during the Trust Period may appoint and in default of such appointment in equal shares provided that

(i) no appointment shall be made or revoked so as to vary the entitlement (whether by increase or decrease or otherwise) of any of the Beneficiaries who has previously attained the Specified Age or died under that age and

(ii) the provisions of Clauses 5 and 6 shall apply to the share or entitlement or presumptive share or entitlement in or to the Trust Fund of any of the Beneficiaries (whether under or in default of appointment) such share or entitlement or presumptive share or entitlement being in those clauses called 'the Share' and that one of the Beneficiaries who is primarily interested in the Share being called 'the Primary Beneficiary'

B–06 5 Trusts for beneficiaries under the Specified Age B–06

THE following provisions shall apply to the Share during the Trust Period while the Primary Beneficiary is living and under the Specified Age

(a) The Trustees may pay or apply any income of the Share for or towards the maintenance or education or otherwise for the benefit of the Primary Beneficiary or any other or others of the Beneficiaries who are for the time being living and under the Specified Age

(b) The Trustees may also pay or apply any capital of the Share for or towards the maintenance or education or otherwise for the benefit of the Primary Beneficiary provided that capital shall not be so applied in a way that would or might prevent the Primary Beneficiary from becoming entitled to or to an interest in possession in the capital so applied on or before attaining the Specified Age nor in such a way that that income of the Share might in the meantime be dealt with except by being applied for the maintenance education or otherwise for the benefit of one or more of the Beneficiaries for the time being living and under the Specified Age or by being accumulated

(c) Subject as above during the Accumulation Period the income of the Share shall be accumulated as an accretion to the capital of the Share

(d) Subject as above section 31 of the Trustee Act 1925 (as modified below) shall apply to the income of the Share

(e) Notwithstanding the above the Trustees may at any time or times by deed or deeds revocable during the Trust Period or irrevocable and executed during the Trust Period direct in relation to all or any part of the Share that the trusts declared by Clause 6 shall take effect (and the trusts declared by Clause 5 determine) from the date of such deed or on the attainment by the Primary Beneficiary of an age less than the Specified Age or on the occurrence of any other event (not being earlier than the date of the deed) prior to the Primary Beneficiary attaining the Specified Age

B–07 6 Trusts for beneficiaries over the Specified Age B–07

ON the Primary Beneficiary attaining the Specified Age before the end of the Trust Period or being alive and under that age at the end of the Trust Period or dying under that age before the end of the Trust Period leaving a child or children the Share shall not vest absolutely in the Primary Beneficiary but shall be retained by the Trustees upon with and subject to the following trusts powers and provisions (or such of the same as are subsisting and capable of taking effect) that is to say

(a) The income of the Share shall be paid to the Primary Beneficiary

(b) The Trustees may at any time or times during the Trust Period as to the whole or any part of the share transfer or raise and pay the same to or for the absolute use and benefit of the Primary Beneficiary or raise and pay or apply the same for the advancement or otherwise for the benefit of the Primary Beneficiary in such manner as the Trustees shall in their absolute discretion think fit

(c) The Primary Beneficiary shall have power to appoint by deed or deeds revocable during the Trust Period or irrevocable and executed during the Trust Period or by will or codicil to take effect during the Trust Period that all or any part or parts of the Share in which the Primary Beneficiary is entitled to an interest in possession at death shall after the death of the Primary Beneficiary (in priority to the trusts declared by subclauses (d) (e) and (f)) be held upon trust to pay the income to the surviving spouse of the Primary Beneficiary during the life of such spouse or for any less period

(d) Subject as above the capital and income of the Share shall be held in trust for all or such one or more of the children and remoter issue of the Primary Beneficiary and if more than one in such shares and upon such trusts and with and subject to such powers and provisions (including protective or discretionary trusts or powers operative or exercisable at the discretion of the Trustees or any other person or persons) and in such manner generally as the Primary Beneficiary (subject to the application (if any) of the rule against perpetuities) by deed or deeds revocable during the Trust Period or irrevocable and executed during the Trust Period or by will or codicil to take effect during the Trust Period shall appoint provided that no appointment shall take effect unless the Primary Beneficiary shall previously have attained the Specified Age or become entitled to an interest in possession in the Share

(e) Subject as above the capital and income of the Share shall be held upon trust for such of the children of the Primary Beneficiary as attain the age of 21 years before the end of the Trust Period or are living and are under that age at the end of the Trust Period and if more than one in equal shares absolutely

(f) Subject as above the Share (together with any accrual to it) shall accrue to the other Share or Shares the trusts of which shall not previously have failed or determined (otherwise than by absolute vesting) and if more than one rateably between them and every such accrual shall be held upon with and subject to the same trusts powers and provisions as the original Share or Shares to which the same accrues

B–08 **7 Ultimate default trusts** B–08

(a) SUBJECT as above during the Accumulation Period (no Beneficiary having previously attained the Specified Age) and so long as a further Beneficiary or further Beneficiaries may come into existence the income of the Trust Fund shall be accumulated

(b) Subject as above and if and so far as not wholly disposed of for any reason whatever by the above provisions the capital and income of the Trust Fund shall be held upon trust for [such of the Beneficiaries as are living at the date of this Settlement in equal shares] absolutely

–09 **8 Administrative powers** B–09

THE Trustees shall in addition and without prejudice to all statutory powers have the powers and immunities set out in the First Schedule provided that the Trustees shall not exercise any of their powers so as to conflict with the beneficial provisions of this Settlement

–10 **9 Extended power of maintenance** B–10

SECTION 31 of the Trustee Act 1925 shall be deemed to apply as if the words 'may in all the circumstances be reasonable' had been omitted from paragraph (i) of subsection (1) and in substitution there had been inserted the words 'the Trustees may think fit' and as if the proviso at the end of subsection (1) had been omitted

–11 **10 Extended power of advancement** B–11

SECTION 32 of the Trustee Act 1925 shall be deemed to apply as if the proviso (a) of subsection (1) had been omitted

–12 **11 Restrictions on certain powers** B–12

DURING such period as these trusts qualify as accumulation and maintenance trusts in that they comply with the provisions of section 71 of the Inheritance Tax Act 1984 or any statutory modification or re-enactment of such section or would so qualify but for the existence of the powers conferred on the Trustees by Clauses 8 to 10 inclusive and Clause 15 such powers shall not be exercised in such a way that would or might prevent a Beneficiary who is under the Specified Age and has not become entitled to or to an interest in possession in all or part of the Trust Fund from becoming entitled to such an interest on or before attaining the Specified Age or in such a way that the income of all or part of the Trust Fund might in the meantime be dealt with except by being applied for the maintenance education or otherwise for the benefit of one or more of the Beneficiaries for the time being living and under the Specified Age or by being accumulated

–13 **12 Trustee charging clause** B–13

(a) ANY trustee which shall be a trust corporation or company authorised to undertake trust business shall be entitled in addition to reimbursement of its proper expenses to remuneration for its services in accordance with its published terms and conditions for trust business in force from time to time and in the absence of any such published terms and conditions in accordance with such terms and conditions as may from time to time be agreed between such trustee and the Settlor or (if the Settlor is unfit unable or unwilling to act) the person or persons by whom the power of appointing new trustees is for the time being exercisable

(b) Any trustee who is a solicitor or other person engaged in a profession or business shall be entitled to charge and be paid all normal professional or other charges for business done services rendered or time spent personally or by such trustee's firm in the administration of these trusts including acts which a trustee not engaged in any profession or business could have done personally

B–14 **13 Appointment of new trustees**

(a) DURING the lifetime of the Settlor the power of appointing new trustees shall be vested in the Settlor

(b) A person may be appointed to be a trustee notwithstanding that such person is not resident in the United Kingdom and remaining out of the United Kingdom for more than 12 months shall not be a ground for the removal of a trustee

B–15 **14 Clause headings**

THE clause headings are included for reference only and do not affect the interpretation of this Settlement

B–16 **15 Proper law forum and place of administration**

(a) THE proper law of this Settlement shall be that of England and Wales and all rights under this Settlement and its construction and effect shall be subject to the jurisdiction of and construed according to the laws of England and Wales

(b) The courts of England and Wales shall be the forum for the administration of these trusts

(c) Notwithstanding the provisions of subclauses (a) and (b)

- (i) The Trustees shall have power (subject to the application (if any) of the rule against perpetuities) to carry on the general administration of these trusts in any jurisdiction in the world whether or not such jurisdiction is for the time being the proper law of this Settlement or the courts of such jurisdiction are for the time being the forum for the administration of these trusts and whether or not the Trustees or any of them are for the time being resident or domiciled in or otherwise connected with such jurisdiction
- (ii) The Trustees may at any time declare in writing that from the date of such declaration the proper law of this Settlement shall be that of any specified jurisdiction (not being a jurisdiction under the law of which this Settlement would be capable of revocation) and that all rights under this Settlement and its construction and effect shall be subject to and construed according to the laws of that jurisdiction
- (iii) The Trustees may at any time declare in writing that from the date of such declaration the forum for the administration of these trusts shall be the courts of any specified jurisdiction

B–17 **16 Exclusion of settlor and spouse**

(a) NO discretion or power by this Settlement or by law conferred on the Trustees or any other person shall be exercised and no provision of this

Settlement shall operate directly or indirectly so as to cause or permit any part of the capital or income of the Trust Fund to become in any way payable to or applicable for the benefit of the Settlor or any person or persons who shall previously have added property to the Trust Fund or the spouse for the time being of the Settlor or any such person or persons

(b) The prohibition in this clause shall apply notwithstanding anything else contained or implied in this Settlement

17 Stamp duty certificate

THE Settlor hereby certifies that this instrument falls within category L in the Schedule to the Stamp Duty (Exempt Instruments) Regulations 1987.

IN WITNESS whereof the parties hereto have hereunto set their hands and seals the day and year first above written

THE FIRST SCHEDULE B–18

[*Administrative powers*]

[*See* A1–19 to A1–41]

THE SECOND SCHEDULE B–19

[*The initial trust fund*]

SIGNED SEALED and DELIVERED etc

APPENDIX 2

The Inheritance Tax (Double Charges Relief) Regulations 1987

(1987 No. 1130)

Made on June 30, 1987 and coming into force July 22, 1987

The Commissioners of Inland Revenue, in exercise of the powers conferred on them by section 104 of the Finance Act 1986, hereby make the following Regulations.

Citation and commencement

1. These Regulations may be cited as the Inheritance Tax (Double Charges Relief) Regulations 1987 and shall come into force on 22nd July 1987.

Interpretation

2. In these Regulations unless the context otherwise requires—
"PET" means potentially exempt transfer;
"property" includes part of any property;
"the 1984 Act" means the Inheritance Tax Act 1984;
"the 1986 Act" means Part V of the Finance Act 1986;
"section" means section of the 1984 Act.

Introductory

3. These Regulations provide for the avoidance, to the extent specified, of double charges to tax arising with respect to specified transfers of value made, and other events occurring, on or after 18th March 1986.

Double charges—potentially exempt transfers and death

4.—(1) This regulation applies in the circumstances to which paragraph (a) of section 104(1) of the 1986 Act refers where the conditions ("specified conditions") of paragraph (2) are fulfilled.

(2) The specified conditions to which paragraph (1) refers are—

(a) an individual ("the deceased") makes a transfer of value to a person ("the transferee") which is a PET,

(b) the transfer is made on or after 18th March 1986,

(c) the transfer proves to be a chargeable transfer, and

(d) the deceased immediately before his death was beneficially entitled to property to which paragraph (3) refers.

(3) The property to which paragraph (2)(d) refers is property—

(a) which the deceased, after making the PET to which paragraph (2)(a) refers, acquired from the transferee otherwise than for full consideration in money or money's worth,

(b) which is property which was transferred to the transferee by the PET to which paragraph (2)(a) refers or which is property directly or indirectly representing that property, and

(c) which is property comprised in the estate of the deceased immediately before his death (within the meaning of section 5(1)), value attributable to which is transferred by a chargeable transfer (under section 4).

(4) Where the specified conditions are fulfilled there shall be calculated, separately in accordance with sub-paragraphs (a) and (b), the total tax chargeable as a consequence of the death of the deceased—

(a) disregarding so much of the value transferred by the PET to which paragraph (2)(a) refers as is attributable to the property, value of which is transferred by the chargeable transfer to which paragraph (3)(c) refers, and

(b) disregarding so much of the value transferred by the chargeable transfer to which paragraph (3)(c) refers as is attributable to the property, value of which is transferred by the PET to which paragraph (2)(a) refers.

(5)(a) Whichever of the two amounts of tax calculated under paragraph (4)(a) or (b) is the lower amount shall be treated as reduced to nil but, subject to sub-paragraph (b), the higher amount shall be payable,

(b) where the amount calculated under paragraph (4)(a) is higher than the amount calculated under paragraph (4)(b)—

(i) so much of the tax chargeable on the value transferred by the chargeable transfer to which paragraph (2)(c) refers as is attributable to the amount of that value which falls to be disregarded by virtue of paragraph (ii) shall be treated as a nil amount, and

(ii) for all the purposes of the 1984 Act so much of the value transferred by the PET to which paragraph (2)(a) refers as is attributable to the property to which paragraph (3)(c) refers shall be disregarded.

(6) Part I of the Schedule to these Regulations provides an example of the operation of this regulation.

Double charges—gifts with reservation and death

5.—(1) This regulation applies in the circumstances to which paragraph (b) of section 104(1) of the 1986 Act refers where the conditions ("specified conditions") of paragraph (2) are fulfilled.

(2) The specified conditions to which paragraph (1) refers are—

(a) an individual ("the deceased") makes a transfer of value by way of gift of property,
(b) the transfer is made on or after 18th March 1986,
(c) the transfer is or proves to be a chargeable transfer,
(d) the deceased dies on or after 18th March 1986,
(e) the property in relation to the gift and the deceased is property subject to a reservation (within the meaning of section 102 of the 1986 Act),
(f) (i) the property is by virtue of section 102(3) of the 1986 Act treated for the purposes of the 1984 Act as property to which the deceased was beneficially entitled immediately before his death, or,
(ii) the property ceases to be property subject to a reservation and is the subject of a PET by virtue of section 102(4) of the 1986 Act, and
(g) (i) the property is comprised in the estate of the deceased immediately before his death (within the meaning of section 5(1)) and value attributable to it is transferred by a chargeable transfer (under section 4), or
(ii) the property is property transferred by the PET to which sub-paragraph (f)(ii) refers, value attributable to which is transferred by a chargeable transfer.

(3) Where the specified conditions are fulfilled there shall be calculated, separately in accordance with sub-paragraphs (a) and (b), the total tax chargeable as a consequence of the death of the deceased—
(a) disregarding so much of the value transferred by the transfer of value to which paragraph (2)(a) refers as is attributable to property to which paragraph (2)(g) refers, and
(b) disregarding so much of the value of property to which paragraph (2)(g) refers as is attributable to property to which paragraph (2)(a) refers.

(4) Where the amount calculated under paragraph (3)(a) is higher than the amount calculated under paragraph (3)(b)—
(a) only so much of that higher amount shall be payable as remains after deducting, as a credit, from the amount comprised in that higher amount which is attributable to the value of the property to which paragraph (2)(g) refers, a sum (not exceeding the amount so attributable) equal to so much of the tax paid—
(i) as became payable before the death of the deceased, and
(ii) as is attributable to the value disregarded under paragraph (3)(a), and
(b) so much of the value transferred by the transfer of value to which paragraph (2)(a) refers as is attributable to the property to which paragraph (2)(g) refers shall (except in relation to chargeable transfers which were chargeable to tax, when made by the deceased, for the purposes of an occasion which occurred before the death of the deceased on which tax was chargeable under section 64 or 65) be treated as reduced to a nil amount for all the purposes of the 1984 Act.

(5) Where the amount calculated under paragraph (3)(a) is less than the amount calculated under paragraph (3)(b) the value of the property to which paragraph (2)(g) refers shall be reduced to nil for all the purposes of the 1984 Act.

(6) For the purposes of the interpretation and application of this regulation section 102 of and Schedule 20 to the 1984 Act shall apply.

(7) Part II of the Schedule to these Regulations provides examples of the operation of this regulation.

Double charges—liabilities subject to abatement and death

6.—(1) This regulation applies in the circumstances to which paragraph (c) of section 104(1) of the 1986 Act refers where the conditions ("specified conditions") of paragraph (2) are fulfilled.

(2) The specified conditions to which paragraph (1) refers are—

(a) a transfer of value which is or proves to be a chargeable transfer ("the transfer") is made on or after 18th March 1986 by an individual ("the deceased") by virtue of which the estate of the transferee is increased or by virtue of which property becomes comprised in a settlement of which the transferee is a trustee, and

(b) at any time before his death the deceased incurs a liability to the transferee ("the liability") which is a liability subject to abatement under the provisions of section 103 of the 1986 Act in determining the value transferred by a chargeable transfer (under section 4).

(3) Where the specified conditions are fulfilled there shall be calculated, separately in accordance with sub-paragraphs (a) and (b), the total tax chargeable as a consequence of the death of the deceased—

(a) disregarding so much of the value transferred by the transfer—

(i) as is attributable to the property by reference to which the liability falls to be abated, and

(ii) as is equal to the amount of the abatement of the liability, and

(4)(a) Whichever of the two amounts of tax calculated under paragraph (3)(a) or (b) is the lower amount shall be treated as reduced to nil but, subject to sub-paragraph (b), the higher amount shall be payable,

(b) where the amount calculated under paragraph (3)(a) is higher than the amount calculated under paragraph (3)(b)—

(i) only so much of that higher amount shall be payable as remains after deducting, as a credit, from that amount a sum equal to so much of the tax paid—

(a) as became payable before the death of the deceased, and

(b) as is attributable to the value disregarded under paragraph (3)(a), and

(c) as does not exceed the difference between the amount of tax calculated under paragraph (3)(a) and the amount of tax that would have fallen to be calculated under paragraph (3)(b) if the liability had been taken into account, and

(ii) so much of the value transferred by the transfer to which paragraph (2)(a) refers—

(a) as is attributable to property by reference to which the liability is abated, and

(b) as is equal to the amount of the abatement of the liability,

shall (except in relation to chargeable transfers which were chargeable to tax, when made by the deceased, for the purposes of an occasion which occurred before the death of the deceased on which tax was chargeable under section 64 or 65) be treated as reduced to a nil amount for all the purposes of the 1984 Act.

(5) Where there is a number of transfers made by the deceased which are relevant to the liability to which paragraph (2)(b) applies the provisions of this regulation shall apply to those transfers taking them in reverse order of their making, that is to say, taking the latest first and the earliest last, but only to the extent that in aggregate the value of those transfers does not exceed the amount of the abatement to which paragraph (2)(b) refers.

(6) Part III of the Schedule to these Regulations provides examples of the operation of this regulation.

Double Charges—chargeable transfers and death

7.—(1) This regulation applies in the circumstances specified (by this regulation) for the purposes of paragraph (d) of section 104(1) of the 1986 Act (being circumstances which appear to the Board to be similar to those referred to in paragraphs (a) to (c) of that subsection) where the conditions ("specified conditions") of paragraph (2) are fulfilled.

(2) The specified conditions to which paragraph (1) refers are—

(a) an individual ("the deceased") makes a transfer of value to a person ("the transferee") which is a chargeable transfer,

(b) the transfer is made on or after 18th March 1986,

(c) the deceased dies within 7 years after that chargeable transfer is made, and

(d) the deceased immediately before his death was beneficially entitled to property to which paragraph (3) refers.

(3) The property to which paragraph (2)(d) refers is property—

(a) which the deceased, after making the chargeable transfer to which paragraph (2)(a) refers, acquired from the transferee otherwise than for full consideration in money or money's worth,

(b) which was transferred to the transferee by the chargeable transfer to which paragraph (2)(a) refers or which is property directly or indirectly representing that property, and

(c) which is property comprised in the estate of the deceased immediately before his death (within the meaning of section 5(1)), value attributable to which is transferred by a chargeable transfer (under section 4).

(4) Where the specified conditions are fulfilled there shall be calculated,

separately in accordance with sub-paragraphs (a) and (b), the total tax chargeable as a consequence of the death of the deceased—

(a) disregarding so much of the value transferred by the chargeable transfer to which paragraph (2)(a) refers as is attributable to the property, value of which is transferred by the chargeable transfer to which paragraph (3)(c) refers, and

(b) disregarding so much of the value transferred by the chargeable transfer to which paragraph (3)(c) refers as is attributable to the property, value of which is transferred by the chargeable transfer to which paragraph (2)(a) refers.

(5)(a) Whichever of the two amounts of tax calculated under paragraph (4)(a) or (b) is the lower amount shall be treated as reduced to nil but, subject to sub-paragraph (b), the higher amount shall be payable,

(b) where the amount calculated under paragraph (4)(a) is higher than the amount calculated under paragraph (4)(b)—

(i) only so much of that higher amount shall be payable as remains after deducting, as a credit, from the amount comprised in that higher amount which is attributable to the value of the property to which paragraph (2)(d) refers, a sum (not exceeding the amount so attributable) equal to so much of the tax paid—

(a) as became payable before the death of the deceased, and

(b) as is attributable to the value disregarded under paragraph (4)(a), and

(ii) so much of the value transferred by the chargeable transfer to which paragraph (2)(a) refers as is attributable to the property to which paragraph (3)(c) refers shall (except for the purposes of an occasion which occurred before the death of the deceased on which tax was chargeable under section 64 or 65) be treated as reduced to a nil amount for all the purposes of the 1984 Act.

(6) Part IV of the Schedule to these Regulations provides an example of the operation of this regulation.

Equal calculations of tax—special rule

8. Where the total tax chargeable as a consequence of death under the two separate calculations provided for by any of regulation 4(4), 5(3), 6(3) or 7(4) is equal in amount the first of those calculations shall be treated as producing a higher amount for the purposes of the regulation concerned.

Schedule and saving

9. The Schedule to these Regulations shall have effect only for providing examples of the operation of these Regulations and, in the event of any conflict between the Schedule and the Regulations, the Regulations shall prevail.

Appendix 2

Schedule

Introductory

1. This Schedule provides examples of the operation of the Regulations.

2. In this Schedule—

"cumulation" means the inclusion of the total chargeable transfers made by the transferor in the 7 years preceding the current transfer;

"GWR" means gift with reservation;

"taper relief" means the reduction in tax provided under section 7(4) of the 1984 Act, inserted by paragraph 2(4) of Schedule 19 to the 1986 Act.

3. Except where otherwise stated, the examples assume that—

—tax rates and bands remain as at 18 March 1987;

—the transferor has made no other transfers than those shown in the examples;

—no exemptions (including annual exemption) or reliefs apply to the value transferred by the relevant transfer; and

—"grossing up" does not apply in determining any lifetime tax (the tax is not borne by the transferor).

Part I

Regulation 4: Example

Jul 1987	A makes PET of £100,000 to B.	
Jul 1988	A makes gift into discretionary trust of £95,000.	Tax paid £750
Jan 1989	A makes further gift into same trust of £45,000.	Tax paid £6,750
Jan 1990	B dies and the 1987 PET returns to A.	
Apr 1991	A dies. His death estate of £300,000 includes the 1987 PET returned to him in 1990, which is still worth £100,000.	

First calculation under reg. 4(4)(a)

Charge the returned PET in A's death estate and ignore the PET made in 1987.

		Tax
Jul 1987	PET £100,000 ignored	NIL
Jul 1988	Gift £95,000 Tax £1,500 less £750 already paid	£750
Jan 1989	Gift £45,000 as top slice of £140,000 Tax £13,500 less £6,750 already paid	£6,750
Apr 1991	Death estate £300,000 as top slice of £400,000	£153,000*
	Total tax due as result of A's death	£160,500

* In first calculation the tax of £153,000 on death estate does not allow for any successive charges relief (inder s.141 I.H.T.A. 1984) that might be due in respect of "the returned PET" by reference to any tax charged on that "PET" in connection with B's death.

Second calculation under reg. 4(4)(b)

Charge the 1987 PET and ignore the value of the returned PET in A's death estate.

		Tax
Jul 1987	PET £100,000. Tax with taper relief	£2,400
Jul 1988	Gift £95,000 as top slice of £195,000 Tax £34,000 less £750 already paid	£33,250
Jan 1989	Gift £45,000 as top slice of £240,000 Tax £20,000 less £6,750 already paid	£13,250
Apr 1991	Death estate £200,000 as top slice of £440,000	£111,000
	Total tax due as result of A's death	£159,900

Result*

First calculation gives higher amount of tax. So PET reduced to nil and tax on other transfers is as in first calculation.

*If, after allowing any successive charges relief, the second calculation gives higher amount of tax, 1987 PET will be charged and tax on other transfers will be as in second calculation.

PART II

Regulation 5: Example 1

Jan 1988	A makes PET of £150,000 to B.	
March 1992	A makes gift of land worth £200,000 into a discretionary trust of which he is a potential beneficiary. The gift is a "G.W.R."	Tax paid £19,500
Feb 1995	A dies without having released his interest in the trust. His death estate valued at £400,000, includes the G.W.R. land currently worth £300,000.	

First calculation under reg. 5(3)(a)

Charge the G.W.R. land in A's death estate and ignore the G.W.R.

		Tax
Jan 1988	PET (now exempt)	NIL
Mar 1992	G.W.R. ignored	NIL
Feb 1995	Death estate £400,000 Tax £144,000 less £19,500 already paid on G.W.R.*	£124,500
	Total tax due as result of A's death	£124,500

* Credit for the tax already paid cannot exceed the amount of the death tax attributable to the value of the G.W.R. property.

In this example the tax so attributable is £108,000 (*i.e.* $\frac{144,000}{400,000} \times 300,000$). So credit is given for the full amount of £19,500.

Second calculation under reg. 5(3)(b)
Charge the G.W.R. and ignore the G.W.R. land in the death estate.

		Tax
Jan 1988	PET (now exempt)	NIL
Mar 1992	G.W.R. £200,000 Tax £39,000 less £19,500 already paid	£19,500
Feb 1995	Death estate £100,000 (ignoring G.W.R. property) as top slice of £300,000	£48,000
	Total tax due as result of A's death	£67,500

Result
First calculation yields higher amount of tax. So the value of the G.W.R. transfer is reduced to nil and tax on death is charged as in first calculation with credit for the tax already paid.

PART II

Regulation 5: Example 2

Apr 1987	A makes gift into discretionary trust of £150,000	Tax paid £9,500
Jan 1988	A makes further gift into same trust of £50,000.	Tax paid £10,000
Mar 1993	A makes PET of shares valued at £150,000 to B.	
Feb 1996	A dies. He had continued to enjoy the income of the shares he had given to B (the 1993 PET is a G.W.R.). His death estate, valued at £300,000, includes those shares currently worth £200,000.	

First calculation under reg. 5(3)(a)
Charge the G.W.R. shares in the death estate and ignore the PET.

		Tax
Apr 1987	Gift £150,000. No adjustment to tax as gift made more than 7 years before death	NIL
Jan 1988	Gift £50,000. No adjustment to tax as gift made more than 7 years before death	NIL
Mar 1993	PET £150,000 now reduced to NIL	NIL
Feb 1996	Death estate including G.W.R. shares £300,000. No previous cumulation	£87,000
	Total tax due as result of A's death	£87,000

Second calculation under reg. 5(3)(b)
Charge the PET and ignore the value of the G.W.R. shares in the death estate.

		Tax
Apr 1987	Gift £150,000. No adjustment to tax as gift made more than 7 years before death	NIL
Jan 1988	Gift £50,000. No adjustment to tax as gift made more than 7 years before death	NIL

		Tax
Mar 1993	G.W.R. £150,000 as top slice of £350,000 (*i.e.* previous gifts totalling £200,000+£150,000)	£75,000
Feb 1996	Death estate (excluding G.W.R. shares) £100,000 as top slice of £250,000 (the 1987 and 1988 gifts drop out of cumulation)	£43,000
	Total tax due as result of A's death	£118,000

Result
Second calculation yields higher amount of tax. So tax is charged by reference to the PET and the value of the G.W.R. shares in the death estate is reduced to NIL.

PART III

Regulation 6: Example 1

Nov 1987	X makes a PET of cash of £95,000 to Y.
Dec 1987	Y makes a loan to X of £95,000.
May 1988	X makes a gift into discretionary trust of £20,000.
Apr 1993	X dies. His death estate is worth £182,000. A deduction of £95,000 is claimed for the loan from Y.

First calculation under reg. 6(3)(a)
No charge on November 1987 gift, and no deduction against death estate.

		Tax
Nov 1987	PET ignored	NIL
May 1988	Gift £20,000	NIL
Apr 1993	Death estate £182,000 as top slice of £202,000	£39,800
	Total tax due as result of X's death	£39,800

Second calculation under reg. 6(3)(b)
Charge the November 1987 PET, and allow the deduction against the death estate.

		Tax
Nov 1987	PET £95,000. Tax with taper relief	£600
May 1988	Gift £20,000 as top slice of £115,000. Tax with taper relief	£3,600
Apr 1993	Death estate (£182,000–loan of £95,000) £87,000 as top slice of £202,000	£32,300
	Total tax due as result of X's death	£36,500

Result
First calculation gives higher amount of tax. So debt is disallowed against death estate, but PET of £95,000 is not charged.

PART III

Regulation 6: Example 2

Aug 1988	P makes a PET of cash of £100,000 to Q.	
Sept 1988	Q makes a loan to P of £100,000.	
Oct 1989	P makes gift into discretionary trust of £98,000.	Tax paid £1,200
Nov 1992	P dies. Death estate £110,000 less allowable liabilities of £80,000 (which do not include the debt of £100,000 owed to Q).	

First calculation under reg. 6(3)(a)

No charge on August 1988 PET, and no deduction against death estate for the £100,000 owed to Q.

		Tax
Aug 1988	PET ignored	NIL
Oct 1989	Gift £98,000 Tax (with taper relief) £1,920 less £1,200 already paid	£720
Nov 1992	Death estate £30,000 as top slice of £128,000	£9,000
	Total tax due as result of P's death	£9,720

Second calculation under reg. 6(3)(b)

Charge the August 1988 PET, and allow deduction against death estate for the £100,000 owed to Q.

		Tax
Aug 1988	PET £100,000. Tax with taper relief	£1,800
Oct 1989	Gift £98,000 as top slice of £198,000 Tax (with taper relief) £28,100 less £1,200 already paid	£26,960
Nov 1992	Death estate £30,000–£100,000 (owed to Q)	NIL
	Total tax due as result of P's death	£28,760

Result

Second calculation gives higher amount of tax. So the PET to Q is charged, and deduction is allowed against death estate for the debt to Q.

PART III

Regulation 6: Example 3

1 May 1987	A makes PET to B of £95,000.	
1 Jan 1988	A makes PET to B of £40,000.	
1 Jul 1988	A makes gift into discretionary trust of £100,000.	Tax paid £1,500
1 Jan 1989	A makes PET to B of £30,000.	
1 Jul 1989	B makes loan to A of £100,000.	

Regulation 6: Example 3—*cont.*

1 Dec 1990	A dies. Death estate £200,000, against which deduction is claimed for debt of £100,000 due to B.

First calculation under reg. 6(3)(a)

Disallow the debt and ignore corresponding amounts (£100,000) of PETs from A to B, starting with the latest PET.

		Tax
1 May 1987	PET now reduced to £65,000	NIL
1 Jan 1988	PET now reduced to NIL	NIL
1 Jul 1988	Gift into trust £100,000 as top slice of £165,000 Tax £25,000 less £1,500 already paid	£23,500
1 Jan 1989	PET now reduced to NIL	NIL
1 Dec 1990	Death estate £200,000 as top slice of £365,000	£98,000
	Total tax due as result of A's death	£121,500

Second calculation under reg. 6(3)(b)

Allow the debt and charge PETs to B in full.

		Tax
1 May 1987	PET £95,000. Tax with taper relief	£1,200
1 Jan 1988	PET £40,000 as top slice of £135,000	£12,000
1 Jul 1988	Gift into trust £100,000 as top slice of £235,000 Tax £41,000 less £1,500 already paid	£39,500
1 Jan 1989	PET £30,000 as top slice of £265,000	£15,000
1 Dec 1990	Death estate £100,000 as top slice of £365,000	£53,500
	Total tax due as result of A's death	£121,200

Result

First calculation yields higher amount of tax. So the debt is disallowed and corresponding amounts of PETs to B are ignored in determining the tax due as a result of the death.

PART III

Regulation 6: Example 4

1 Apr 1987	A makes gift into discretionary trust of £100,000.	Tax paid £1,500
1 Jan 1990	A makes PET to B of £60,000.	
1 Jan 1991	A makes further gift into same trust of £50,000.	Tax paid £8,000
1 Jan 1992	Same trust makes a loan to A of £120,000.	
1 Jun 1994	A dies. Death estate is £220,000, against which deduction is claimed for debt of £120,000 due to the trust.	

First calculation under reg. 6(3)(a)

Disallow the debt and ignore corresponding amounts (£120,000) of gifts from A to trust, starting with the latest gift.

		Tax
1 Apr 1987	Gift now reduced to £30,000. No adjustment to tax already paid as gift made more than 7 years before death	NIL
1 Jan 1990	PET £60,000 as top slice of £90,000	NIL
1 Jan 1991	Gift now reduced to NIL. No adjustment to tax already paid	NIL
1 Jun 1994	Death estate £220,000 as top slice of £280,000 (the 1987 gift at £30,000 drops out of cumulation)	£77,000
		£77,000
	Less credit for tax already paid £1,500+£8,000	£9,500
	Total tax due as result of A's death	£67,500

Second calculation under reg. 6(3)(b)

Allow the debt and no adjustment to gifts into the trust.

		Tax
1 Apr 1987	Gift £100,000. No adjustment to tax already paid as gift made more than 7 years before death	NIL
1 Jan 1990	PET £60,000 as top slice of £160,000. Tax with taper relief	£12,000
1 Jan 1991	Gift £50,000 as top slice of £210,000 Tax (with taper relief) £16,000 less £8,000 already paid	£8,000
1 June 1994	Death estate £100,000 as top slice of £210,000. (The 1987 gift drops out of cumulation. No credit for tax paid on that gift.)	£37,000
	Total tax due as result of A's death	£57,000

Result

First calculation yields higher amount tax. So the debt is disallowed and corresponding amounts of gifts into trust are ignored in determining the tax due as a result of the death.

PART IV

Regulation 7: Example

May 1986	S transfers into discretionary trust property worth £150,000. Immediate charge at the rates then in force.	Tax paid £13,750
Oct 1986	S gives T a life interest in shares worth £85,000. Immediate charge at the rates then in force.	Tax paid £19,500
Jan 1991	S makes a PET to R of £20,000.	
Dec 1992	T dies, and the settled shares return to S who is the settlor and therefore no tax charge on the shares on T's death.	

Regulation 7: Example—*cont.*

Aug 1993	S dies. His death estate includes the shares returned from T which are currently worth £75,000, and other assets worth £144,000.

First calculation under reg. 7(4)(a)

Charge the returned shares in the death estate and ignore the October 1986 gift. Tax rates and bands are those in force at the date of S's death.

		Tax
May 1986	Gift into trust made more than 7 years before death. So no adjustment to tax already paid but the gift cumulates in calculating tax on other gifts	NIL
Oct 1986	Gift ignored and no adjustment to tax already paid	NIL
Jan 1991	PET of £20,000 as top slice of (£150,000+£20,000) £170,000	£8,000
Nov 1993	Death estate £219,000 as top slice of £239,000 Tax £56,000 less £19,350 (part of tax already paid)*	£37,150
	Total tax due as a result of S's death	£45,150

* £19,350 represents the amount of the death tax attributable to the value of the returned shares, and is lower than the amount of the lifetime tax charged on those shares. So credit against the death charge for the tax already paid is restricted to the lower amount.

Second calculation under reg. 7(4)(b)

Charge the October 1986 gift and ignore the returned shares in the death estate. Tax rates and bands are those in force at the date of S's death.

		Tax
May 1986	Gifts into trust made more than 7 years before death. So no adjustment to tax already paid but the gift is taken into account in calculating the tax on the other gifts	NIL
Oct 1986	Gifts of £85,000 as top slice of £235,000 Tax (with taper relief) £7,100 less £19,500 already paid	NIL*
Jan 1991	PET of £20,000 as top slice of £255,000	£10,000
Aug 1993	Death estate (excluding the returned shares) £144,000 as top slice of £249,000 (£85,000+£20,000+£144,000)	£57,000
	Total tax due as a result of S's death	£67,000

* Credit for the tax already paid restricted to the (lower) amount of tax payable as result of the death. No repayment of the excess.

Result

Second calculation gives higher amount of tax. So tax is charged as in second calculation by excluding the shares from the death estate.

Appendix 2

Explanatory Note

(This Note is not part of the Regulations)

The Finance Act 1986 by the provisions of section 104 empowered the Board of Inland Revenue to make provision by regulations for avoiding in certain circumstances double charges to inheritance tax in respect of transfers of value and other events occurring on or after 18 March 1986.

These Regulations provide for the avoidance of double charges arising in specified circumstances.

Regulation 1 provides the title and commencement date.

Regulation 2 contains definitions.

Regulation 3 describes the scope of the Regulations.

Regulation 4 provides for the avoidance of a double charge where property given by a potentially exempt transfer (PET) is subsequently returned (otherwise than for full consideration) by the donee to the transferor, and as a result of the transferor's death both that property and the PET become chargeable to tax. If charging the property as part of the death estate produces a higher amount of tax than would be payable if the charge on the PET was taken instead, the value transferred by the original transfer (the PET) is reduced by reference to the amount of the value of that property which is included in the chargeable transfer on the death. Conversely the PET is charged if that produces the higher amount of tax, with a corresponding reduction in the value of that property which is included in the chargeable transfer on the death. To avoid the value of the same property entering twice into the tax calculations this reduction applies for all purposes of the tax.

Regulation 5 provides for the avoidance of a double charge where there is a transfer of value by way of gift of property which is or subsequently becomes a chargeable transfer, and the property is (by virtue of the provisions relating to gifts with reservation) subject to a further transfer which is chargeable as a result of the transferor's death. As under regulation 4, whichever transfer produces the higher amount of tax as a result of the death remains chargeable and the value of the other transfer is reduced by reference to the value of the transfer which produced that amount. However this reduction in value does not apply for the purposes of any discretionary trust charges arising before the transferor's death if the transfer by way of gift was chargeable to tax when it was made. Further, provision is made for credit to be given on account of any tax already paid on the transfer by way of gift against so much of the tax payable on the other transfer as relates to the value of the property in question.

Regulation 6 provides for the avoidance of a double charge where a transfer of value is or subsequently becomes a chargeable transfer, and at the transferor's death his estate owes to the transferee a debt which (under the rules relating to such liabilities) falls to be abated or disallowed in determining the value of the estate chargeable on the death. Two separate calculations of tax payable as a result of the death are made. In the first, the amount of the transfer of value is reduced by the amount of the debt which is disallowed or abated, and in the second, the amount of the transfer of value and of the debt are both taken into account. The higher amount of tax is payable, but relief is given either by reducing the value of the transfer of value or by allowing the debt and charging the transfer of value in full. As under regulation 5, the reduction in value does not apply for the purposes of any charges on discretionary trusts arising before the death if the transfer of value was a chargeable transfer when it was made. Credit is allowed for some or all of the tax already paid on that transfer against the tax payable on the transferor's estate at death.

Regulation 7 provides for the avoidance of a double charge where property given by a transfer of value which is chargeable when made, is returned (otherwise than for full consideration) by the donee to the transferor, and that property is also chargeable as part of the transferor's estate on his death. It provides the same relief as is provided under regulation 4 in the case where the transfer of value was a PET when it was made, but credit is available to tax already paid. The reduction in value does not apply for the purposes of discretionary trust charges arising before the death.

Regulation 8 provides a rule to determine which of two equal amounts under regulation 4(4), 5(3), 6(3) or 7(4) is to be treated as the higher amount for the purposes of each of those regulations.

Regulation 9 introduces the Schedule which provides examples of the operation of these Regulations.

INDEX